The CCSA™ Cram Sheet

This Cram Sheet contains the distilled, key facts about the Check Point Certified Security Administrator exam. Review this information last thing before entering the test room, paying special attention to those areas where you feel you need the most review. You can transfer any of the facts onto a blank piece of paper before beginning the exam.

INSTALLATION PLATFORM REQUIREMENTS

Minimum requirements for installing Check Point FireWall-1 on an NT server.

Component	Minimum Specifications
OS version	Windows NT 4 with Service Pack 4 or higher
Memory	64MB
Disk space	40MB

Minimum requirements for installing Check Point FireWall-1 on a Solaris system.

Component	Minimum Specifications
OS version	Solaris 2.6 and Operating Environment 7
Processor	SPARC and x86
Memory	64MB
Disk space	40MB

INSTALLATION TYPES

1. *Standalone installation*—Installs all the components (Management Server, Firewall Module, Security Server, and so on) onto a single machine.

2. *Distributed installation*—Lets you pick and choose which pieces you want installed onto the server. Through the distributed installation configuration, you can manage multiple firewalls from one Management Server.

KEY INSTALLATION POINTS

3. *Selecting setup type*—Choosing to install FireWall-1 as a standalone installation or a distributed installation.

4. *Selecting product type*—Choosing either VPN-1/FireWall-1 Enterprise Management or VPN-1/FireWall-1 Gateway/Server Module. Based on licensing and product purchased.

5. *Licensing*—Implementing the license that was generated from Check Point's Web site. Host (IP address), expiration date, features, and key must match what was generated on the Web site *exactly* or applying the license will fail.

6. *Creating administrators*—Creating a user account that will be used for managing the Firewall Module.

7. *Host IP address*—Informing the FireWall-1 software of the IP address for the external interface that the Firewall Module will use to protect all internal nodes.

8. *GUI clients*—Informing the firewall of the hostnames of machines that will be allowed to manage the firewall by using the GUI clients. If a host that is not listed on the GUI clients screen attempts to contact the firewall via a GUI client, it will be rejected.

- In a passive SYN gateway, SYNDefender sits as a proxy between a client and a server. When a SYN request is issued from the client to the server, SYNDefender verifies that the three-way handshake can be completed with the host before passing the SYN request to the server.

37. *IP spoofing* is a popular way to generate denial of service attacks by generating packets from a nonexistent IP address and fooling a server into generating a SYN/ACK.

38. The rules for licensing are as follows:
    - For the Single Gateway product, licensing can be purchased in the following bundles:
      - 10 licenses
      - 25 licenses
      - 50 licenses
      - 100 licenses
      - 250 licenses
    - The Enterprise product is purchased with unlimited licensing.

39. Allowing FireWall-1 to control IP forwarding prevents unauthorized access through the gateway when the firewall is down (for example, if the machine is rebooting or the services are stopped).

40. In a Unix installation, **pkadd** is a command-line program that transfers the FireWall-1 files to the machine.

41. In a Unix installation, **InstallU** can be used to install the FireWall-1 files.

OTHER FIREWALL TYPES

42. Packet filtering was one of the earliest forms of firewalls; it was an efficient way of filtering traffic coming into a network.

43. Packet filters simply compare network protocols to a database of rules and forward all packets that meet the predefined criteria.

44. Packet filters are most often seen on routers.

45. The main advantages of packet filtering are:
    - Transparent to end users
    - Very fast compared to proxy servers
    - Relatively inexpensive

46. The main disadvantages of packet filtering are:
    - It offers the least amount of network security.
    - It is unable to manipulate information.
    - It is subject to IP spoofing.

47. A proxy server is a firewall that is implemented on the Application layer.

48. Proxies are an improvement over packet filtering because they examine packets all the way up to the Application layer.

49. Proxies offer better security because they are fully aware of the context of the information that is being passed between the networks.

50. Proxies take the place of the source machine and send the request for information to the intended destination using the proxy server's own IP address. When the data is returned from the intended target, the information is then sent to the initiating source.

CORIOLIS™
Certification Insider Press

22. NAT rules can also be created manually by using the NAT rule base found in the Policy Editor.

23. For NAT to work properly, your firewall must be configured to use the Address Resolution Protocol (ARP). ARP is used to match a MAC address to an IP address. Windows NT requires the file local.arp to be created for ARP entries to work correctly.

AUTHENTICATION

24. *Client authentication*—Used to authenticate users for any service. Users are required to Telnet to the firewall either by using port 259 or by pointing their Web browser to the firewall using HTTP on port 900. *Implicit client authentication* is used to allow access to all client authentication rules once a user has successfully authenticated to the firewall using user or session authentication.

25. *Session authentication*—Is similar to client authentication; however, client software must be installed on the user's workstation in order to use session authentication.

26. *User authentication*—Can be used with only:
- FTP
- HTTP
- HTTPS
- Telnet
- Rlogin

LOG VIEWER

27. Used to review any traffic that was specified for logging in the rule base.

28. There are three Log Viewer modes:
- Security Log
- Accounting Entries
- Active Connections

29. You can extract certain log records by using selection criteria. Criteria can be created by using search strings in any of the available columns of the Log Viewer.

30. You can create a new log file. When creating a new log file, *the informa*

ACCESS CONTROL

31. Access control rights are established in a three-step process, as follows:
1. The GUI client transmits the username, password, and IP address of the client machine to the Management Server specified in the logon screen.
2. If the IP address of the client machine is a valid IP address as specified in the Management Server's configuration, the Management Server will validate the username and password supplied.
3. After the username and password are verified, the Firewall Module passes the security policy, objects, and log database for the client to manipulate.

32. This method of handshaking is important to prevent unwanted changes to a firewall, which in turn may compromise the network's security.

ADDITIONAL IMPORTANT INFORMATION

33. A Management Module can control up to 50 Enforcement Modules.

34. To connect to a firewall, you need to know the username, password, and IP address (or hostname) of the firewall.

35. Traffic passing through an Enforcement Module can be examined in three directions:
- Inbound
- Outbound
- Eitherbound

36. SYNDefender is used to protect the firewall (and internal network) from denial-of-service attacks. SYNDefender can be configured as a SYN gateway or a passive SYN gateway.
- A SYN gateway is used when a SYN request is issued to a server from a client and the firewall passes the packet to the server. When the server sends the SYN/ACK packet back to the client, the firewall passes the SYN/ACK to the client but also sends an ACK to the server. This method ensures that the queue does not get overloaded by SYN floods but still allows for free communications.

9. *Key Hit Session*—Used to generate a random key to be used in internal firewall encryption.

- A light bulb indicates that the characters that are typed have been accepted as part of the random seed.

- A bomb indicates that the characters that are typed have been refused as part of the random seed. Characters are refused if keys are too similar to the ones before it or if keys are pressed too fast.

FIREWALL OBJECTS MANAGED BY THE POLICY EDITOR

10. *Network Object Manager*—A tool used to create workstations, networks, domains, routers, switches, integrated firewalls, groups (of network objects), logical servers, and address ranges.

- The *workstation object* is used not only to define workstations, but also to designate a workstation as a *gateway*, as well as a FireWall-1 Enforcement Module.

- The *network object* is used to designate a network of hosts that will in some way be affected by the firewall.

11. *Services Manager*—A tool used to manage services (such as FTP, Telnet, HTTP, and so on). Common services are already defined in the Services Manager, but additional services of the following types can be created: TCP, UDP, RDP, ICMP, other, groups (of services), and port ranges.

12. *Resources Manager*—A tool used to manage additional resources. A resource is used to match packets and perform actions on those packets when they pass through the firewall. One difference between resources and services is that resources can be used only with FTP, HTTP, and SMTP. Resources can be made of the four following types:

- URI
- SMTP
- FTP
- Group

13. *User Manager*—A tool used to manage users for authentication purposes. Using the User Manager, you can create groups, templates, external groups, or individual users from the templates.

- User properties include name, expiration date, authentication schemes, time and date, encryption type, and location information.

- The different types of authentication schemes are S/Key, SecurID, VPN-1 & FireWall-1 Password, OS Password, RADIUS, AXENT, and TACACS.

14. *Time Manager*—A tool used to define times that a specific rule may or may not be enforced.

SECURITY POLICY

15. A security policy can be created by using the Rule Base Wizard, rule base template, or an empty rule base.

16. The first rule in a security policy should be the *stealth rule*. The stealth rule is used to block all traffic directly to the firewall, therefore making it seem transparent.

17. All other rules below the stealth rule are applied *in order*.

18. The last rule in the rule base should be the *cleanup rule*. The cleanup rule is used to track any traffic that is not defined in the rules above and is to be *explicitly dropped*.

19. If the cleanup rule does not exist, any remaining traffic not *explicitly* defined in the security policy will be *implicitly* dropped using the *implicit drop rule*.

NETWORK ADDRESS TRANSLATION (NAT)

20. The three types of network address translation are:

- *Hide mode*—Hides multiple internal (invalid) IP addresses behind a single external (valid) IP address.

- *Static destination mode*—Translates external (valid) IP addresses to internal (invalid) IP addresses as packets enter the firewall.

- *Static source mode*—Translates internal (invalid) IP addresses to external (valid) IP addresses as packets leave the firewall.

21. NAT can be applied to network objects using the NAT tab of an object's properties screen.

CCSA™

Tony Piltzecker

CCSA™ Exam Cram

Limits of Liability and Disclaimer of Warranty

The author and publisher of this book have used their best efforts in preparing the book and the programs contained in it. These efforts include the development, research, and testing of the theories and programs to determine their effectiveness. The author and publisher make no warranty of any kind, expressed or implied, with regard to these programs or the documentation contained in this book.

The author and publisher shall not be liable in the event of incidental or consequential damages in connection with, or arising out of, the furnishing, performance, or use of the programs, associated instructions, and/or claims of productivity gains.

Trademarks

Trademarked names appear throughout this book. Rather than list the names and entities that own the trademarks or insert a trademark symbol with each mention of the trademarked name, the publisher states that it is using the names for editorial purposes only and to the benefit of the trademark owner, with no intention of infringing upon that trademark.

The Coriolis Group, LLC
14455 N. Hayden Road
Suite 220
Scottsdale, Arizona 85260

(480)483-0192
FAX (480)483-0193
www.coriolis.com

Library of Congress Cataloging-in-Publication Data
Piltzecker, Tony, 1975-
    CCSA / Tony Piltzecker.
        p.   cm. -- (Exam cram)
    Includes index.
    ISBN 1-57610-916-X
    1. Electronic data processing personnel--Certification.   2. Computer security--Examinations--Study guides.   I. Title.   II. Series.
QA76.3 .P55   2001
005.8--dc21

                                    2001047422
                                    CIP

President and CEO
Roland Elgey

Publisher
Al Valvano

Associate Publisher
Katherine R. Hartlove

Acquisitions Editor
Sharon Linsenbach

Product Marketing Manager
Jeff Johnson

Project Editors
Meredith Brittain
Tom Lamoureux

Technical Reviewer
Kevin McCarter

Production Coordinator
Todd Halvorsen

Cover Designer
Laura Wellander

Printed in the United States of America
10 9 8 7 6 5 4 3 2 1

⊘ CORIOLIS™

The Coriolis Group, LLC • 14455 North Hayden Road, Suite 220 • Scottsdale, Arizona 85260

A Note from Coriolis

Our goal has always been to provide you with the best study tools on the planet to help you achieve your certification in record time. Time is so valuable these days that none of us can afford to waste a second of it, especially when it comes to exam preparation.

Over the past few years, we've created an extensive line of *Exam Cram* and *Exam Prep* study guides, practice exams, and interactive training. To help you study even better, we have now created an e-learning and certification destination called **ExamCram.com**. (You can access the site at **www.examcram.com**.) Now, with every study product you purchase from us, you'll be connected to a large community of people like yourself who are actively studying for their certifications, developing their careers, seeking advice, and sharing their insights and stories.

We believe that the future is all about collaborative learning. Our **ExamCram.com** destination is our approach to creating a highly interactive, easily accessible collaborative environment, where you can take practice exams and discuss your experiences with others, sign up for features like "Questions of the Day," plan your certifications using our interactive planners, create your own personal study pages, and keep up with all of the latest study tips and techniques.

We hope that whatever study products you purchase from us—*Exam Cram* or *Exam Prep* study guides, *Personal Trainers*, *Personal Test Centers*, or one of our interactive Web courses—will make your studying fun and productive. Our commitment is to build the kind of learning tools that will allow you to study the way you want to, whenever you want to.

Visit ExamCram.com now to enhance your study program.

Help us continue to provide the very best certification study materials possible. Write us or email us at **learn@examcram.com** and let us know how our study products have helped you study. Tell us about new features that you'd like us to add. Send us a story about how we've helped you. We're listening!

Good luck with your certification exam and your career. Thank you for allowing us to help you achieve your goals.

ExamCram.com *Connects You to the Ultimate Study Center!*

Look for these other products from The Coriolis Group:

CISSP Exam Cram
by Mandy Andress

Windows 2000 Security Little Black Book
by Ian McLean

MCSE ISA Server 2000 Exam Cram
by Diana Bartley and Gregory W. Smith

MCSE ISA Server 2000 Exam Prep
by Kimberly Simmons and Masaru Ryumae

MCSE Windows 2000 Security Design Exam Cram
by Phillip G. Schein

Also recently published by Coriolis Certification Insider Press:

MCSE SQL Server 2000 Database Design Exam Cram
by Richard McMahon and Sean Chase

Oracle8i DBA: Backup and Recovery Exam Cram
by Debbie Wong

Server+ Exam Cram
by Deborah Haralson and Jeff Haralson

CIW Foundations Exam Cram
by Carol Miller

I would like to dedicate this book to my family and friends,
who have all been so supportive during the past few months.
Your strength and support has carried me
through the times when I did not think I would make it.
A special thanks to my wife, Melanie, and daughter, Kaitlyn,
for standing by me when things got really tough
and I seemed to have lost my way.
Thank you for being my light!

About the Author

Tony Piltzecker is a Senior Networking Consultant with Integrated Information Systems in Tempe, Arizona. With more than five years of networking experience, Tony has become an authority in network technologies, with a specialty in routing and network security. He holds several field certifications, including Check Point Certified Security Administrator (CCSA), Microsoft Certified Systems Engineer (MCSE), Cisco Certified Network Associate (CCNA), and Citrix Certified Administrator (CCA).

In his spare time, Tony enjoys rollerblading, playing football, and spending time with his family. He lives in Chandler, Arizona, with his wife, Melanie, and his daughter, Kaitlyn, but he is a Bostonian at heart.

Acknowledgments

I would like to thank my family for all of their support throughout the years. To my parents, who were always there to give me a hand when I needed it, and even sometimes when I did not! To my sister, who has always been a great friend and supporter. To my brother, who sparked my interest in computers oh-so-many years ago. To my beautiful baby girl Kaitlyn, you are an inspiration to me, and you bring a smile to my face every morning.

A special thanks to my wife, Melanie. You have stuck with me through thick and thin, and I cannot tell you how much that has meant to me. Thank you for being my wife, and my best friend.

I would also like to acknowledge my co-workers and managers at Integrated Information Systems. Thank you for giving me the time and flexibility to write this book. Everyone's support and understanding made writing this book less difficult than I initially anticipated.

Finally, I would like to acknowledge the team at Coriolis that helped in getting this book published. Thanks to Sharon Linsenbach, acquisitions editor, who was so crucially important in bringing this book to life. To Meredith Brittain and Tom Lamoureux, project editors, for their excellent work in editing each of these chapters and picking up the pieces that I might have dropped. I would also like to thank the rest of the Coriolis team—Todd Halvorsen, production coordinator; Jeff Johnson, product marketing manager; and Laura Wellander, cover designer— for their hard work and dedication behind the scenes.

Contents at a Glance

Table of Contents

Chapter 4
Implementing Network Objects 69

Introduction

Welcome to *CCSA Exam Cram*! Whether this is your first or your fifteenth *Exam Cram* book, you'll find information here and in Chapter 1 that will help ensure your success as you pursue knowledge, experience, and certification. This book aims to help you get ready to take—and pass—the Check Point certification Exam 156-205, titled "Check Point Certified Security Administrator." This Introduction explains Check Point's certification programs in general and talks about how the *Exam Cram* series can help you prepare for certification exams.

Exam Cram books help you understand and appreciate the subjects and materials you need to pass certification exams. *Exam Cram* books are aimed strictly at test preparation and review. They do not teach you everything you need to know about a topic. Instead, I present and dissect the questions and problems I've found that you're likely to encounter on a test. I've worked to bring together as much information as possible about Check Point certification exams.

Nevertheless, to completely prepare yourself for any Check Point test, I recommend that you begin by taking the Self-Assessment included in this book immediately following this Introduction. The Self-Assessment tool will help you evaluate your knowledge base against the requirements for a CCSA under both ideal and real circumstances.

Based on what you learn from the Self-Assessment, you might decide to begin your studies with some classroom training or some background reading. On the other hand, you might decide to pick up and read one of the many study guides available from Check Point or third-party vendors on certain topics. Further, I recommend that you supplement your study program with visits to **ExamCram.com** to receive certification information and advice.

I also strongly recommend that you install, configure, and experiment with the software that you'll be tested on, because nothing beats hands-on experience and familiarity when it comes to understanding the questions you're likely to encounter on a certification test. Book learning is essential, but hands-on experience is the best teacher of all!

The Check Point Certifications

Check Point currently offers several levels of certification, which vary based on the level of expertise and the products currently offered by Check Point. As this book goes to press, Check Point offers the following six certifications:

➤ *CCSA CP 2000 (Check Point Certified Security Administrator)*—The CCSA CP 2000 exam is the topic of this *Exam Cram* book. You must have a thorough understanding of configuring all aspects of a FireWall-1 gateway. Passing the 156-205 exam is the only requirement for obtaining the CCSA CP 2000 certification.

➤ *CCSA NG (Check Point Certified Security Administrator)*—The requirements for the CCSA NG exam are the same as those for the CCSA exam; however, the criteria are based on Check Point FireWall-1 Next Generation, whereas the basic CCSA certification is based on FireWall-1 version 4.1. Passing the 156-210 exam is the only requirement for obtaining a CCSA NG certification.

➤ *CCSE CP 2000 (Check Point Certified Security Engineer)*—The CCSE CP 2000 exam is geared toward experienced FireWall-1 administrators who work with the product in large, enterprise environments. A CCSE must be able to manage complex installations of FireWall-1 and have in-depth knowledge of VPNs (virtual private networks). To achieve CCSE CP 2000 certification, you must pass the 156-205 and 156-305 exams.

➤ *CCSE NG (Check Point Certified Security Engineer)*—The CCSE NG exam is geared toward experienced FireWall-1 administrators who work with the product in large, enterprise environments. Like the CCSA NG exam, this test is based on the Next Generation version of FireWall-1. A CCSE NG must be able to manage complex installations of FireWall-1 and have in-depth knowledge of VPNs. To achieve CCSE NG certification, you must pass the 156-210 and 156-310 exams.

➤ *CCAE (Check Point Certified Addressing Engineer)*—The CCAE exam is for administrators who will be managing a Check Point product known as MetaIP. A CCAE must have a very strong understanding of TCP/IP and MetaIP to pass this exam. The CCAE is a new exam offered by Check Point, and it does not have an exam number at this time.

➤ *CCQE (Check Point Certified Quality of Service Engineer)*—The CCQE exam is for administrators who will be managing a Check Point product known as FloodGate-1. A CCQE must know how to install, navigate, and coordinate FloodGate-1 with FireWall-1 and VPN-1. THE CCQE is a new exam, and it does not have an exam number at this time.

*Note: Refer to the Check Point Education Services Web page at **www.checkpoint.com/ services/education** on a regular basis to access updated information about Check Point certifications and exam numbers.*

Taking a Certification Exam

After you've prepared for your exam, you need to register with a testing center. Each computer-based Check Point exam costs $150, and if you don't pass, you can retest for an additional $150 for each additional try. In the United States and Canada, tests are administered by Virtual University Enterprises (VUE). You can sign up for a test or get the phone numbers for local testing centers by visiting the VUE Web page at **www.vue.com**.

To sign up for a test, you must possess a valid credit card or contact VUE for mailing instructions to send a check (in the United States). After payment is verified or a check has cleared, you can register for a test.

To schedule an exam, call the number or visit the Web page at least one day in advance. To cancel or reschedule an exam, you must call before 7 P.M. pacific standard time the day before the scheduled test time (or you might be charged, even if you don't appear to take the test). When you want to schedule a test, have the following information ready:

➤ Your name, organization, and mailing address.

➤ Your Check Point Test ID. Inside the United States, this means your Social Security number; citizens of other nations should call ahead to find out what type of identification number is required to register for a test.

➤ The name and number of the exam you want to take.

➤ A method of payment. As I've already mentioned, a credit card is the most convenient method of payment, but alternate means of payment can be arranged in advance, if necessary.

After you sign up for a test, you'll be informed as to when and where the test is scheduled. Try to arrive at least 15 minutes early. You must supply two forms of identification—one of which must be a photo ID—to be admitted into the testing room.

All exams are completely closed-book. In fact, you will not be permitted to take anything with you into the testing area, but you will be furnished with a blank sheet of paper and a pen or, in some cases, an erasable plastic sheet and an erasable pen. I suggest that you immediately write down on the sheet of paper all the information you've memorized for the test. In *Exam Cram* books, key information appears on a tear-out sheet inside the front cover of each book. You will have some time to compose yourself, record the information, and take a sample orientation exam before you begin the real test. I suggest you take the orientation test before taking your first exam, but because they're all more or less identical in layout, behavior, and controls, you probably won't need to do this more than once.

When you complete a Check Point certification exam, the software will tell you whether you've passed or failed. If you need to retake an exam, you'll have to schedule a new test with VUE and pay another $150.

The first time you fail a test, you can retake the test the next day. However, if you fail a second time, you must wait 14 days before retaking the test. The 14-day waiting period remains in effect for all retakes after the second failure.

Check Point generates transcripts that indicate which exams you have passed. You can view a copy of your transcript at any time by going to the Check Point Professional secured site at **www.checkpoint.com/services/education/cpo/ index.html**. This tool allows you to print a copy of your current transcript and confirm your certification status.

Tracking Certification Status

After you pass the necessary exam or set of exams, you'll be certified. Official certification normally takes anywhere from six to eight weeks, so don't expect to get your credentials overnight. When the package for a qualified certification arrives, it includes a Welcome Kit that contains a number of elements (see Check Point's Web site for other benefits of specific certifications), including:

➤ A certificate suitable for framing, along with a wallet card and lapel pin.

➤ A license to use the CCSA (or other certification) logo, thereby allowing you to use the logo in advertisements, promotions, and documents, and on letterhead, business cards, and so on. Along with the license comes a CCSA logo sheet, which includes camera-ready artwork. (Note: Before using any of the artwork, you must sign and return a licensing agreement that indicates that you'll abide by its terms and conditions.)

Many people believe that the benefits of CCSA certification go well beyond the perks that Check Point provides to newly anointed members of this elite group. I'm starting to see more job listings that request or require applicants to have a CCSA, CCSE, and so on, and many individuals who complete the program can qualify for increases in pay and/or responsibility. As an official recognition of hard work and broad knowledge, one of the CCSA credentials is a badge of honor in many IT organizations.

How to Prepare for an Exam

Preparing for any Check Point related test (including "Check Point Certified Security Administrator") requires that you obtain and study materials designed to provide comprehensive information about the products (and their capabilities) that will appear on the specific exam for which you are preparing. The following list of materials will help you study and prepare:

➤ The Check Point FireWall-1 product CD includes comprehensive online documentation and related materials; it should be a primary resource when you are preparing for the test.

➤ The exam preparation materials, practice tests, and self-assessment exams on the Check Point Educational Services page at **www.checkpoint.com/services/ education**.

➤ The exam preparation advice, practice tests, questions of the day, and discussion groups on the **ExamCram.com** e-learning and certification destination Web site (**www.examcram.com**).

In addition, you'll probably find any or all of the following materials useful in your quest for Check Point FireWall-1 expertise:

➤ *Check Point Authorized Product Training*—Hands-on classroom training for the Check Point certifications. Check Point has several ATCs (authorized training centers) available across the United States and the rest of the world for teaching Check Point material.

➤ *Study guides*—More and more publishers—including The Coriolis Group— offer certification titles. The Coriolis Group series includes the following:

➤ *The Exam Cram series*—These books give you information about the material you need to know to pass the tests.

➤ *The Exam Prep series*—These books provide a greater level of detail than the *Exam Cram* books and are designed to teach you everything you need to know from an exam perspective. Each book comes with a CD that contains interactive practice exams in a variety of testing formats.

Together, the two series make an ideal pair.

➤ *Classroom training*—Check Point Authorized Training Centers (ATCs), available throughout the world, offer extensive training classes for Check Point products. To locate an ATC in your area, visit Check Point's ATC Web site at **www.checkpoint.com/services/education/atcprogram/atc_locations/ locations.html**.

➤ *Other publications*—The resource sections at the end of each chapter should give you an idea of where I think you should look for further discussion.

This set of required and recommended materials represents a nonpareil collection of sources and resources for Check Point FireWall-1 and related topics. I anticipate that you'll find that this book belongs in this company.

About this Book

Each topical *Exam Cram* chapter follows a regular structure, along with graphical cues about important or useful information. Here's the structure of a typical chapter:

➤ *Opening hotlists*—Each chapter begins with a list of the terms, tools, and techniques that you must learn and understand before you can be fully conversant with the chapter's subject matter. I follow the hotlists with one or two introductory paragraphs to set the stage for the rest of the chapter.

➤ *Topical coverage*—After the opening hotlists, each chapter covers a series of topics related to the chapter's subject title. Throughout this section, I highlight topics or concepts likely to appear on a test using a special Exam Alert layout, like this:

 This is what an Exam Alert looks like. Normally, an Exam Alert stresses concepts, terms, software, or activities that are likely to relate to one or more certification test questions. For that reason, I think any information found offset in Exam Alert format is worthy of unusual attentiveness on your part.

Pay close attention to material flagged as an Exam Alert; although all the information in this book pertains to what you need to know to pass the exam, I flag certain items that are especially important. You'll find what appears in the meat of each chapter to be worth knowing, too, when preparing for the test. Because this book's material is very condensed, I recommend that you use this book along with other resources to achieve the maximum benefit.

In addition to the Exam Alerts, I have provided tips that will help you build a better foundation for Check Point FireWall-1 knowledge. Although the information might not be on the exam, it is certainly related and will help you become a better test-taker.

This is how tips are formatted. Keep your eyes open for these, and you'll become a Check Point FireWall-1 guru in no time!

➤ *Practice questions*—Although I talk about test questions and topics throughout the book, a section at the end of each chapter presents a series of mock test questions and explanations of both correct and incorrect answers. I also try to point out especially tricky questions by using a special icon, like this:

Ordinarily, this icon flags the presence of a particularly devious inquiry, if not an outright trick question. Trick questions are calculated to be answered incorrectly if not read carefully more than once. Although they're not ubiquitous, such questions make occasional appearances on the Check Point tests. That's why I say test questions are as much about reading comprehension as they are about knowing your material inside out and backwards.

➤ *Details and resources*—Every chapter ends with a section titled "Need to Know More?". This section provides direct pointers to Check Point and third-party resources offering more details on the chapter's subject. In addition, this section tries to rank or at least rate the quality and thoroughness of the topic's coverage by each resource. If you find a resource you like in this collection, use it, but don't feel compelled to use all the resources. On the other hand, I recommend only resources I use on a regular basis, so none of my recommendations will be a waste of your time or money (but purchasing them all at once probably represents an expense that many professionals might find hard to justify).

The bulk of the book follows this chapter structure slavishly, but there are a few other elements that I'd like to point out. Chapter 12 is a sample test that provides a good review of the material presented throughout the book to ensure you're ready for the exam. Chapter 13 is an answer key to the sample test that appears in Chapter 12. In addition, you'll find a handy glossary and an index.

Finally, the tear-out Cram Sheet attached next to the inside front cover of this *Exam Cram* book represents a condensed and compiled collection of facts and tips that I think you should memorize before taking the test. Because you can dump this information out of your head onto a piece of paper before taking the exam, you can master this information by brute force—you need to remember it only long enough to write it down when you walk into the test room. You might even want to look at it in the car or in the lobby of the testing center just before you walk in to take the test.

How to Use this Book

I've structured the topics in this book to build on one another. Therefore, some topics in later chapters make more sense after you've read earlier chapters. That's why I suggest you read this book from front to back for your initial test preparation. If you need to brush up on a topic or you have to bone up for a second try, use the index or table of contents to go straight to the topics and questions that you need to study. Beyond helping you prepare for the test, I think you'll find this book useful as a tightly focused reference to some of the most important aspects of Check Point FireWall-1.

Given all the book's elements and its specialized focus, I've tried to create a tool that will help you prepare for—and pass—Check Point Exam 156-205. Please share your feedback about the book, especially if you have ideas about how I can improve it for future test-takers.

Send your questions or comments to **learn@examcram.com**. Please remember to include the title of the book in your message; otherwise, it won't be clear book you're writing about. Also, be sure to check out the Web pages at **www.examcram.com**, where you'll find information updates, commentary, and certification information.

Thanks, and enjoy the book!

Self-Assessment

The reason I included a Self-Assessment in this *Exam Cram* book is to help you evaluate your readiness to tackle CCSA certification. It should also help you understand what you need to know to master the topic of this book—namely, Exam 156-205, "Check Point Certified System Administrator." But before you tackle this Self-Assessment, let's talk about concerns you may face when pursuing a CCSA for Check Point FireWall-1, and what an ideal CCSA candidate might look like.

CCSAs in the Real World

In the next section, I describe an ideal CCSA candidate, knowing full well that only a few real candidates will meet this ideal. In fact, the description of the ideal candidate might seem downright scary, especially with the changes that have been made to the program to support Check Point FireWall-1. But take heart. Although the requirements to obtain a CCSA might seem formidable, they are by no means impossible to meet. However, be keenly aware that it does take time, involves some expense, and requires real effort to get through the process.

Increasing numbers of people are attaining Check Point certifications, so the goal is within reach. You can get all the real-world motivation you need from knowing that many others have gone before you, so you will be able to follow in their footsteps. If you're willing to tackle the process seriously and do what it takes to obtain the necessary experience and knowledge, you can take—and pass—the certification test necessary to obtain a CCSA. In fact, *Exam Crams* and the companion *Exam Preps* are designed to make it as easy on you as possible to prepare for these exams. Coriolis has also greatly expanded its Web site, **www.examcram.com**, to provide a host of resources to help you prepare for the complexities of various certifications.

Besides CCSA, other Check Point certifications include:

➤ CCSE, which is aimed at Check Point administrators who want to take the next step in certification. To become a CCSE, you need to pass one exam in addition to the CCSA exam.

➤ Other Check Point certifications, whose requirements vary depending on the certification you wish to achieve.

The Ideal Check Point CCSA Candidate

Just to give you some idea of what an ideal CCSA candidate is like, here are some relevant statistics about the background and experience such an individual might have. Don't worry if you don't meet or even come close to meeting the following qualifications—this is a far from ideal world, and where you fall short is simply where you'll have more work to do:

➤ Academic or professional training in network theory, concepts, and operations. This includes everything from networking media and transmission techniques to network operating systems, services, and applications.

➤ Three-plus years of professional networking experience, including experience with Ethernet, Token Ring, modems, and other networking media. This must include installation, configuration, upgrading, and troubleshooting experience.

➤ At least one year of network security experience, either hands-on or in theory, and an understanding of how firewalls and network security are implemented into a wide area network (WAN).

➤ A strong knowledge of installing Windows NT, Solaris, or other Unix operating systems.

➤ A thorough understanding of key networking protocols, addressing, and name resolution, most importantly TCP/IP.

➤ Familiarity with TCP/IP-based services, including HTTP (Web servers), FTP, Telnet, DNS, and HTTPS.

➤ Some hands-on experience working with the Check Point GUIs (graphical user interfaces), including creating objects, creating rules, viewing log files, and examining the system status. An ideal candidate knows how FireWall-1 works and is familiar with the Check Point product lines.

Fundamentally, this boils down to a bachelor's degree in computer science plus three years' experience working in a position involving network design, installation, configuration, and maintenance. I believe that well under half of all certification candidates meet these requirements, and, in fact, most meet less than half of these requirements—at least, when they begin the certification process. But because all the people who already have been certified have survived this ordeal, you can survive it, too—especially if you heed what this Self-Assessment can tell you about what you already know and what you need to learn.

Put Yourself to the Test

The following series of questions and observations is designed to help you figure out how much work you must do to attain Check Point certification and the kinds of resources you might consult on your quest. Be absolutely honest in your answers, or you'll end up wasting money on exams you're not yet ready to take. There are no right or wrong answers, only steps along the path to certification. Only you can decide where you really belong in the broad spectrum of aspiring candidates.

Two points should be clear from the outset, however:

➤ Even a modest background in computer science will be helpful.

➤ Hands-on experience with Check Point products and technologies is an essential ingredient to certification success.

Educational Background

1. Have you ever taken any computer-related classes? [Yes or No]

   If Yes, proceed to Question 2; if No, proceed to Question 4.

2. Have you taken any classes on computer operating systems? [Yes or No]

   If Yes, you will probably be able to handle Check Point's installation and configuration options. You will be able to install the software, management clients, and other programs, as well as troubleshoot these programs after installation.

   If No, consider some basic reading in this area. I strongly recommend a good general operating systems book, such as *Operating System Concepts, 6th Edition*, by Abraham Silberschatz, Peter Baer Galvin, and Greg Gagne (John Wiley & Sons, 2001, ISBN 0-471-36414-2). If this title doesn't appeal to you, check out reviews for other, similar titles at your favorite online bookstore.

3. Have you taken any networking concepts or technologies classes? [Yes or No]

   If Yes, you will probably be able to handle Check Point's networking terminology, concepts, and technologies (brace yourself for frequent departures from normal usage). If you're rusty, brush up on basic networking concepts and terminology, especially networking media, transmission types, the OSI Reference Model, and networking technologies, such as Ethernet, Fast Ethernet, and WAN links.

If No, you might want to read one or two books in this topic area. The two best books that I know of are *Computer Networks*, *3rd Edition*, by Andrew S. Tanenbaum (Prentice-Hall, 1996, ISBN 0-13-349945-6) and *Computer Networks and Internets*, *2nd Edition*, by Douglas E. Comer and Ralph E. Droms (Prentice-Hall, 1999, ISBN 0-130-83617-6).

4. Have you ever read any material about network security and firewalls? [Yes or No]

If Yes, review these materials; early in this book, I cover a lot of the general concepts related to firewalls and network security. If you understand how firewalls work and have evolved, you will have a head start on understanding FireWall-1.

If No, you might want to read at least one title in the network security area. A title that I recommend is *Firewalls 24seven*, by Matthew Strebe and Charles L. Perkins (Sybex, 1999, ISBN 0-7821-2529-8).

Hands-on Experience

The most important key to success on all of the Check Point tests is hands-on experience. If I leave you with only one realization after taking this Self-Assessment, it should be that there's no substitute for time spent installing, configuring, and using the various Check Point products upon which you'll be tested repeatedly and in depth.

5. Have you installed, configured, and worked with:

➤ Windows NT? [Yes or No]

If Yes, make sure you are familiar with the Control Panel, especially Add/Remove Programs and Services.

If No, you should obtain a copy of this software and install it on a computer. It would also be beneficial to have a second computer available; the second computer can function as a host behind the firewall for testing purposes.

➤ Sun Solaris? [Yes or No]

If Yes, make sure you understand navigation in the command line and some of the basic command-line utilities.

If No, you might be able to obtain a copy of Solaris. Solaris is free, unlike Microsoft NT, but it takes a bit of skill and experience to install and configure properly. If you have never used Solaris or any other Unix operating systems, it might be easier to use this book with Windows NT instead of Solaris.

If you have the funds, or your employer will pay your way, consider taking a class at an authorized training center (ATC). In addition to classroom exposure to the topic of your choice, you get a copy of the software that is the focus of your course, along with a trial version of whatever operating system it needs, with the training materials for that class.

Before you even think about taking any Check Point exam, make sure you've spent enough time with the related software to understand how it is installed and configured, how to maintain such an installation, and how to troubleshoot the software when things go wrong. This will help you in the exam and in real life!

Testing Your Exam-Readiness

Whether you attend a formal class on a specific topic to get ready for an exam or use written materials to study on your own, some preparation for the Check Point certification exams is essential. At $150 a try, pass or fail, you want to do everything you can to pass on your first try. That's where studying comes in.

I have included a practice exam in this book; if you don't score that well on the practice test, you can study more and then tackle the test again. If you still don't hit a score of at least 80 percent on the practice test, you'll want to investigate other practice test resources.

For any given subject, consider taking a class if you've tackled self-study materials, taken the exam, and failed anyway. Sometimes, the opportunity to interact with an instructor and fellow students can make all the difference in the world, if you can afford that privilege. For information about Check Point classes, visit the Check Point Authorized Training Center (ATC) Program page at **www.checkpoint.com/services/education/atcprogram** for Check Point authorized training centers.

If you can't afford to take a class, visit the Check Point Study Aids page at **www.checkpoint.com/services/education/certification/studyaids.html**. This page offers supplemental training information that Check Point has offered free of charge to people who want to take advantage of it.

6. Have you taken a practice exam on your chosen test subject? [Yes or No]

If Yes, and you scored 80 percent or better, you're probably ready to tackle the real thing. If your score isn't above that threshold, keep at it until you break that barrier.

If No, obtain all the free and low-budget practice tests you can find and get to work. Keep at it until you can break the 80 percent threshold comfortably.

When it comes to assessing your test readiness, there is no better way than to take a good-quality practice exam and pass with a score of 80 percent or better. When I'm preparing myself, I shoot for 80-plus percent, just to leave room for the "weirdness factor" that sometimes shows up on exams.

Assessing Readiness for Exam 156-205

In addition to the general exam-readiness information in the previous section, you can take a number of actions to prepare for the Check Point Certified Security Administrator exam. Consider signing up for the *Exam Cram Insider* newsletter at **www.examcram.com** (or you can sign up by sending a blank email message to **subscribe-ec@mars.coriolis.com**). I also suggest that you join an active CCSA mailing list. One of the better ones is an email discussion group that you can join by sending an email to **checkpointstudy@egroups.com**.

You can also cruise the Web looking for *brain dumps* (recollections of test topics and experiences recorded by others) to help you anticipate topics you're likely to encounter on the test. The CCSA mailing list is a good place to ask where useful brain dumps are located.

You can't be sure that a brain dump's author can provide correct answers. Thus, use the questions to guide your studies, but don't rely on the answers in a brain dump to lead you to the truth. Double-check everything you find in any brain dump.

Check Point exam mavens also recommend checking the Check Point Knowledge Base, which is available at **support.checkpoint.com,** for technical support issues that relate to your exam's topics. Although Check Point does offer Knowledge Base support to the public, detailed support requires either purchasing support or being a certified Check Point professional.

Onward, through the Fog!

After you've assessed your readiness, undertaken the right background studies, obtained the hands-on experience that will help you understand the products and technologies at work, and reviewed the many sources of information to help you prepare for an exam, you'll be ready to take a round of practice tests. When your scores come back positive enough to get you through the exam, you're ready to go after the real thing. If you follow this assessment regime, you'll not only know what you need to study, but you'll be able to gauge when you're ready to schedule a test date with VUE. Good luck!

Check Point
Certification Exams

Terms you'll need to understand:

✓ Radio button
✓ Checkbox
✓ Multiple-choice question formats
✓ Fixed-length tests
✓ Process of elimination

Techniques you'll need to master:

✓ Assessing your exam-readiness
✓ Preparing to take a certification exam
✓ Practicing (to make perfect)
✓ Making the best use of the testing software
✓ Budgeting your time
✓ Saving the hardest questions until last
✓ Guessing (as a last resort)

Exam taking is not something that most people anticipate eagerly, no matter how well prepared they might be. In most cases, familiarity helps offset test anxiety. In plain English, this means you probably won't be as nervous when you take your fourth or fifth Check Point certification exam as you'll be when you take your first one.

Whether it's your first certification exam or your tenth, understanding the details of taking the exam (how much time to spend on questions, the environment you'll be in, and so on) will help you concentrate on the material rather than on the setting. Likewise, mastering a few basic exam-taking skills should help you recognize—and perhaps even outfox—some of the tricks and snares you're bound to find in some exam questions.

This chapter, besides explaining the exam environment and software, describes some proven exam-taking strategies that you should be able to use to your advantage.

Assessing Exam-Readiness

I strongly recommend that you read through and take the Self-Assessment included with this book (it appears just before this chapter, in fact). This will help you compare your knowledge base to the requirements for obtaining a CCSA, and it will also help you identify parts of your background or experience that might be in need of improvement, enhancement, or further learning. If you get the right set of basics under your belt, obtaining Check Point certification will be that much easier.

Once you've gone through the Self-Assessment, you can remedy any topical areas where your background or experience might not measure up to an ideal certification candidate. But you can also tackle subject matter for individual tests at the same time, so you can continue making progress while you're catching up in some areas.

After you've worked through an *Exam Cram*, read the supplementary materials, and taken the practice test at the end of the book, you'll have a pretty clear idea of when you should be ready to take the real exam. Although I strongly recommend that you keep practicing until your score tops the 75 percent mark, 80 percent would be a good goal to give yourself some margin for error in a real exam situation (where stress will play more of a role than when you practice). Once you hit that point, you should be ready to go. But if you get through the practice exam in this book without attaining that score, you should keep taking practice tests and studying the materials until you get there. You'll find more pointers on how to study and prepare in the Self-Assessment. But now, on to the exam itself!

The Exam Situation

When you arrive at the testing center where you scheduled your exam, you'll need to sign in with an exam coordinator. He or she will ask you to show two forms of identification, one of which must be a photo ID. After you've signed in and your time slot arrives, you'll be asked to deposit any books, bags, or other items you brought with you. Then, you'll be escorted into a closed room. All exams are completely closed book. In fact, you will not be permitted to take anything with you into the testing area, but you will be furnished with a blank sheet of paper and a pen or, in some cases, an erasable plastic sheet and an erasable pen. Before the exam, you should memorize as much of the important material as you can, so you can write that information on the blank sheet as soon as you are seated in front of the computer. You can refer to this piece of paper anytime you like during the test, but you'll have to surrender the sheet when you leave the room.

You will have some time to compose yourself, to record this information, and to take a sample orientation exam before you begin the real thing. I suggest you take the orientation test before taking your first exam, but because they're all more or less identical in layout, behavior, and controls, you probably won't need to do this more than once.

Typically, the room will be furnished with anywhere from one to half a dozen computers, and each workstation will be separated from the others by dividers designed to keep you from seeing what's happening on someone else's computer. Most test rooms feature a wall with a large picture window. This permits the exam coordinator to monitor the room, to prevent exam-takers from talking to one another, and to observe anything out of the ordinary that might go on. The exam coordinator will have preloaded the appropriate Check Point certification exam—for this book, that's Exam 156-205—and you'll be permitted to start as soon as you're seated in front of the computer.

All Check Point certification exams allow a certain maximum amount of time in which to complete your work (this time is indicated on the exam by an on-screen counter/clock, so you can check the time remaining whenever you like). All Check Point certification exams are computer generated. The questions are constructed not only to check your mastery of basic facts and figures about Check Point FireWall-1, but they also require you to evaluate one or more sets of circumstances or requirements. Often, you'll be asked to give more than one answer to a question. Likewise, you might be asked to select the best or most effective solution to a problem from a range of choices, all of which technically are correct. Taking the exam is quite an adventure, and it involves real thinking. This book shows you what to expect and how to deal with the potential problems, puzzles, and predicaments.

In the next section, you'll learn more about how Check Point test questions look and how they must be answered.

Exam Layout and Design

Check Point certification exams consist of multiple-choice questions. A multiple-choice question might have up to five or six potential answers, or it might simply be a true or false question. A typical test question is depicted in Question 1. It's a multiple-choice question that requires you to select a single correct answer. Following the question is a brief summary of each potential answer and why it is either right or wrong.

Question 1

What subfolder must the sync.conf file be placed in?

○ a. bin

○ b. conf

○ c. 4.1

○ d. state

○ e. tmp

○ f. database

Answer b is correct. The sync.conf file must be placed in the %systemroot%/ FW1/4.1/conf directory in a Windows NT environment. In a Unix environment, the sync.conf file must be placed in the $FWIR/conf directory. The conf directory holds all of the firewall configuration information. The rest of the subdirectories are valid FireWall-1 directories, but they serve different purposes. Answer a is incorrect because the bin folder holds the executable files of FireWall-1. Answer c is incorrect because the 4.1 folder is used as a parent folder to such subfolders as bin and conf. Answers d, e, and f are incorrect because the state, tmp, and database folders hold firewall state, temporary files, and database files, respectively.

This sample question format corresponds closely to the Check Point certification exam format—the only difference on the exam is that questions are not followed by answer keys. To select an answer, you would position the cursor over the radio button next to the answer. Then, click the mouse button to select the answer.

Let's examine a question where one or more answers are possible. This type of question provides checkboxes rather than radio buttons for marking all appropriate selections.

Question 2

Jane needs to add a mail server behind her network. She installs her mail server using the IP address of 10.0.0.105. Jane has assigned a valid IP address to the mail server, created an object for the mail server, and created the MX record in her DNS server. What else must Jane do to begin sending and receiving mail? [Check all correct answers]

❏ a. Nothing

❏ b. Enable NAT on the mail server object

❏ c. Set the NAT mode to hide

❏ d. Set the NAT mode to static

❏ e. Insert the valid IP address into the NAT field of the object

❏ f. Restart the mail server

❏ g. Reinstall the rule base

Answers b, d, e, and g are correct. Before the mail server will be able to communicate with the Internet, Jane must first enable NAT for the object, set the NAT mode to static so that it has its own IP address, type the valid IP address that the object will use, and reinstall the rule base. Answer a is incorrect because there are additional steps that must take place. Answer c is incorrect because using hide mode will not give the mail server a one-to-one (one invalid to one valid) IP address translation. Answer f is incorrect because the mail server does not require a restart.

For this particular question, four answers are required. Notice that picking the right answers also means knowing why the other answers are wrong.

Check Point's Testing Format

Currently, Check Point exams employ a very straightforward testing approach—the fixed-length test approach. The Check Point Certified Security Administrator exam consists of a total of 99 questions. If you take this test in any of the following countries, you have a total of 90 minutes to complete the exam: Australia, Bermuda, Canada, Japan, New Zealand, Ireland, South Africa, United Kingdom, and the United States. In all other countries, a total of 120 minutes is given to complete the exam.

Question-Handling Strategies

A well-known principle when taking fixed-length exams is to first read over the entire exam from start to finish while answering only those questions you feel absolutely sure about. On subsequent passes, you can dive into more complex questions more deeply, knowing how many such questions you have left.

Fortunately, the Check Point exam software for fixed-length tests makes the multiple-visit approach easy to implement. At the top-left corner of each question is a checkbox that permits you to mark the question for a later visit.

Note: Marking questions makes review easier, but you can return to any question by clicking the Forward or Back button repeatedly.

As you read each question, if you answer only those you're sure of and mark for review those that you're not sure of, you can keep working through a decreasing list of questions as you answer the trickier ones in order.

 There's at least one potential benefit to reading the exam over completely before answering the trickier questions: Sometimes, information supplied in later questions sheds light on earlier questions. At other times, information you read in later questions might jog your memory about Check Point FireWall-1 facts, figures, or behavior that helps you answer earlier questions. Either way, you'll come out ahead if you defer those questions about which you're not absolutely sure.

Here are some question-handling strategies that apply to fixed-length tests. Use them if you have the chance:

➤ When returning to a question after your initial read-through, read every word again—otherwise, your mind can fall quickly into a rut. Sometimes, revisiting a question after turning your attention elsewhere lets you see something you missed, but the strong tendency is to see what you've seen before. Try to avoid that tendency at all costs.

➤ If you return to a question more than twice, try to articulate to yourself what you don't understand about the question, why answers don't appear to make sense, or what appears to be missing. If you chew on the subject awhile, your subconscious might provide the details you lack, or you might notice a "trick" that points to the right answer.

As you work your way through the exam, another counter that Check Point provides will come in handy—the number of questions completed and questions outstanding. For fixed-length and short-form tests, it's wise to budget your time by making sure that you've completed one-quarter of the questions one-quarter of the way through the exam period, and three-quarters of the questions three-quarters of the way through.

If you're not finished when only five minutes remain, use that time to guess your way through any remaining questions. Remember, guessing is potentially more valuable than not answering, because blank answers are always wrong, but a guess might turn out to be right. If you don't have a clue about any of the remaining questions, pick answers at random, or choose all a's, b's, and so on. The ultimate goal is to submit an exam for scoring that has an answer for every question.

At the very end of your exam period, you're better off guessing than leaving questions unanswered.

For questions that take only a single answer, usually two or three of the answers will be obviously incorrect, and two of the answers will be plausible—of course, only one can be correct. Unless the answer leaps out at you (if it does, reread the question to look for a trick; sometimes, those are the ones you're most likely to get wrong), begin the process of answering by eliminating the answers that are most obviously wrong.

Almost always, at least one answer out of the possible choices for a question can be eliminated immediately because it matches one of the following conditions:

➤ The answer does not apply to the situation.

➤ The answer describes a nonexistent issue, an invalid option, or an imaginary state.

After you eliminate all answers that are obviously wrong, you can apply your retained knowledge to eliminate further answers. Look for items that sound correct but refer to actions, commands, or features that are not present or not available in the situation that the question describes.

If you're still faced with a blind guess among two or more potentially correct answers, reread the question. Try to picture how each of the possible remaining answers would alter the situation. Be especially sensitive to terminology; sometimes, the choice of words (*remove* instead of *disable*) can make the difference between a right answer and a wrong one.

Only when you've exhausted your ability to eliminate answers, but remain unclear about which of the remaining possibilities is correct, should you guess at an answer. An unanswered question offers you no points, but guessing gives you at least some chance of getting a question right; just don't be too hasty when making a blind guess. Wait until the last round of reviewing marked questions (just as you're about to run out of time or out of unanswered questions) before you start making guesses. Guessing should be your technique of last resort!

Numerous questions assume that the default behavior of a particular utility is in effect. If you know the defaults and understand what they mean, this knowledge will help you cut through many Gordian knots.

Mastering the Inner Game

In the final analysis, knowledge breeds confidence, and confidence breeds success. If you study the materials in this book carefully and review all the practice questions at the end of each chapter, you should become aware of those areas where additional learning and study are required.

After you work your way through the book, take the practice exam in the back of the book. Taking this test will provide a reality check and help you identify areas to study further. Make sure you follow up and review materials related to the questions you miss on the practice exam before scheduling a real exam. Only when you've covered that ground and feel comfortable with the whole scope of the practice exam should you set an exam appointment. Only if you score 80 percent or better should you proceed to the real thing (otherwise, obtain some additional practice tests so you can keep trying until you hit this magic number).

If you take a practice exam and don't score at least 80 to 85 percent correct, you'll want to practice further. Check Point provides links to practice exam providers and also offers self-assessment exams at **www.checkpoint.com/services/education/certification**. You should also check out **ExamCram.com** for downloadable practice questions.

Armed with the information in this book and with the determination to augment your knowledge, you should be able to pass the certification exam. However, you need to work at it, or you'll spend the exam fee more than once before you finally pass. If you prepare seriously, you should do well. I are confident that you can do it!

The next section covers other sources you can use to prepare for the Check Point certification exams.

Additional Resources

A good source of information about Check Point certification exams comes from Check Point itself. Because its products and technologies—and the exams that go with them—change frequently, the best place to go for exam-related information is online.

If you haven't already visited the Check Point Educational Services site, do so right now. The Check Point Educational Services home page resides at **www.checkpoint.com/services/education** (see Figure 1.1).

Note: This page might not be there by the time you read this, or it might be replaced by something new and different, because information changes regularly on the Check Point site. If this happens, please read the sidebar titled "Coping with Change on the Web."

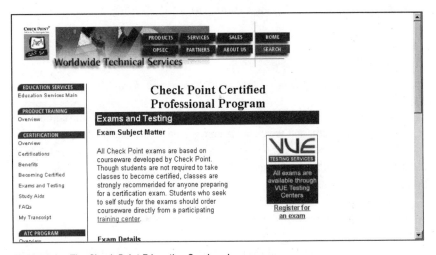

Figure 1.1   The Check Point Education Services home page.

Coping with Change on the Web

Sooner or later, all the information I've shared with you about the Check Point Educational Services pages and the other Web-based resources mentioned throughout the rest of this book will go stale or be replaced by newer information. In some cases, the URLs you find here might lead you to their replacements; in other cases, the URLs will go nowhere, leaving you with the dreaded "404 File not found" error message. When that happens, don't give up.

There's always a way to find what you want on the Web if you're willing to invest some time and energy. Most large or complex Web sites—and Check Point's qualifies on both counts—offer a search engine. On all of Check Point's Web pages, a

Search button appears along the top edge of the page. As long as you can get to Check Point's site (it should stay at **www.checkpoint.com** for a long time), use this tool to help you find what you need.

The more focused you can make a search request, the more likely the results will include information you can use. For example, you can search for the string

```
"training and certification"
```

to produce a lot of data about the subject in general, but if you're looking for the preparation guide for Exam 156-205, "Check Point Certified Security Administrator," you'll be more likely to get there quickly if you use a search string similar to the following:

```
"Exam 156-205" AND "preparation guide"
```

Likewise, if you want to find the training and certification downloads, try a search string such as this:

```
"training and certification" AND "download page"
```

Finally, feel free to use general search tools—such as **www.search.com**, **www.altavista.com**, and **www.excite.com**—to look for related information. Although Check Point offers great information about its certification exams online, there are plenty of third-party sources of information and assistance that need not follow Check Point's party line. Therefore, if you can't find something where this book says it lives, intensify your search.

Introduction to FireWall-1

Terms you'll need to understand:

✓ Packet filtering

✓ Application gateway (proxy)

✓ Stateful inspection

✓ INSPECT Engine

✓ Firewall daemon

✓ Communication-derived state

✓ Application-derived state

✓ Information manipulation

✓ Management Module

✓ Network address translation (NAT)

Techniques you'll need to master:

✓ Understanding the pros and cons of packet filtering and application gateways

✓ Knowing the benefits and features of stateful inspection

✓ Understanding the components of the INSPECT Engine

✓ Understanding why a packet is allowed, rejected, or dropped

✓ Learning the functions of the Firewall and Management Modules

✓ Learning how Check Point licensing works

✓ Knowing what happens when you exceed your license limit

Rarely can you pick up a paper or watch the news without hearing something about another company being attacked by hackers, crackers, "script kiddies," and the like. Port scanning, software bugs, and forcible entry are just a few of the ways attackers can penetrate networks. Types of attacks vary, but common ones are denial of service (overloading a server with traffic), defacing Web sites, viruses, and Trojan horses. A common mistake with many smaller to mid-size companies is the "not us" mentality. Many small to mid-size companies believe that they are too small to interest attackers; however, companies that take that stance are often the target of hacker attempts precisely because of their belief.

Over the years, network security has been a cat-and-mouse game—for every door that's secured, someone's picking the lock of another. Therefore, corporate environments must stay abreast of the latest security leaks and patches or face the possibility of intrusion. Many methods have been developed in an attempt to keep out unwanted "guests." Of all the different methods of intrusion protection, the implementation of firewalls has become the most popular. In this chapter, I cover the most popular methods of network firewall implementations, several types of attacks that are used by hackers, how FireWall-1 handles these attacks, and what other features are available using FireWall-1. I also discuss in brief how licensing works for FireWall-1.

Defining Firewalls

A *firewall* can best be defined as a protective shield around an internal network. One way to look at it is to compare a firewall to the walls of a castle. The castle walls protect the inside of the castle and only folks deemed "friendly" are allowed to pass. The same can be said of a firewall—only traffic that has been *explicitly* allowed can pass into the internal network.

Basically, a firewall examines each network packet to determine whether to forward it toward its destination. A firewall is often installed in a specially designated computer separate from the rest of the network so that no incoming request can gain direct access to private network resources. This computer is often defined in networking terms as a *gateway*.

On a network, traffic can come in many formats. Firewall rules can be built based on protocols, users, networks, specific IP addresses, ports, and other firewalls as well as other criteria, such as time of day. How, when, and why traffic is allowed to pass is based on an administrator's decisions. With this in mind, you should create a strong rule base when you configure a firewall. Each rule must be implemented carefully to ensure that each rule does not create any type of security hazard.

There are several protocols used for network communications, however most firewalls focus on one particular protocol—TCP/IP. TCP/IP is the most popular network protocol used to connect to the Internet and other corporate networks. TCP/IP works by using *data packet* transmittals. A *packet* is a unit of data that is routed between an origin and a destination on the Internet or any other packet-switched network. In addition to containing the data, the packet is also responsible for passing the intended destination address of the data. Devices connected to the network must decide whether to accept or refuse a packet based on its address, also known as the *IP address*. Understanding what types of attacks a firewall can prevent and the limitations of a firewall are important in understanding how much planning and effort goes into securing a network. In the next section, I discuss some of the attacks that can occur.

Note: It is important to have a good understanding of how IP data packets are transferred. In addition, you need to understand the OSI (Open Systems Interconnect) Reference Model and how it is structured.

Types of Attacks

Although an entire book could be written about the various methods of penetrating a network (and there are many books out there on the topic), this section briefly discusses some common types of attacks. In particular, let's take a look at port scanning, denial of service (DoS), impersonation, and man-in-the-middle.

Port Scanning

Many tools are available to hackers that enable them to determine which sockets are open for network connection requests. These tools try each port incrementally and create a report for the hacker that indicates which ports are open and which ports are refusing connection. *Port scanning* reveals several bits of information—it can tell you what type of operating system is in use; whether TCP/IP services, such as Telnet and FTP, are open; and which applications (for certain applications) use specific ports, such as Citrix. Armed with that type of information, a hacker can begin to dig into a network.

Denial of Service (DoS)

Denial of service is fairly self-explanatory. In this type of attack, a hacker finds a method of crippling communications to a network. There are several methods of issuing a denial of service attack; some common ones include:

➤ Ping of death

➤ DNS redirection

➤ SNMP reconfiguration

➤ ICMP flooding

Note: See the first, third, and fourth references in the "Need to Know More?" section at the end of this chapter for resources that contain more in-depth information about DoS attacks.

Impersonation

Impersonation is a method of attack that takes the identity of another computer that is trusted by a network. The purpose of this type of attack is to convince the other machines on a network to pass private information based on the fact that they assume the impersonated workstation can be trusted.

Man-in-the-Middle

Man-in-the-middle is another form of the impersonation attack. In this case, the hacker sits between two computers that are in communication. When one of the computers opens communications with the other, the hacker intercepts the traffic. The hacker then opens up its own line of communication to the intended host, acting as if it were the source of the communication.

Limitations of Firewalls

Short of disconnecting yourself, there is no way that a network can make itself completely secure. There is a common misconception that once a firewall has been put up between a private network and the rest of the world, all potential security problems have been alleviated. Although many administrators would like this to be true, the hard fact is that it is not.

As discussed, the purpose of a firewall is to allow traffic into a network that has been specifically designated in a rule base. Think about that for a second—allowing traffic into a network that has been specifically designated. Now, consider the types of traffic you can allow into your network. For instance, here are some common forms of traffic, such as:

➤ FTP (File Transfer Protocol)

➤ SMTP (Simple Mail Transfer Protocol)

➤ DNS (Domain Name System)

For illustrative purposes, let's look at FTP. In FireWall-1, you can specify the IP addresses of workstations and networks as *network objects*. Let's say you have a server that needs to be accessed by one of your partners. So, you create a rule in your rule base allowing only the IP address of your partner's network to access your FTP server.

Do you see the potential security hazards here? What if someone on your partner's network happens to stumble upon this and is not authorized (by his or her employer) to connect to your server? What would stop them? Worse yet, what about a hacker sitting on the Internet watching the traffic passing between your respective networks? The hacker could very easily spoof your partner's network and access the FTP server.

The point is that although firewalls offer a huge advantage in network security, they can't save networks from every form of attack. Your job as an administrator is to stay on top of new possible security breaches and solutions so that you can keep security attacks from occurring on your network. Fortunately, many organizations, user groups, and newsletters are available to help you to stay on top of the latest security issues and to keep your network secure.

Firewall Methods

As an administrator, you need to know about the following three major firewall technologies:

➤ Packet filtering

➤ Proxy servers (also knows as Application layer gateways)

➤ Stateful inspection firewalls

Different firewalls work on different layers of the IP protocol stack, thereby offering varying layers of security and manageability. Each type of firewall offers its own set of pros and cons. Therefore, the next few sections describe what each firewall can offer you as an administrator as well as point out each type's weaknesses.

Packet Filtering

Packet filtering was one of the earliest forms of firewalls; it was an efficient way of filtering traffic coming into a network. Packet filters simply compare network protocols to a database of rules and forward all packets that meet the predefined criteria. The main advantages of packet filtering are that it is transparent to end-users, very fast compared to proxy servers, and relatively inexpensive. Because packet filtering does not depend on the Application layer, it often outperforms proxy servers. A packet-filtering firewall will examine a packet only through the first three layers (Physical, Data Link, and Network). As new forms of attacking a network developed, packet filters slowly became obsolete.

Packet filters are most often seen on routers. Because packet filters stop their analysis of the packet at the Network layer, they are incapable of understanding the purpose of a specific packet. This lack of understanding makes it easy for a hacker to penetrate the network because of the packet filter's inability to understand the context of the packets being transferred.

The main disadvantages of packet filtering are that it offers the least amount of network security, is unable to manipulate information, and is subject to IP spoofing. Packet filters became a security risk after it was realized that they could not filter traffic above port 1023. From an administrator's perspective, a packet-filtering firewall is not manageable because it is difficult to configure and monitor, and it offers very little in terms of logging.

Because it is a relatively primitive form of a firewall, the data transmittal process is pretty simple, as described in the following steps:

1. A user opens a browser and decides to visit the Coriolis Web site. The user types **www.coriolis.com**.

2. The workstation of the user sends a TCP message to the intended recipient (let's ignore the DNS portion for this example). The TCP packet will include the IP address, the port number it is trying to reach, and the port where it expects to receive a reply.

3. The packet filter takes note of the IP of the internal host, the destination host, and the associated ports.

4. Assuming a connection is made, the recipient sends the requested data back to the originator on the expected port.

5. After the source and destination host close the connection, the information is removed from the state table.

Unfortunately, with packet-filtering firewalls, the weaknesses far outweigh the advantages. Let's review some of the weaknesses of a packet-filtering firewall:

➤ *Packet filters do not offer any form of user authentication.* This is another form of security that both proxy servers and stateful inspection firewalls can offer to users. User authentication limits who inside of your network can pass through the firewall to an intended destination. This feature is useful for users who have abused company policy regarding Internet usage as well as to protect unwanted people from surfing the Internet on your connection.

➤ *Packet filters offer very poor auditing.* One of the most important aspects of your job as an administrator is to be able to monitor and audit your network. When you are speaking in terms of network security, the importance of monitoring and auditing increases tenfold. Without these capabilities, the task of administering a packet-filtering firewall can be incredibly painful.

➤ *Because packet filters are aware of protocols only up to the Network layer, they are vulnerable to attacks above it.* This leaves your network wide open to several types of attacks, and it limits your ability to properly secure your network.

➤ *A packet filter is difficult to configure.* With the preceding three cons in mind, this disadvantage should be no surprise. Most packet filters are command driven and do not notify you of potential conflicts or errors in configuration. This can cause hours of headaches and make your job that much more difficult.

In its prime, packet filters were a great way to protect a network from attacks. However, as the Internet grew and the would-be hacker became smarter, it was necessary to develop a new way to protect an internal network. The next step in this evolution was the Application layer gateway.

Application Layer Gateways (Proxies)

A proxy server is a firewall that is implemented on the Application layer. Proxies are an improvement over packet filtering because they examine packets all the way up to the Application layer. Proxies offer better security because they are fully aware of the context of the information that is being passed between the networks. Proxies take the place of the source machine and send the request for information to the intended destination using its (the proxy server's) own IP address. When the data is returned from the intended target, the information is then sent to the initiating source. Sound familiar? This is the same general concept behind the man-in-the-middle attack described earlier in this chapter.

Although more secure than packet filtering, proxy servers have many downsides. Each proxy requires a different daemon (application process), making it incredibly difficult to support new applications. Think about all the new software packages that are added to the market each day. An upgrade, or *service pack*, would need to be released almost on a weekly basis to keep up! Proxies are also considerably slower than packet filtering, because proxies require two connections.

Proxies, being application-aware, are also capable of stripping information from certain applications. For instance, an HTTP proxy could potentially be able to strip Java codes from Web pages, thus preventing unwanted Java bombs and Trojan horses. This type of security is why Application layer gateways rose in popularity with the growth of the Internet and the new technologies that came with it.

Now that you know how a proxy server works, let's look at the steps a proxy server runs through. To begin, a connection is required from the client to the firewall and from the firewall to the requested service. Then, the data-transfer process works like this:

1. A proxy server receives a request for an Internet service (such as a Web page request) from a user.

2. If it passes filtering requirements, the proxy server looks in its local cache of previously downloaded Web pages. If it finds the page, it returns the page to the user without needing to forward the request to the Internet.

3. If the page is not in the cache, the proxy server, acting as a client on behalf of the user, uses one of its own IP addresses to request the page from the server on the Internet.

4. When the page is returned, the proxy server relates it to the original request and forwards it on to the user.

The main disadvantages of proxy servers include:

➤ Each service requires its own Application layer gateway, so scalability is poor.

➤ Most proxies are not transparent to users.

➤ Proxies are vulnerable to bugs.

➤ Proxies are expensive.

➤ Proxies do not provide for RPC (remote procedure call) and UDP (User Datagram Protocol).

➤ Proxies overlook information at the lower layers.

Application layer gateways were a step in the right direction. However, their bottlenecks and inability to scale made the use of Application layer gateways very unpleasant. There had to be a better and faster way to get the job done. The next step was through stateful inspection.

Stateful Inspection

If you take one tidbit of information away from this section about stateful inspection, it should be that stateful inspection firewalls remember the state of their connections by recording the information of the communication session and storing it. One key factor is that while most packet filters allow all traffic above port 1024, a stateful inspection firewall will not. *A stateful inspection firewall will allow only traffic that it is programmed to allow.*

The biggest selling point of the Check Point FireWall-1 engine is that it is able to use the communications that pass through for tracking and decision-making purposes. I discuss how the engine works later in this chapter. How the firewall ultimately handles data is based on the firewall's ability to properly handle the data. The biggest advantage of stateful inspection is that it not only uses the information on the communications layers, but also that it uses the information from the applications themselves. Stateful inspection works in much the same way as any typical decision-making process. As you know, you need to know all the facts before you can make an educated decision. Likewise, the firewall must have all the "facts" before it can proceed.

A Check Point firewall obtains the following four kinds of information:

➤ *Communication information*—Information that comes from all the layers of the packet

➤ *Communication-derived state*—Information obtained from previous communications

➤ *Application-derived state*—The state information derived from other applications

➤ *Information manipulation*—Information obtained by analyzing the data from the preceding states

A stateful inspection firewall can give you the highest level of security, without sacrificing speed and flexibility. Let's take a deeper look into the advantages of stateful inspection firewalls.

Stateful inspection firewalls offer several advantages, but the ones you will need to know for the test are:

➤ Scalability

➤ High performance

➤ Transparency

➤ Strong security

➤ Full application awareness

Scalability

Scalability is just what you would expect—the ability to grow dynamically as the needs and requirements of network security change. This is a huge advantage over proxy servers, because this is one of the most glaring shortcomings of proxy servers. A stateful inspection firewall does not require an individual proxy for each application; therefore, it does not rely on software updates to make it aware of changes.

High Performance

In a stateful inspection firewall, the performance of the firewall is greatly increased because there is little overhead. This is achieved by the Inspection Module running within the OS kernel as well as by taking some measures—such as caching and hash tables—in order to speed up data access. Compared to an Application layer gateway, a stateful inspection firewall works at incredible speeds.

Transparency

FireWall-1 is much like a packet-filtering firewall in that it is transparent to the user. With a FireWall-1 setup, a client does not have to be installed on the internal workstations as is required by proxy servers. The comparison ends there, though, because the security features in a stateful inspection firewall are much greater.

Note: Session authentication requires client software; however, the actual connection to the firewall is still transparent to the user.

Strong Security

Strong security is another advantage of stateful inspection firewalls. This advantage stems from the fact that information is taken from all the layers of the packet, the application-derived information, and the previously processed communications. I look at some of the other features that make this much stronger than other firewall options throughout this book.

Full Application Awareness

Because FireWall-1 is aware of the information being passed up and down the OSI model, it creates greater reliability and security. Knowing the intended purpose of a packet makes it much easier to know how to handle the packet versus a packet-filtering setup, which simply follows a set of rules based on IP addresses.

Stateful Inspection and FireWall-1

With all the advantages of stateful inspection, it's easy to understand why Check Point has built its technology on this architecture. Now that you understand how stateful inspection works in concept, the next step is to see exactly how Check Point has implemented the technology. The workhorse of FireWall-1 is the Inspection Engine, which is contained within the Inspection Module.

Note: You will also see the Inspection Engine referred to as the INSPECT Engine.

The Inspection Engine can be thought of as the bouncer at a popular club. Unless you are "on the list," you will be discarded. After a packet is verified and meets the criteria of the security policy, it is allowed to pass further up the protocol stack. The Inspection Engine is loaded onto the OS kernel and resides between the Data Link and Network layers, as illustrated in Figure 2.1. The Inspection Engine resides here because the Network layer is the first layer of the actual protocol stack (the Data Link layer is the physical network interface card, or NIC). The reason behind this arrangement is to ensure that no packet will be able to pass higher into the stack unless it meets the Inspection Engine's criteria.

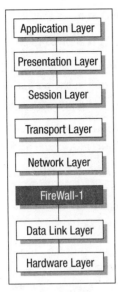

Figure 2.1   Positioning of the Inspection Engine.

Packets can be inspected in one of three directions:

➤ *Inbound*—Inbound packets are packets that are inspected as they pass through the firewall into the internal network.

➤ *Outbound*—Outbound packets are packets that are generated inside of the firewall and are inspected as they pass through the firewall to the outside world.

➤ *Eitherbound*—Eitherbound packets are packets that are inspected when both entering and exiting the internal network. The concept of eitherbound will become clear when you work with the Policy Editor in Chapter 6.

The INSPECT Engine analyzes packets by using a combination of the compiled code derived from the security policy and rule base. At this point, you're probably wondering how the engine compares the rules to the data packet. Well, within the Inspection Module is an INSPECT script that does just that. This script continually examines the data packets, comparing them to the INSPECT code and making decisions based on the rules put into place.

As the Inspection Engine continues to analyze packets as they pass through the firewall, it begins to build a list of the data it has analyzed. This action makes it possible for FireWall-1 to move much more quickly through the information over time. The other advantage to processing and storing information at such a low level in the stack is that it uses little resources, thereby freeing resources up for applications above the kernel.

The actual decision-making process is fairly simple, as depicted here:

➤ If the packet passed the FireWall-1 inspection, the packet is allowed to continue to its destination, as illustrated in Figure 2.2.

➤ If the packet does not pass the FireWall-1 inspection criteria, the packet is dropped or rejected based on the rule base, as illustrated in Figure 2.3.

Note: You need to understand the difference between a dropped packed and a rejected packet. A dropped packet does not send notification to the user, while a rejected packet does.

FireWall-1 is also capable of controlling stateless protocols, such as RPC and UDP, by storing context data. The Inspection Module is configured so that it can allow or disallow connections as necessary. With this configuration, the Inspection Module provides a high level of security for complex protocols.

FireWall-1 secures UDP processes by maintaining a virtual connection on top of the UDP connection. As each UDP packet is permitted through the firewall to its destination, it is recorded. As a packet is transferred back to its original source, the packet is verified against the list of open UDP sessions to ensure that the transmittal is authorized. All packets that match up against the list are allowed to pass to their destination, while all others are dropped.

For remote procedure calls, FireWall-1 and the Inspection Engine transparently track PRC port numbers using *port mappers*. Each time an Inspection Engine

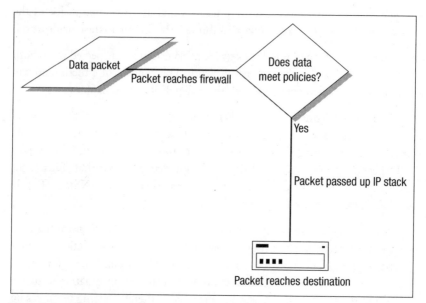

Figure 2.2 Allowing a packet to continue to its destination.

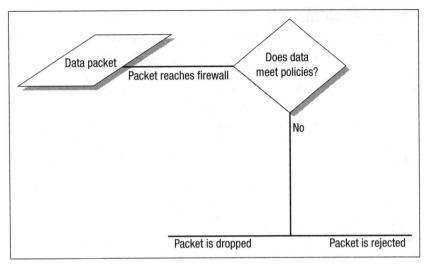

Figure 2.3   Denying a packet.

looks at a rule involving RPC services, it looks at a cache that is built to map RPC program numbers to their respective port numbers. If a program number matches the port that is specified in the rule base, the traffic is allowed to pass. If the association does not exist in the cache, the Inspection Engine will work as a proxy to send a request to the port mapper and then verify the information returned.

Components of FireWall-1

FireWall-1 is broken up into separate modules to make management easier, as shown in Table 2.1. The main modules are the Firewall and Management Modules. FireWall-1 is designed so that the different sets of modules can reside on separate computers. However, before the modules can be installed on separate computers, an Enterprise license needs to be purchased. Licensing is discussed a little later in this chapter.

Table 2.1 The FireWall-1 components.	
Component	**Function**
Firewall Module	Inspects packets and provides authentication, NAT, and content security.
Management Module	Controls and monitors the Firewall Module.
Connect Control Module	Provides load balancing.
Encryption Module	Secures data transmissions on a firewall-to-firewall or client-to-firewall basis.

The Firewall Module

Calling this module the Firewall Module can be a bit deceiving. Why? Your first thought might be that this is where all the decision making for passing packets is made. Well, you're right, but this module does a lot more than that. The Firewall Module is also responsible for client, user, and session authentication. I discuss the different types of authentications in Chapter 10 but, for now, knowing that the Firewall Module handles authentication is enough. The Firewall module is also responsible for network address translation, synchronization, content security, and auditing.

Note: NAT is a key element in hiding an internal network from the outside world. It is also key to keeping address conflicts from occurring between networks.

The Firewall Module is a combination of three separate pieces:

➤ Inspection Module

➤ FireWall-1 daemon

➤ Security server

Let's look at the separate pieces of the firewall module and what roles they play in handling the transfer of packets.

Inspection Module

I've already discussed the Inspection Module at length, but let's recap the functions to drive the point home. The Inspection Module is responsible for providing authentication, auditing the firewall, performing network address translation, and controlling the transfer of traffic in and out of the firewall.

FireWall-1 Daemon

A *daemon* is a program that runs continuously and exists for the purpose of handling periodic service requests that a computer system expects to receive. In the case of FireWall-1, the purpose of the daemon is to pass communications between the clients, hosts, and other modules.

The daemon handles the communications in a number of steps. In a situation where the components of the firewall are broken up onto different machines, the *Daemon Communicator* is responsible for authenticating the services as they talk to one another. The *Daemon Command Handler* then takes the information passed with the Daemon Communicator and executes the set of directives. The information is then logged to a management station by the *Daemon Logger*.

Security Server

The security server is responsible for handling authentication based on particular services or protocols. This is where the decision-making process is controlled for HTTP, FTP, and other like-services. The security server is positioned above the INSPECT Engine in the kernel. This can be very high-level or very granular, depending on the security needs of the administrator.

The Management Module

The Management Module, made up of the Management Server and the GUI interfaces, is where the bulk of the administration is done. The Management Server manages all of the objects within the firewall and is modified by using the GUI interfaces for the task you are trying to accomplish. You will need to become very comfortable with the Management Module, because 90 percent of your time will be spent working with the GUIs.

 The actual GUI software and Management Server can reside on separate machines as long as the client computer has been granted access to administer the Management Server.

The Management Module runs under both Windows and X/Motif. The Management Module is used to configure the firewall security policy, view the firewall logs, and monitor the system status. I will refer to the management GUIs throughout this book.

As the administrator of your firewall, you will be manipulating the policies of the firewall through the GUI interfaces. Although the changes occur through the use of the GUIs, the changes are never actually made directly onto the firewall. The server acts as a middle man between the administrator and the actual Management Module. When an administrator requests a policy change to be made, the server passes the request along and then returns the results to the GUI.

Additional Check Point Products

Check Point is best known for its FireWall-1 product, but it also has several other products available on the market. As you can see during the installation process (see Chapter 3), you can install several of these products from the FireWall-1 CD-ROM. Of course, licensing is necessary for these additional products. Let's take a quick look at some of the additional products.

VPN-1 Gateway

VPN-1 Gateway combines the functionality of the FireWall-1 suite with advanced VPN (virtual private network) technologies. VPN-1 Gateway provides connections to corporate networks, off-site users, and remote offices. VPN-1 uses industry-standard technologies, such as Internet Protocol Security (IPSec) and Public Key Infrastructure (PKI), to allow for the configuration of extranets.

An extranet is a private network that uses the Internet protocol and the public telecommunication system to securely share part of a business's information or operations with suppliers, vendors, partners, customers, or other businesses. An extranet can be viewed as part of a company's intranet that is extended to users outside the company.

VPN-1 SecuRemote

SecuRemote is the client-side portion of Check Point's virtual private network implementation. VPN-1 SecuRemote is used to connect remote users to their corporate network through the Internet over a secure connection. SecuRemote can also be installed on internal workstations to create secure internal connections that can help to protect sensitive data. VPN-1 SecuRemote encrypts and decrypts data to protect data transmittal over lines of communications.

FloodGate-1

FloodGate-1 is a bandwidth-management solution used to resolve network congestion due to bandwidth-intensive traffic. FloodGate-1 works by prioritizing certain, more critical types of traffic over less important traffic. On top of managing the traffic, FloodGate-1 can help to identify sources of network congestion.

FloodGate-1 supports over 100 Internet services and applications. When integrated with VPN-1, FloodGate-1 is able to securely classify encrypted traffic, both in aggregate and within the VPN tunnel.

Meta-IP

Meta-IP is a central administration point for control over IP services and network naming conventions. It automates IP addressing and eliminates duplicate IP address errors with DHCP (Dynamic Host Configuration Protocol), provides failover by replicating DHCP, and provides for increased security and stability. Meta-IP is responsible for managing all DNS and DHCP servers across a corporate infrastructure. It takes the information that is discovered throughout the network and integrates it into an LDAP (Lightweight Directory Access Protocol) database. Meta-IP is useful in environments that require a central management point for a large IP network.

Other Advantages of FireWall-1

I've already discussed the biggest advantage of a Check Point FireWall-1 firewall earlier in this chapter—stateful inspection. It should now be obvious that the three main advantages of a stateful inspection firewall are security, speed, and ease of management. Let's take a look at some of the other features of FireWall-1: NAT, content vectoring, firewall synchronization, and ease of management.

Network Address Translation (NAT)

NAT should not be a new concept to any seasoned administrator or engineer. Simply put, NAT is the translation of an IP address used inside of a private network to an IP address that is acknowledged as a valid Internet address. This method secures (or hides) the internal machine because each outgoing or incoming request must be translated for the intended recipient. NAT was developed to deal with the issue of running out of valid Internet IP addresses as well as to provide additional security. See Chapter 9 for more information.

Content Vectoring

Content vectoring is a method of scanning the content of all traffic going across the network. Content vectoring is useful for searching for viruses, searching for Java bombs, scanning email messages, and filtering URLs. Content vectoring can also be used to strip attachments and scripts. There are many third-party content vectoring programs on the market, but Check Point offers this service with the FireWall-1 suite.

Firewall Synchronization

FireWall-1 can allow each firewall in a network infrastructure to pass state information between each other through firewall synchronization. This is a good way to achieve load-balancing across a set of firewalls with little additional administration or user intervention. See Chapter 8 for more information.

Ease of Management

From a conceptual perspective, FireWall-1 is one of the easiest packages on the market to understand. Because everything is handled through the GUI consoles, setting up your firewall rules are pretty simplistic. Everything in FireWall-1 is menu-driven and allows for a lot of manipulation and documentation. Creating a rule is incredibly simple, considering that all you have to do is click the portion of the rule that you want to change, then add or remove as necessary. FireWall-1 also prevents user errors by warning you about rule conflicts and potential errors. What could be easier? See Chapters 4, 5, and 6 for more information.

FireWall-1 Licensing

Anyone who has ever installed and configured FireWall-1 will tell you that the licensing can be the most difficult part of the entire installation process. It's not that getting the license or understanding the license is difficult; it's the complexity of the actual license string! Many of the problems with this are simply human error. The key points to keep in mind when you register your product to generate the license are to know:

➤ The OS you will be running

➤ The IP that you will be assigning the firewall to

➤ The features you are expecting to implement

➤ The number of users you will need to protect behind the firewall

Note: It's important to know the IP and interface that you will install the firewall on. This is a key part of generating the key, which will not work if you assign it incorrectly.

Determining the Number of Licenses Needed

The number of licenses is determined by the number of devices behind the firewall. This includes every piece of equipment sitting on the internal network that has an IP address and that needs to have a secure connection to the Internet. Figure 2.4 shows how FireWall-1 determines a licensed node that it is protecting. This has its pluses and minuses, but, in the end, you'll find out that it works out for the best. So, it goes without saying that it is important to keep in mind the growth of your internal network.

The firewall makes a listing of all the internal devices that it sees and continues to function normally until the limit is reached. Here's the nice part (thank you, Check Point!): the firewall will continue to run after this threshold is reached. At the point when you reach your limit, a message is sent to the root account and adds itself to the syslog if you are using Solaris. If you are installing FireWall-1 on NT, the message is stored in Event Viewer. In both cases, you can also see this warning in the Check Point Log Viewer GUI. Although FW-1 will not lock you out once you reach your licensing threshold, it will continue to warn you that you need to add more licenses. It is important to understand that violating your license agreement could result in the loss of your licensing.

The first step in generating a license for your firewall is to purchase a certificate key from an authorized FireWall-1 reseller (I'll discuss the purchasing options in a moment). The certificate key given depends on the FireWall-1 options that you have decided to purchase. After you have received the certificate key from the

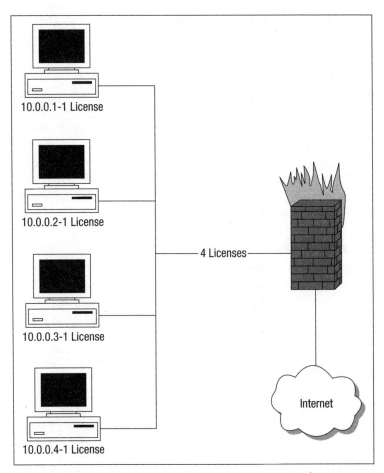

Figure 2.4   How FireWall-1 sees a licensed node.

vendor, open your Web browser and go to **http://license.checkpoint.com**. Check Point will ask you a series of questions relating to the installation of the software as well as some basic contact information for tracking purposes. After you have entered all of the information, Check Point will email you the newly generated license.

Purchasing FireWall-1 Products

Check Point offers a database of authorized Check Point resellers on its Web site; these resellers can assist you in purchasing the correct product for your environment. You might also want to speak with a Check Point pre-sales representative prior to making your purchase. FireWall-1 can be purchased as an Enterprise product or by purchasing the individual products. Check Point offers this flexibility so that it can offer various price breakpoints for ease of purchasing. The

Enterprise product also offers several feature differences that the Single Gateway product does not, as described next.

The Enterprise Product

The Enterprise product offers several options that the Single Gateway product does not. These differences include the ability to manage several firewalls from a single management console and centralized management of third-party routers, such as Nortel, Cisco, and 3Com. The most visible difference between the Enterprise product and the Single Gateway product is the ability to break out the Management Modules onto separate machines. This gives you the potential to manage multiple firewalls from remote sites. Also, a license for this product allows for an unlimited number of users.

The Single Gateway Product

The Single Gateway product still offers the Firewall and Management Modules; however, it does not give you the ability to separate the Management Modules onto separate machines. The other difference between the Enterprise product and the Single Gateway product is that the Single Gateway product allows licensing to only 25, 50, 100, or 250 users.

Other Single Products

Check Point also offers the ability to purchase the Firewall Module and Inspection Modules separately. The Firewall Module can be installed on a gateway that is managed remotely. The Firewall Module includes the high availability features as well as the security server.

The other single product option is the Inspection Module. The Inspection Module can also be installed on a gateway that is remotely managed; however, it does not offer the high availability features or the security server.

Both of these options allow for an unlimited number of users.

Practice Questions

Question 1

What are the biggest advantages of packet filtering? [Check all correct answers]

 a. Speed

 b. Transparency

❑ c. Data manipulation

☑ d. Price

Answers a, b, and d are correct. A packet filter was most popular in its prime due to the fact that it was much faster than Application layer gateways, was transparent to the end user because no client software was necessary, and was relatively inexpensive compared to other solutions. Answer c is incorrect because packet filters are unaware of the data being transmitted and, therefore, cannot manipulate it.

Question 2

What are the disadvantages of an Application layer gateway (proxy server)? [Check all correct answers]

 a. Each service requires its own Application layer gateway

❑ b. Poor security

☑ c. Overlooks information on lower layers

❑ d. None of the above

Answers a and c are correct. Each service requires its own Application layer gateway (or proxy), which makes scalability difficult. Application layer gateways also overlook information being passed beneath the Application layer, creating security issues. Answer b is incorrect because Application layer gateways offer a very high level of network security.

Question 3

> What is the communication-derived state?
>
> ○ a. Where information is passed between the communication layers
>
> ○ b. The state derived from previous communications
>
> ○ c. The information derived from other applications
>
> ○ d. The point in time before the firewall policy is administered

Answer b is correct. The communication-derived state is created from previous communications, such as outgoing FTP information that will be used to verify the incoming FTP information. Answer a is incorrect because it a location where information is passed. Answer c relates to the application-derived state; therefore, it is incorrect. Answer d is incorrect because the communication-derived state has nothing to do with the administration of the policy.

Question 4

> Which of the following is contained in the Firewall Module?
>
> ○ a. Inspection Module
>
> ○ b. FireWall-1 daemon
>
> ○ c. Security server
>
> ☒ d. All of the above

Answer d is correct. The Inspection Module, FireWall-1 daemon, and security server are all components of the Firewall Module.

Question 5

What are the benefits of Check Point FireWall-1? [Check all correct answers]

- ☒ a. Performance
- ☒ b. Scalability
- ☒ c. Application-awareness
- ☐ d. Inexpensive
- ☐ e. Resides on the Application layer
- ☒ f. Strong security
- ☒ g. Transparent

Answers a, b, c, f, and g are all correct. They are all key benefits offered by FireWall-1. Answer d is incorrect; a stateful inspection firewall is expensive compared to a packet filter. Answer e is incorrect because FireWall-1 resides on the kernel layer.

Question 6

Which of the following is not a form of a denial of service attack?

- ○ a. Man-in-the-middle
- ○ b. Ping of death
- ○ c. DNS redirection
- ○ d. SNMP reconfiguration
- ○ e. None of the above

Answer a is correct. A man-in-the-middle attack is a form of an impersonation attack in which the hacker intercepts communications between the communications between two machines. Therefore, answers b, c, d, and e are incorrect.

Question 7

An Application layer gateway can be compared to what type of network attack?

○ a. Ping of death

○ b. DNS redirection

◉ c. Man-in-the-middle

○ d. Port scan

○ e. All of the above

○ f. None of the above

Answer c is correct. An Application layer gateway sits between the two machines who are attempting to communicate, in the same way a man-in-the-middle attack sits between two machines to intercept traffic. The difference is that the Application gateway is used to protect the internal machine, not to impersonate it. Answers, a, b, and d all forms on network attacks, but they do not share similarities to an Application layer gateway.

Question 8

Which are not valid licensing options for FireWall-1? [Check all correct answers]

❑ a. 5 users

❑ b. 25 users

❑ c. 50 users

❑ d. Unlimited users

❑ e. 500 users

Answers a and e are correct because licensing for Check Point FireWall-1 is only available for purchasing as 25, 50, 100, 250, or unlimited user licensing. Therefore, answers b, c, and d are not correct answers because they are all valid licensing options.

Question 9

For which of the following is the Inspection Module responsible? [Check all correct answers]

- ❏ a. Data encryption
- ☑ b. Access control
- ☑ c. Application load balancing
- ☑ d. Client authentication
- ☑ e. Session authentication
- ☑ f. Network address translation
- ❏ g. Third-party management
- ☑ h. Auditing

Answers b, d, e, f, and h are correct. The Inspection Module is responsible for access control, client and session authentication, NAT, and auditing. Data encryption, such as DES and FWZ, is handled by the Encryption Module, so answer a is incorrect. Load balancing is a function of the Connect Control Module, so answer c is incorrect. Third-party management, such as the management of Cisco, 3Com, Nortel, and other router and firewall developers is controlled through the Open Security Manager, so answer g is incorrect.

Need to Know More?

 Brenton, Chris. *Mastering Network Security*. Sybex Books, San Francisco, CA, 1998. ISBN 0-78-212343-0. The book serves as a practical security guide for network and systems administrators.

 Goncalves, Marcus and Steven Brown. *Check Point FireWall-1 Administration Guide*. McGraw-Hill, New York, NY, 1999. ISBN 0-07-134229-X. This book is a good bookshelf reference for FireWall-1.

 Scambray, Joel, Stuart McClure, and George Kurtz. *Hacking Exposed: Second Edition*. McGraw-Hill Professional Publishing, New York, NY, 1992. ISBN 0-07-212748-1. The authors do a great job of looking at network security from a hacker's perspective.

 www.sans.org is the SANS Institute's site, which is a fantastic site that offers a great amount of network security information, recommendations, and evaluations.

Installing and Configuring FireWall-1

Terms you'll need to understand:

✓ Standalone installation

✓ Distributed installation

✓ Management Server

✓ External interface

✓ Key hit session

✓ Enforcement point

✓ IP forwarding

Techniques you'll need to master:

✓ Knowing the minimum requirements for an NT installation

✓ Knowing the minimum requirements for a Solaris installation

✓ Installing and uninstalling FireWall-1 on Windows NT

✓ Installing and uninstalling FireWall-1 on Solaris

✓ Installing the GUI client onto a separate machine

✓ Understanding the difference between a distributed and standalone installation

✓ Licensing your software

In this chapter, I discuss the initial installation process of our firewall. I also discuss the different methods of installations, and how they vary from one another. However, before I jump into the installation process, I need to cover the requirements of FireWall-1.

Preinstallation Checklist

You're at the point in the book where we are going to get into the meat of Check Point FireWall-1. The details and requirements to follow are a key part of the CCSA exam, and you will need to have a good understanding of the steps you need to perform to install FireWall-1. As with any software package, minimum requirements have been predetermined to ensure proper operation. Table 3.1 shows the requirements Check Point states that you need to meet if you're using Windows NT as your operating system.

FireWall-1 will work on many Unix flavors; however, in this chapter, I'll be focusing only on installing it onto a Solaris operating system. The minimum requirements for a Unix installation are almost identical to those of Windows NT. Table 3.2 shows the requirements for Solaris, Table 3.3 shows the requirements for Red Hat Linux, and Table 3.4 shows the requirements for HP-UX.

Note: FireWall-1 is a very memory-intensive program. Although it will run on a minimum of 64MB, higher memory will give you better performance.

Table 3.1	Minimum requirements for installing Check Point FireWall-1 on an NT server.	
Component	**Minimum Specifications**	
OS version	Windows NT 4 with Service Pack 4 or higher	
Memory	64MB	
Disk space	40MB	

Table 3.2	Minimum requirements for installing Check Point FireWall-1 on a Solaris system.	
Component	**Minimum Specifications**	
OS version	Solaris 2.6 and Operating Environment 7	
Processor	SPARC and x86	
Memory	64MB	
Disk space	40MB	

Table 3.3	Minimum requirements for installing Check Point FireWall-1 on a Red Hat Linux system.
Component	**Minimum Specifications**
OS version	Red Hat Linux 6.1 or higher
Memory	64MB
Disk space	40MB

Table 3.4	Minimum requirements for installing Check Point FireWall-1 on an HP-UX system.
Component	**Minimum Specifications**
OS version	10.20 or 11 (32-bit installation mode)
Memory	64MB
Disk space	40MB

You'll want to address some issues prior to installing the firewall software. Here is a checklist of actions you should complete prior to installation:

➤ Verify that the host can communicate with both the internal and external networks.

➤ Verify that the latest drivers for your interface cards have been installed and that both cards are functioning properly.

➤ Make sure that your OS meets the minimum stated requirements and that any applicable service packs have been loaded.

➤ Ensure that DNS is running either internally or externally for name resolution.

➤ Make sure that IP forwarding is turned off in the Solaris kernel and that IP routing is enabled on NT systems.

➤ Verify that the IP addresses you will be using for your firewall (both internal and external) are available.

In case you're curious, FireWall-1 *will* work on Windows 2000; however, you must download and install Service Pack 2. If you attempt to install FireWall-1 straight off of the CD, you will receive an error message and the installation will halt. For the purposes of the CCSA exam, you don't need to know how to install FireWall-1 in a Windows 2000 environment.

Now that I've covered the preliminaries, you're ready to begin installing the firewall!

Installing FireWall-1 on a Windows NT Server

To begin the installation, you should be logged into the server using an administrator account with full rights to the machine. You will also want to stop any other programs that are currently running on the server, to ensure no conflicts or errors arise during the installation. To get started, follow these steps:

1. Insert the CD into the CD-ROM drive. If the setup program does not start automatically, click Start|Run and type "x:\wrappers\windows\demo32.exe".

2. Click Next.

3. Click Yes to accept the license agreement.

4. At the Product Menu, select Server/Gateway Components, and click Next.

5. Because we are going to be specifically focusing on the FireWall-1 and VPN-1 components, deselect everything except VPN-1/FireWall-1.

6. After clearing the other component options, click Next.

Choosing an Installation Type

At this point, you need to decide on the type of installation you want. The Stand Alone Installation option installs all the components onto the machine, whereas the Distributed Installation option lets you pick and choose which pieces you want installed onto the server. For our purposes at this time, we will be using the Stand Alone Installation option. To continue the installation process, follow these steps:

Note: The Distributed Installation option is discussed later in this chapter.

1. Click Stand Alone Installation (see Figure 3.1), and then click Next.

2. In the Information box, verify that Stand Alone Installation was selected, and click Next.

3. Tell Check Point what type of licensing will be used for the server. This example uses the Unlimited Hosts option. Select the licensing type, and click Next.

Note: Evaluation licenses are available at www.checkpoint.com.

4. When asked if you want to manage previous versions of the software, choose Install Without Backward Compatibility, and click Next.

5. Verify the destination folder, and click Next. This example uses the default folder.

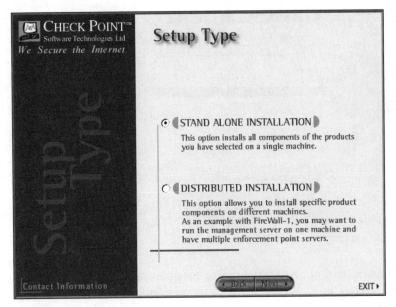

Figure 3.1   Choosing an installation type.

6. Click Next. FireWall-1 will begin the installation process. When the setup is complete, you will be notified that the installation will be completed upon the next reboot.

7. Click OK.

8. Check Point will automatically begin the installation of Service Pack 1.

After the installation of the firewall software, the installation of the management clients will automatically kick off.

Installing the Management Clients

The management clients can be installed on multiple machines, but, in a standalone installation, you are automatically prompted to install the client on the machine. To install the management clients, follow these steps:

1. Choose a destination location. The default location for the management tools is C:\Checkpoint\Policy Editor. Verify the destination folder, and click Next.

2. Select the components you want to install. For this example, let's go ahead and choose all of the components. Policy Editor, Log Viewer, and System Status should already be checked. Check Real Time Monitor, as shown in Figure 3.2, and click Next.

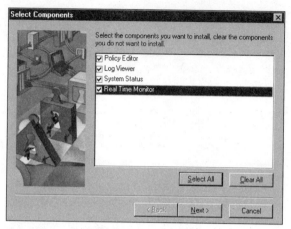

Figure 3.2 Selecting management clients.

3. The management clients will begin to install. At the end of the installation, you will be asked if you want to integrate the management client with Meta-IP; click No.

Note: Meta-IP is a central administration point of control over IP services and network naming conventions.

Applying the License

At this point in the installation, you need to add the license that you should have already registered online. If you have not yet registered and received a license, you will need to do so now. It is also important to note that this is where the number of licenses registered comes into effect. If you purchased a license for a limited number of clients and completed the installation for unlimited licenses as described earlier in this chapter, you will not be able to continue. To add the license to the firewall, follow these steps:

1. On the Licenses screen, click Add to enter a new license into the Add License dialog box (see Figure 3.3).

2. You will now need to enter the information that you entered during your license registration.

 Be sure to enter the license information *exactly as you entered it during registration*. One incorrect keystroke can cause the license to be rejected.

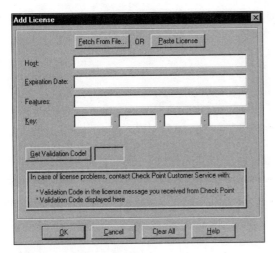

Figure 3.3   Adding a license.

3. Once you have entered the license information, click the Get Validation Code! button.

4. Click OK. If the license is good, the newly entered license will appear in the New Licenses box on the Licenses screen.

5. Click Next to continue the installation.

Note: You can also import license information from a file. To do so, click the Fetch From File button and select the license file.

The next step in the FireWall-1 installation process is to grant administrator permissions.

Creating Administrators

An *administrator* is any user who will need to view and/or manage the firewall settings. Keep in mind that although an administrator might not need to view the rule base, he or she might need to view the Log Viewer for auditing purposes. Administrators can have different levels of permissions, which can be customized based on the needs of each administrator. The three options for permissions are:

➤ *Read/Write All*—The Read/Write All permissions allow an administrator to have full control over the firewall. Only administrators with this permission level are allowed to edit the policy objects. This level of security should only be given to people who are experienced with configuring FireWall-1 and have a need to make changes to the configuration. To ensure the highest security, this account should not be used on a day-to-day basis. If you, as an administrator, need to access the firewall management tools on a daily basis, you should create a separate account with more restrictive permissions.

The Read/Write All permissions is the only permission level that allows editing of policy objects.

➤ *Customized*—The Customized permissions option enables you to grant or deny permissions based on the selections made. You would use this option if you want to grant permissions to certain areas of the firewall, but you also want to restrict access to others. For example, this could be a useful option for a help desk where help desk agents would need to create firewall users in the user database. The permissions that can be customized are:

➤ Edit User Database

➤ Security Rules

➤ Bandwidth Rules

➤ Compression Rules

➤ Log Viewer

➤ System Status

➤ *No Permissions*—No permissions is pretty straightforward. When you use this permission setting, administrators are not allowed access to any of the products.

Now that you're familiar with the permissions options, let's create an administrator with Read/Write All permissions, as described here:

1. Click the Add button in the Administrators screen. A dialog box will open to add your new administrator (see Figure 3.4).

2. Type a username for the administrator. In this example, we will use *admin*.

3. Type a password and confirm that you entered the password correctly.

4. Click the Read/Write All radio button.

5. Click OK to add the new administrator.

6. When you return to the Administrators screen, you will see your new entry in the Administrator's Permissions table. To add additional administrators, click the Add button again and repeat Steps 2 through 5. If you are done adding administrators, click Next to continue.

The next step will be to verify the IP address for the external interface of the firewall.

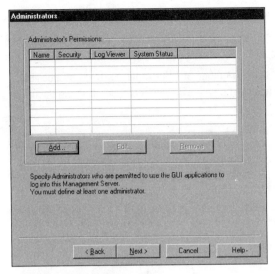

Figure 3.4   Administrators screen.

Configuring the External Interface

The external interface is the interface that will be on the public side of your network. You need to make sure that you are using the correct address here, or the firewall will not work properly. Using the wrong interface can have adverse effects on your firewall. If configured incorrectly, the firewall assumes that the IP addresses that should be considered *external* are actually *internal* and offers no protection to your network. Furthermore, an incorrect configuration will wreak havoc on your firewall log because it will consider every IP address on the Internet to be an *internal* address. To configure your external interface, enter the IP address and then click Next.

Note: If you enter an incorrect IP address, click Change IP and enter the correct address.

Now you are ready to select which machines you want to be able to control your firewall through: the GUI clients.

Configuring GUI Clients

You're at the stage where you need to enter the IP addresses of the machines that will be allowed to log into the Management Server. GUI clients are specific machines where the administrators that you assigned previously will be able to view and/or change settings on your firewall. Choosing your GUI machines should follow the same rule of thumb as choosing your administrators—only assign IP addresses that are tied statically to specific administrator workstations. You also want to make sure that you are assigning only static IP addresses and not addresses that are part of a DHCP scope. In a standalone installation, the Management Station is allowed as a GUI client by default.

> You should restrict the number of GUI clients as much as possible. Indiscriminately adding multiple GUI clients can create a big security hazard.

In the example installation, the GUI management tools will be used from the Management Station, but let's enter a GUI client for practice, as described here:

1. Enter the IP address into the Remote Hostname field. In this example, we'll use 10.0.0.2.

2. Click the Add button.

3. Click Next to continue.

Next, you'll need to specify which remote Enforcement Modules your Management Server will control.

Specifying Remote Enforcement Modules

Check Point calls the Management Server a *Master Server* because it is where the Firewall Module (also known as the Enforcement Module) will get the security policy, and where the alerts and logs will be sent. When specifying an Enforcement Module to manage, follow these steps:

1. Enter the name or IP address of your firewall. Because we will only have one firewall at this stage, we will only enter this address. In our example, the IP is 192.168.1.1.

2. Click Add to add the server to the list. The Add Module pop-up window appears.

3. Enter a password. The password must be at least four characters long. In this example, we will use the word *password* as the password.

4. Click OK, and then click Next to continue.

The next step in this process is to determine how IP forwarding will be handled. We need to decide if we want FireWall-1 to control it, or leave this to the OS.

IP Forwarding

FireWall-1 will now ask you to specify whether you want the firewall to control IP forwarding (see Figure 3.5). If you choose not to allow the firewall to control

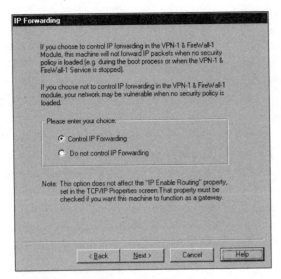

Figure 3.5   Controlling IP forwarding.

IP forwarding, you are indicating that you want to allow traffic to be passed when a security policy is not loaded. This presents some pretty big security holes; it means that any time you do not have the firewall modules running, all traffic can be passed between the two networks freely.

Note: You must enable IP forwarding in the Network Settings in NT.

Because we want to be as secure as possible (this is a firewall, after all!), we will allow the firewall to control IP forwarding by completing the following steps:

1. Click the Control IP Forwarding radio button.

2. Click Next.

We're almost done with our installation. The last step is to complete the key hit session.

Key Hit Session

The last step in the installation process before rebooting is to generate a random string (or *seed*) for future encryption purposes (see Figure 3.6). To complete the Key Hit Session screen, follow these steps:

1. Start typing; you will notice that either a light bulb or a bomb will appear. If you see a light bulb, your keystroke was accepted. If you see a bomb, try a different key. If a keystroke is too fast or is the same as the previous character, the keystroke is denied. When you have entered enough characters, the status bar will be full and you will not be allowed to enter any more characters.

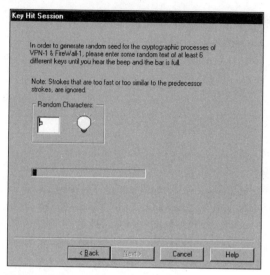

Figure 3.6 Creating the random seed.

2. Click Next to proceed. The setup process is complete. The computer must now be restarted for the changes to take effect.

3. Click the Finish button.

The Check Point software restarts your computer, and the installation takes effect.

Uninstalling from Windows NT

Now that we have completed the installation of our firewall, let's look at how to properly uninstall it. Uninstalling a firewall may be necessary when replacing hardware, troubleshooting system issues, or for a variety of different reasons. Uninstalling Check Point FireWall-1 is simple when it has been installed on Windows NT. To uninstall FireWall-1 from a Windows NT machine, follow these steps:

1. Close any open FireWall-1 windows.

2. Click Start|Settings|Control Panel.

3. Select Add/Remove Programs in the Control Panel window.

4. Remove the three Check Point FireWall-1 components.

5. Restart the computer.

You can either remove the entire FireWall-1 package or you can remove certain portions of the software. Clicking the installed components will show you the options you can choose from for removal of your software.

Installing FireWall-1 on Solaris

Similar to the Windows NT installation described in the first portion of this chapter, we'll now walk through a Stand Alone Installation of the FireWall-1 software on a Solaris machine. The first step in installing FireWall-1 onto a Solaris machine is to transfer the files from the CD. In this example, we'll accomplish the file transfer by using the **InstallU** command-line utility. Optionally, you can use the **pkgadd** command to install just the installation files for FireWall-1.

Beginning the Installation

Like the Windows NT installation, you need full administrative authority over the machine before you can install the software. Next, you will need to log onto the server using the superuser (su) account. Make sure that all other applications are closed before you proceed. You will also need to verify that the **FW_BOOT_ DIR** variable is not defined. To start the installation, follow these steps:

1. Change drives to your CD-ROM.

2. At the command prompt, type "./InstallU".

3. When the Actions menu appears, press "N".

4. The next menu to appear will be the Products menu. Select option number 1, VPN-1 / FireWall-1 Modules, and press "N" to continue.

5. The next menu is the Setup Type menu. On this menu, choose option 1, which is the Stand Alone Installation. This will install all of the components onto the machine. Press "N" to continue.

6. At the Confirmation screen, confirm that you will be doing a Stand Alone Installation of FireWall-1, and press "N" to continue.

7. FireWall-1 will now attempt to create the installation directory where the software will reside. You will be prompted to accept the directory. Press "Y" to continue.

8. Solaris will warn you that the software contains several scripts that will be installed using the superuser account. You will then be prompted to continue with the installation. Because you know what is going to happen, you can press "Y" to continue.

At this point, the installation process will begin by moving the files to the newly created installation directory.

Post-Installation Steps

Once the software has been installed, you will be instructed to complete the following manual steps:

1. Add the line **setenv FWDIR /opt/CPfw1-41** to the .cshrc file or **FWDIR=/ opt/CPfw-41; export FWDOR** to the .profile file.

2. Add **$FWDIR/bin** to the path file.

Next, you will be notified that in order to enable backward compatibility, you will need to install the CKPfw package. In this example, I assume that you will not be supporting any firewalls other than the latest version. Therefore, we have nothing to worry about here. So, let's continue with the installation.

Installing the GUI Clients

Now that the installation steps are complete, we need to install the GUI clients so that we can manage our firewall:

1. When the list of software packages returns, press "8" to begin the installation of the GUI.

2. You will now be prompted to create the installation directory for the GUI client. Press "Y" to accept the directory.

3. Again, you will be notified that scripts are included in the installation software and will be installed under the superuser account. Press "Y" to continue.

4. The installation of the GUI software is complete. You should see the software packages screen. Press "Q" to exit the software packages screen.

The next step is choosing the type of installation you will be using and how it will be licensed.

Choosing and Licensing an Installation Type

The configuration for FireWall-1 on the Solaris platform is very straightforward. After exiting the software packages screen, you will be returned to a console prompt. To begin the configuration process, follow these steps:

1. Select the type of installation you will be implementing on the server. To begin a Stand Alone Installation, press "1".

2. FireWall-1 will prompt you for the type of licensing you will be using for your firewall. This example uses the Unlimited Hosts licensing. Press "2" to select Unlimited Hosts, and press Enter to continue.

3. You will now be prompted to start FireWall-1 automatically at boot. Press "Y" to start automatically.

4. You will now need to enter the license for your software. Press "Y" to add a new license.

5. Using the registration information you received from Check Point, enter the host, expiration data, license string, and feature code.

6. You will be asked if you want to install any additional licenses. Press "N" to continue.

The next step in the installation process is to grant administrator permissions.

Creating Administrators

Administrators can have different levels of permissions, which can be customized based on the needs of each administrator. As stated in the NT installation section earlier in this chapter, who you define as an administrator can have serious effects on the level of security of your firewall. Make sure that you are very careful regarding who receives administrator permissions and the permissions level each administrator is granted. Let's quickly recap the levels of administration (which are described in more detail earlier in this chapter):

➤ *Read/Write All*—Full control

➤ *Customized*—Permissions based on selections made

➤ *No Permissions*—No access

Keep in mind that you will always need at least one administrator with the Read/Write All permissions. To configure the administrators, follow these steps:

1. When you are asked if you want to add a user as an administrator, press "Y" to continue.

2. A prompt will require you to type in the name of the administrator. This example uses *admin* as the administrator account.

3. You need to enter the password for the account you just entered. Enter a password, and press Enter to continue.

4. Retype the password for verification, and press Enter again.

5. At this point, you need to decide the level of rights. For this example, we will be using the Read/Write permissions. Press "W" to select Read/Write, and press Enter.

6. Once the account is created, you will be prompted to create another account. Press "N" to continue on to the next section.

Next, we need to let the firewall know the IP addresses of the GUI clients that will be allowed for configuration.

Configuring GUI Clients

You now need to select the host machines that will be allowed to control the firewall as GUI clients. Limiting the number of machines that can function as GUI clients is as important as the number and level of administrators created. Let's configure a client for practice, as described here:

1. When asked if you want to add a GUI client, press "Y".

2. You will be prompted to enter in the hostname or IP address of each GUI client, one per line.

3. On an empty line, press Ctrl+D to save your changes.

4. You will be asked to verify your changes. Press "Y".

The next area of configuration is for the SMTP server and enabling the SNMP daemon.

SMTP and SNMP Configuration

The next steps relate to configuring an SMTP server and enabling the SNMP daemon. The example setup does not use these options in its configuration. There-fore, to bypass these options and move on to the next step, follow these actions:

1. You will be presented with the current values for the SMTP server. When prompted to modify the configuration, press "N" to skip the modifications and to continue.

2. The next prompt will be to enable the SNMP daemon. When prompted, press "N" to skip enabling the daemon and to continue.

The next configuration menu is for configuring groups.

Configuring Groups

Groups can be given permission to execute the firewall. Without groups, only the superuser will be allowed to execute the FireWall-1 engine. For this configura-tion, groups will not be necessary; therefore, at the group name prompt, complete these actions:

1. When prompted to specify the group name, press Enter.

2. You will be prompted to verify that no group permissions will be granted. Press "Y" to accept.

The next configuration option addresses IP forwarding.

IP Forwarding

The same rules apply to the Solaris configuration regarding IP forwarding as in the NT configuration. If you want FireWall-1 to control IP forwarding and to disable IP forwarding when the firewall engine is not started, you will be further securing your firewall. To disable IP forwarding on boot, press "Y".

We're almost done with our installation. The last step is to complete the key hit session.

Key Hit Session

The last step before reboot is to generate a random string for future encryption purposes. To complete this step, do the following:

1. Start typing; you will notice that either a light bulb or a bomb will appear. If you see a light bulb, your keystroke was accepted. If you see a bomb, try a different key. If a keystroke is too fast or is the same as the previous character, the keystroke is denied. When you have entered enough characters, the status bar will be full and Check Point will complete the configuration.

2. Now that the configuration is complete, you will need to reboot the server to start the FireWall-1 engine. When prompted to reboot the computer, press "Y".

As with the Windows NT installation, it may become necessary to uninstall our firewall. Let's take a look at how this is done in Solaris.

Uninstalling from Solaris

Like the Windows NT installation, uninstalling FireWall-1 from the Solaris Operating system is painless. To uninstall FireWall-1 from a Solaris system, follow these steps:

1. Type "pkgrm" at the command prompt to begin the removal process. The following list of components will appear:

   ➤ Check Point FireWall-1 4.1

   ➤ Check Point FireWall-1 GUI 4.1

2. Choose the installed option that you want to remove from your system. After you select the package that you want to remove, you will be asked to confirm your decision to remove the component. Press "Y" to remove the selected component from your system.

3. As with the installation of the software, you will be given a warning that the package contains scripts that will be executed using the superuser permissions

during removal of this package. Press "Y" to continue with the removal of the software.

Solaris will notify you of the steps it is taking during the removal of the FireWall-1 component you have selected. Once the removal is complete, Solaris will notify you that the removal of the component was successful.

Distributed Installation

The Distributed Installation option doesn't vary much from the Stand Alone Installation option. The difference between the two installations is that a distributed installation allows you to install specific components onto different machines. This is how many administrators who control several firewalls set up their environment. Through the distributed installation configuration, you can manage multiple firewalls from one Management Server. Let's take a look at a distributed installation using Windows NT. To begin the installation, you should be logged into the server using an administrator account with full rights to the machine. You will also want to stop any other programs that are currently running on the server to ensure that there are no conflicts or errors during the installation. When you're ready, follow these steps to begin installation:

1. Insert the CD into the CD-ROM drive. If the setup program does not start automatically, click Start|Run, and type "*x*:\wrappers\windows\demo32.exe".

2. Click Next.

3. Click Yes to accept the license agreement.

4. At the Product Menu, select Server/Gateway Components, and click Next.

5. For this example, we are going to be specifically focusing on the FireWall-1 and VPN-1 components, so deselect everything except the VPN-1/FireWall-1 option.

6. After clearing the other component options, click Next.

At this point, you need to decide on the type of installation you want.

Choosing an Installation Type

The Stand Alone Installation installs all of the components on the machine, while the Distributed Installation lets you pick and choose which pieces you want installed onto the server. In this example, you're creating a distribution setup, so follow these steps:

1. Click Distributed Installation and then Next. This is where the distributed installation begins to differ from the Stand Alone Installation. You will now

be prompted to choose which components you want to install on the machine. This server will serve as your Management Server and Enforcement Point.

2. Check Management Server/Enforcement Point Software, and click Next.

3. Check Point will notify you that you have selected the Management Server/ Enforcement Point software. Click Next to continue.

4. The next screen is the VPN-1/FireWall-1 product page (see Figure 3.7). On this page, you can choose if you want to install the VPN-1/FireWall-1 Enterprise Management component, the VPN-1/FireWall-1 Gateway/Server Module, or both. Check the VPN-1/FireWall-1 Gateway/Server Module.

5. Click Next.

6. The next step is to tell Check Point what type of licensing will be used for the server. In this example, we will be using the Unlimited Hosts option (see Figure 3.8). Select the licensing type, and click Next.

7. Check Point will now prompt you with the default installation folder for the software. You can accept the default folder or click the Browse button to select another folder. Once you have chosen an installation folder, click Next.

8. After the installation is complete, you will be notified that your computer will need to be restarted before the changes take affect. When prompted, click OK to continue.

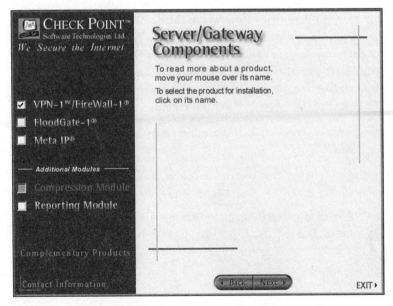

Figure 3.7 Selecting components.

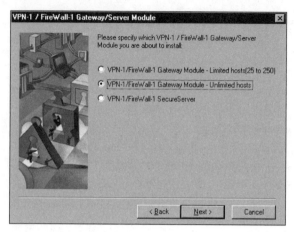

Figure 3.8 Specifying a licensing type.

9. Check Point will present you with the option to integrate the VPN-1/ FireWall-1 software with Meta-IP. Just as described in the Stand Alone Installation, choose No to continue.

At this point, you need to add the license that you should have already registered online.

Applying the License

If you have not yet registered and received a license, you will need to do so now. It is also important to note that this is where the number of licenses registered comes into effect. If you purchased a license for a limited number of clients and completed the installation for unlimited licenses, you will not be able to continue. If you do not have a license, you will need to purchase one from an authorized Check Point reseller or request an evaluation license from Check Point directly. To add the license to the firewall, follow these steps:

1. On the Licenses screen, click Add to enter a new license. The Add License dialog box will appear.

2. Enter the information that you entered during your license registration.

 Be sure to enter the information *exactly as you entered it during regis-tration*. One incorrect keystroke can cause the license to be rejected.

3. After you have entered the information, click the Get Validation Code! button.

4. Click OK. If the license is good, the newly entered license will appear in the New Licenses box on the Licenses screen.

5. Click Next to continue with the installation.

Note: You can also import the information from a file. To do so, click the Fetch From File button and select the license file.

6. You now need to identify the host IP address for the firewall. The IP address you used in the licensing portion should appear here. If it does not, click the Change IP button and enter the correct IP address.

7. Click Next to move onto the Masters screen.

The next step in this installation will be to specify the IP address of the Management Server that will control this firewall.

Specifying Management Servers

You now need to specify which Management Server will control the firewall. The Management Server screen is presented for you to enter the IP address of the Management Server that will be in charge of managing the firewall. In this example, the Management Server is a separate machine from the firewall on an internal network. To select a Management Server, follow these steps:

1. Enter in the name or IP address of your Management Server. In this example, the IP is 10.0.0.2.

2. Click Add to add the server to the list. The Add Module pop-up window appears.

3. Enter a password. The password must be at least four characters long. For this example, we will use the word *password* as our password.

4. Click OK to continue.

5. Click Next to continue the installation.

Next, we need to determine if the firewall will be handling the forwarding of IP information, just as we did in the Stand Alone installation.

IP Forwarding

The next configuration option is to address IP forwarding (see Figure 3.9). If you want FireWall-1 to control IP forwarding and to disable IP forwarding when the firewall engine is not started, you will be further securing your firewall. To disable IP forwarding on boot and let FireWall-1 control IP forwarding, click on the radio button next to "Control IP Forwarding" and click Next to continue.

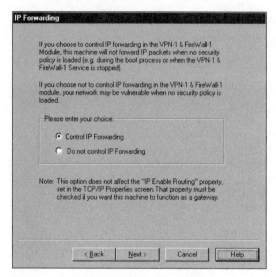

Figure 3.9 Controlling IP forwarding.

High Availability

The last screen of the installation process asks if your server is part of a High Availability cluster. In our example, the installation is not, so follow these steps:

1. Click Finish. The setup is now complete.

2. Click Yes, I Want To Restart My Computer, and then click Finish again.

After the machine has been rebooted, we need to select a machine that we want to serve as our GUI client and Management Server.

Installing the GUI Client and Management Module

Installing the GUI client and Management Server onto a separate NT machine is fairly simple. I'll run through this rather quickly, because you've performed most of these steps in the Stand Alone Installation procedure earlier in this chapter:

1. Insert the CD into the CD-ROM drive.

2. Click Next at the Welcome screen.

3. Click Yes to accept the license agreement.

4. Select the Server/Gateway Components option.

5. Check only the VPN-1/FireWall-1 option, and click Next.

6. On the Setup Type menu, select Distributed Installation, and click Next.

7. On the Distributed Installation screen, check both the Management Server/ Enforcement Point Software and Administration GUI options, and click Next.

8. Click Next again to verify your installation choices. The components you have selected will begin to install. After the installation has completed, you will need to choose the Enterprise product you want to install.

9. Check *only* the VPN-1/FireWall-1 Enterprise Management option, and click Next.

10. Click the Install Without Backward Compatibility option, and click Next.

11. Select a destination folder for the installation, or use the default folder and click Next.

12. Choose a destination location for the management tools. The default location for the management tools is C:\Checkpoint\Policy Editor. Verify the destination folder, and click Next.

13. Select the components you want install. For this example, let's choose all of the components. Policy Editor, Log Viewer, and System Status should already be checked. Click Next.

The management clients will begin to install. Next, you'll need to set up the Enforcement Modules.

Configuring the GUI Client and Management Module

Once the installation of the GUI client and Management Modules is complete, the next step is to configure them to work with your Enforcement Modules, as described in the following steps:

1. On the Licenses screen, click Add to enter a new license.

2. Enter the information that you entered during your license registration.

3. Click the Get Validation Code! button.

4. Click OK. If the license is good, the newly entered license will appear in the New Licenses box in the Licenses screen.

5. Click Next to continue with the installation.

Now that we have added the licensing, we need to create administrator accounts on the firewall.

Creating Administrators

Setting up administrators for a distributed installation is similar to the type of configuration you performed during the standalone installation. If you are unsure regarding how to select rights for an administrator, return to the standalone installation section earlier in this chapter and reread the descriptions of the permissions options. After you've selected which administrators should receive which permissions, complete the following steps:

1. When you are asked if you want to add a user as an administrator, press "Y" or click Yes to continue.

2. The next prompt will be to type in the name of the administrator. In this example, we will use *admin* as our administrator account.

3. You will now be prompted to enter the password for the account you just entered. Enter a password, and press Enter to continue.

4. Retype the password for verification, and press Enter again.

5. Here's where you decide the level of rights. For this example's account, we will use the Read/Write permissions. Press "W" to select Read/Write, and press Enter.

6. Once the account is created, you will be prompted to create another account. Press "N" to continue onto the next section.

As with the Stand Alone installation, we need to specify the IP addresses of the GUI clients that have access to modify the firewall settings. Let's move forward and look at how to configure the GUI clients.

Configuring GUI Clients

Choosing your GUI machines should follow the same rule of thumb as choosing your administrators—only assign IP addresses that are tied statically to specific administrator workstations. You also want to make sure that you assign only static IP addresses and not addresses that are part of a DHCP scope. To configure GUI clients, follow these steps:

1. Enter the IP address into the Remote Hostname field. In this example, we'll use 10.0.0.2.

2. Click the Add button.

3. Click Next to continue.

You now need to specify which remote Enforcement Modules the Management Server will control.

Specifying Remote Enforcement Modules

Check Point calls the Management Server a *Master Server* because it is where the Enforcement Module will get the security policy, and where the alerts and logs will be sent. We will be using the valid IP of our firewall, which is 192.168.1.1. To specify the remote Enforcement Module, follow these steps:

1. Enter the name or IP address of your firewall. Because we will only have one firewall at this stage, we will only enter this address. In our example, the IP is 192.168.1.1.

2. Click Add to add the server to the list. The Add Module pop-up window appears.

3. Enter a password. The password must be at least four characters long. In this example, we will use the word *password* as our password.

4. Click OK to continue.

5. Click Next to continue the installation.

Once again, we've arrived at the last step. Let's go ahead and begin the key hit session.

Key Hit Session

The last step before reboot is to generate a random string (or *seed*) for future encryption purposes (see Figure 3.10). To complete this procedure, follow these steps:

1. Start typing; you will notice that either a light bulb or a bomb will appear. If you see a light bulb, your keystroke was accepted. If you see a bomb, try a different key. If a keystroke is too fast or is the same as the previous character, the keystroke is denied. When you have entered enough characters, the status bar will be full and you will not be allowed to enter any more characters.

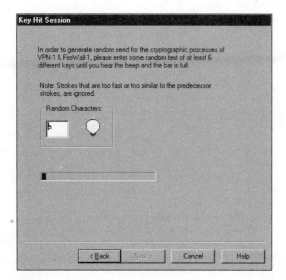

Figure 3.10 Creating the random seed.

2. Click Finish to proceed. The setup process is complete.

3. The computer must now be restarted in order for the changes to take effect. Click the Finish button to allow Check Point to restart your computer.

Once the machine has restarted, your distributed installation is complete. As you can see in this chapter, the installation of FireWall-1 is fairly straightforward. The keys to a successful installation include:

➤ Planning your installation.

➤ Purchasing the proper license.

➤ Knowing the IP addresses for the Enforcement Module, GUI clients, and Management Servers.

➤ Understanding the differences between distributed and standalone installations.

Many administrators would agree that the most difficult part of installing FireWall-1 is over after you've installed the software. You should keep in mind that the installation instructions given in this chapter are guidelines. Installations will vary from system to system, and steps can vary even further due to the revision of the software you have purchased. Check Point offers great technical support for their product, and I recommend that you purchase their support options for the peace of mind it can give you.

So, now that the hard part is over, you get to have some fun defining objects and developing a rule base, as described in Chapters 4 and 5.

Practice Questions

Question 1

What figure will appear if you type the same character twice during the key hit session?

○ a. Light bulb

○ b. Stop sign

○ c. Yield sign

○ d. Bomb

Answer d is correct. A bomb will appear in the key hit box if you type the same key twice or you are entering characters too quickly. Answer a is incorrect because a light bulb will appear if the character is accepted. Answers b and c are incorrect because these signs do not appear anywhere in the key hit session.

Question 2

Which installation type allows you to separate the modules of the firewall onto different machines?

○ a. Distributed Installation

○ b. Stand Alone Installation

○ c. Both installations

○ d. None of the above

Answer a is correct. Only a distributed installation will allow you to install the different modules onto separate machines. Therefore, answers b, c, and d are incorrect.

Question 3

> What two commands can you use on Solaris to install FireWall-1? [Check all correct answers]
>
> ☐ a. **UInstall**
>
> ☐ b. **pkgadd**
>
> ☐ c. **InstallU**
>
> ☐ d. **cpconfig**

Answers b and c are correct. Both **InstallU** and **pkgadd** can be used to install the software onto a Solaris system. Answer a is incorrect because there is no command called **UInstall**. Answer d is incorrect because **cpconfig** can be used to update an installation of FireWall-1, not install it.

Question 4

> What will happen if you do not specify a group name in a Solaris installation?
>
> ○ a. The installation will halt.
>
> ○ b. Only the superuser will be able to access the FireWall-1 module.
>
> ○ c. You must specify a group name.
>
> ○ d. Nothing.

Answer b is correct. If you do not select a group name during installation, only the superuser account will be allowed to execute and access the FireWall-1 and VPN-1 modules. Therefore, answers a, c, and d are incorrect because these results will not occur if you do not specify a group name.

Question 5

Which of the following is not a client GUI module?

- ○ a. NAT Manager
- ○ b. Log Viewer
- ○ c. Policy Editor
- ○ d. System Status
- ○ e. Real Time Monitor
- ○ f. None of the above

Answer a is correct. The NAT Manager is not a client GUI module; in fact no such manager exists. NAT is handled in the Policy Editor, as you will see in Chapter 9. Answers b, c, d, and e are incorrect because the Log Viewer, Policy Editor, System Status, and Real Time Monitor are all client GUI modules that can be installed during the installation process. Answer f is incorrect because the NAT Manager (answer a) is not a client GUI module.

Question 6

Which elements need to be configured during the installation process? [Check all correct answers]

- ❏ a. GUI clients
- ❏ b. Administrators
- ❏ c. Key hit/random key generation
- ❏ d. IP forwarding
- ❏ e. Rule base
- ❏ f. Remote modules

Answers a, b, c, d, and f are all correct. The installation process involves configuring GUI clients, administrators, key hit/random key generation, IP forwarding, and remote modules. Answer e is incorrect because the rule base is not configured until after the firewall installation is complete.

Question 7

> Why would you want FireWall-1 to control IP forwarding?
>
> ○ a. It will prevent IP packets from being forwarded when the firewall is not started.
>
> ○ b. It has better control of IP packets.
>
> ○ c. NT and Solaris cannot control IP forwarding on their own.
>
> ○ d. You do not want FireWall-1 to control IP forwarding.

Answer a is correct. If you choose not to have FireWall-1 control your IP forwarding, you leave your network open to intrusions. Answer b is incorrect because it does not necessarily have better control of IP packets. Answer c is incorrect because both the NT and Solaris operating systems can control IP forwarding. Answer d is incorrect; you would likely want FireWall-1 to control IP forwading so that it can prevent forwarding before the firewall module is loaded.

Question 8

> Which of the following is not a field in the Add License section of the initial FireWall-1 configuration?
>
> ○ a. Host
>
> ○ b. Expiration Date
>
> ○ c. Password
>
> ○ d. Key
>
> ○ e. Features

Answer c is correct. You do not have to complete a password field when adding a license to your firewall. Answers a, b, d, and e are incorrect because the host, expiration date, key, and features must all be valid and entered when adding a license.

Question 9

> Which is not a valid operating system to install FireWall-1 on?
>
> ○ a. Windows NT (SP3 or higher)
>
> ○ b. Red Hat Linux 6.1
>
> ○ c. Solaris 2.6
>
> ○ d. HP-UX
>
> ○ e. None of the above

Answer a is correct. Windows NT is a valid operating system on which to run the firewall module; however, it must have Service Pack 4 or higher installed. Answers b, c, and d are incorrect because Red Hat Linux 6.1, Solaris 2.6, and HP-UX are all operating systems that can run FireWall-1. Answer e is incorrect because the correct answer is provided.

Question 10

> Which of the following are levels of administrator access? [Check all correct answers]
>
> ❏ a. Log Viewer
>
> ❏ b. Edit User Database
>
> ❏ c. No Permissions
>
> ❏ d. Customized
>
> ❏ e. Read Only
>
> ❏ f. Read/Write All

Answers c, d, and f are correct. Read/Write All, Customized, and No Permissions are the three levels that can be assigned to an administrator account. Answers a and b are incorrect because the Log Viewer and Edit User Database settings are options in the Customized configuration. Answer e is incorrect because there is no option in the administrator access screen for Read Only.

Need to Know More?

 Check Point Security Software: Introduction to FireWall-1. Official Check Point courseware.

 Goncalves, Marcus and Steven Brown. *Check Point FireWall-1 Administration Guide.* McGraw-Hill, New York, NY, 1999. ISBN 0-07-134229-X. This book serves as a good bookshelf reference for FireWall-1.

 www.checkpoint.com, the Check Point Web site, offers some basic installation information regarding the various types of installations and OS platforms.

Implementing
Network Objects

Terms you'll need to understand:

✓ Policy Editor

✓ Firewall object

✓ Logical server

✓ Groups

✓ Network object

✓ Workstation object

✓ Domain object

✓ VLAN (virtual local area network)

✓ Address range object

Techniques you'll need to master:

✓ Defining encryption methods

✓ Configuring the various network objects

✓ Managing network objects

✓ Managing external communication devices

✓ Defining a color scheme

✓ Accessing the Policy Editor

✓ Understanding the various object tabs

✓ Choosing encryption types

In Chapter 3, I stepped you through installing and configuring your firewall on your machine. In this chapter, I start looking at the different types of objects that can be created and modified using the FireWall-1 Policy Editor. I also cover some of the details that go into creating a solid security policy, such as color schemes, comments, descriptions, and properly determining the location of an object.

Let's get started by opening the Policy Editor GUI.

Managing Your Firewall

Most firewall administration tasks take place inside the Policy Editor GUI. The Policy Editor is where you define your rules, users, workstations, networks, services, other firewalls that will affect your firewall, and, more importantly, your internal network. In Chapter 3, I showed you how to define your administrators and your GUI clients. In this chapter, I assume that you'll be working with the Stand Alone Installation setup, so I use the Enforcement Module as the GUI client in the examples. However, if you would like to use another workstation as your GUI, you'll be able to easily see where necessary modifications need to occur relative to the text. Now, let's get busy.

To access the firewall, you need the username of an administrator that was defined during the installation, the password that was assigned to the administrator, and the IP address (or hostname) of the Enforcement Module that you will be working on (see Figure 4.1). The administrator that you use must have read/write privileges to make the changes that you will be implementing in this chapter.

 If more that one administrator is logged in at the same time, the second person to sign in will be granted only read access.

Before I get into how to manage your objects, I need to discuss a topic that will make administration of your firewall a much easier task—color schemes.

Welcome to **Check Point**
Policy Editor version *4.1*

User Name: admin
Password:
Management Server: 192.168.1.1
Read Only ☐

OK Quit

Figure 4.1 Policy Editor GUI sign-in screen.

Developing a Color Scheme

Experienced administrators are always looking for ways to make their jobs easier. Anyone working in a large environment is familiar with the hassles of working with servers or other equipment from the same vendor. Trying to distinguish one server from another can be a real headache unless you have properly labeled or grouped the servers. In FireWall-1, Check Point gives you the ability to group objects into categories by developing a color scheme.

If a firewall is using a simple configuration with only a few objects and rules, using a color scheme might not seem necessary. However, if you are developing a firewall that will have dozens of rules and hundreds of objects, you will certainly appreciate having a color scheme. Check Point recommends the following as a potential basic color scheme:

➤ *Green*—Internal objects

➤ *Blue*—External objects

➤ *Red*—Firewall objects

I will use other colors for other objects throughout this book, but the preceding three color assignments are used as a standard by most administrators.

Managing Objects

Immediately upon entering the Policy Editor, you will notice that the security policy is empty, as shown in Figure 4.2. Because you created a brand new Enforcement Module, no security policy is enforced. I define all of the security policy's buttons, tabs, and menu options in Chapter 7, when I show you how to implement the rule base. In this chapter, you will be using the Manage option on the menu bar to access the objects.

In order for you to use an object in your firewall configuration, you must first create the object so that it can be managed by the firewall. There are eight management tools that you will use to define the various types of objects. The tools are:

➤ Network Objects Manager

➤ Services Manager

➤ Resources Manager

➤ Server Manager

➤ User Manager

➤ Users On Account Unit

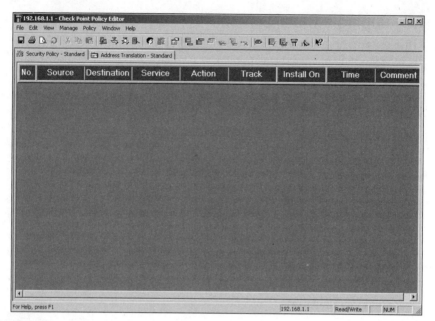

Figure 4.2   Empty security policy.

➤ Time Manager

➤ Key Manager

This chapter focuses on the Network Objects tool. Chapter 5 covers the rest of the management tools. Because most of the objects that you will need to define and manage on your firewall are created in the Network Objects tool, it is worthy of an entire chapter.

Managing Network Objects

The *Network Objects Manager* (also known as the *Network Objects tool*) is where you define the objects that have some sort of presence on your network. That might seem like a strange way to define these types of objects, but the intention is to keep you away from assuming that a network object is a physical object. Namely, a network object can be any of the following:

➤ Workstation

➤ Network

➤ Domain

➤ Router

➤ Switch

➤ Integrated firewall

➤ Groups

➤ Logical servers

➤ Address range

Each of these objects has their own unique characteristics and configuration objects, and you will need to become familiar with these for the exam. In the next few sections, we will create one of each of the network objects listed above. Let's start creating some objects. The first object we will create is a workstation object.

Workstation Object

A workstation object is a server or workstation, or, more generically, any object that has an IP address specifically assigned to it. With that said, a workstation could actually be a networked printer, dumb terminal, or any other device with a network interface card (NIC). To help you become more familiar with workstation objects, let's create a new workstation object by performing the following steps:

1. Click Manage on the menu bar in the Policy Editor.

2. Click Network Objects on the Manage menu.

3. Click the New button on the Network Object menu.

4. Select Workstation on the drop-down menu.

You will now have a blank Workstation Properties dialog box on your screen (see Figure 4.3). As you can see in Figure 4.3, the Workstation Properties dialog box includes several tabs. Each tab contains a different set of values that may or may not need to be changed, depending on how you want the firewall to handle each object. The tabs, in order, are:

➤ General

➤ Interfaces

➤ SNMP

➤ NAT

➤ VPN

In the following sections, we'll configure the tabs for the workstation object we're creating in this chapter. The first tab to appear when creating a new workstation object is the General tab, so this will be a good place to start.

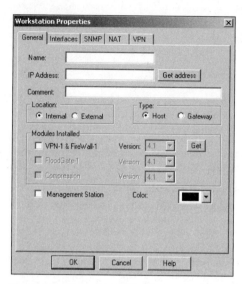

Figure 4.3 General tab in the Workstation Properties dialog box.

General Tab

The General tab is where you define the basic properties for a workstation object. To configure this tab, follow these steps:

1. In the Name field, insert the name of a workstation on your internal network. For this example, we'll name the workstation *Workstation1*.

2. Enter an IP address for the workstation. In this example, we'll use *10.0.0.2*.

3. A description is not necessary for the Comment field, but, as with the color scheme, a description can become very helpful as your rules and objects grow. For this example, we will type "My workstation".

4. In the Location area, you specify the location of the workstation. The location of the workstation is in reference to your firewall. If a workstation is managed by the Management Server, it is an *internal* device. If it is managed by another firewall, it is an *external* device. In this example, our workstation will be controlled by the Management Server, so we will leave it as an internal device, and ensure that the Internal option is selected.

Note: In Step 4 on the General tab, you want to make sure that you assign the location of the workstation properly, so be careful when you are at this step during a configuration.

5. I discussed the color scheme earlier in this chapter, and, based on the Check Point recommendations, we will mark this workstation object as a green object because it is internal.

6. The Type field determines the type of workstation. A workstation can be configured as a *host* or a *gateway*. A host is a device with only one IP address assigned to it. A gateway is a device that handles traffic from two separate networks, such as another firewall. In this example, our workstation is a host.

7. If a workstation was running a Check Point product, you would click the product and version number to let our rule base know of its existence. We will configure a workstation with FireWall-1 later. For now, we don't need to select any options in the Modules Installed section.

8. The last option on this page is the Management Station checkbox. If this station was serving as a Management Server, you would check this checkbox, which would create additional tabs for configuration.

We've now completed configuring the General tab in the Workstation Properties dialog box. Let's move on to the next tab—the Interfaces tab.

Interfaces Tab

The Interfaces tab is used for listing the name of the NIC, IP address, and subnet mask (also called network mask); see Figure 4.4. In this example, we will have only one interface on the workstation, so let's go ahead and enter the information, as follows:

1. Click the Add button.

2. Type the name of the interface. This option applies more to a Unix installation than to an NT installation, but you can still name the interface.

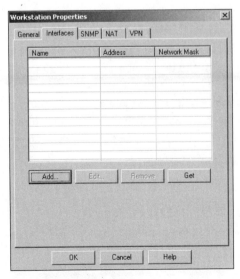

Figure 4.4   Interfaces tab.

3. Type the IP address of the interface, just as you did on the General tab.

4. Type the subnet mask for the IP address.

5. Click OK.

Now, let's move on to the SNMP tab.

SNMP Tab

The SNMP tab allows you to set SNMP (Simple Network Management Protocol) information for your workstation object. I won't be covering SNMP in this book because it is not on the CCSA exam, but you should know that SNMP can be configured here.

NAT Tab

NAT (network address translation) is covered at length in Chapter 9. At this point, just know that the NAT tab is used for selecting if and how this workstation will handle NAT.

VPN Tab

If you are using this workstation as park of a VPN (virtual private network), the VPN tab would be used to specify the encryption type. VPNs and encryption are discussed further in Chapter 10.

To complete the configuration of the workstation, click OK on the bottom of the Workstation Properties dialog box. Your workstation will now appear in the Network Objects dialog box.

Defining a Workstation as a Gateway

As mentioned in the previous section, a workstation can be either a host or a gateway. As a gateway, the workstation can also be running a Check Point product, such as VPN-1, FireWall-1, or FloodGate-1. In this chapter's example setup, we know that our Enforcement Module is both a server and a gateway running the FireWall-1 product. Therefore, we will want to define our firewall in our objects list, so we can specify rules involving it. Let's create a new workstation object as a gateway, as follows:

1. Click Manage on the menu bar in the Policy Editor.

2. Click Network Objects on the Manage menu.

3. Click the New button on the Network Object menu.

4. Select Workstation on the drop-down menu.

Let's start again with the General tab, because this is where we will specify our workstation as a gateway.

General Tab

The General tab is the same at this point as it was the last time we created a workstation object. However, we're going to make one change that is going to set off a whole chain of events.

1. In the Name field, insert the name of your firewall. In this example, we'll name the firewall *Arizona*.

2. Enter an IP address for the workstation. In our example, we will use *192.168.1.1,* the IP we assigned to our firewall in the installation.

Note: We are using invalid addresses in our examples because this is not a real-world configuration. When I use the 192.168.x.x address, I am referring to the external side of the firewall.

3. Enter a description in the Comment field. We'll enter *My Firewall.*

4. Because our firewall is managed by the Management Server, we will leave it as an *internal* device. We will be marking this device as a red object, because it is firewall. You can decide if you want to make this green or red, because it is both a firewall and an internal device.

Note: Even though we are using the external address of the firewall, the gateway is still managed by the Management Server, so it is still listed as internal.

5. The Type field determines the type of workstation. A firewall is, by definition, a gateway, so click the Gateway radio button.

6. Because we know that we are running the FireWall-1 module on the workstation we are defining, I selected the VPN-1 & FireWall-1 option in the Modules Installed section. Notice that there are two new tabs in the dialog box—Certificates and Authentication.

7. Verify that the version is 4.1, and enter a checkmark in the Management Station checkbox.

After you've completed the General tab, click the Interfaces tab to continue setting up your firewall. We will need to identify our interfaces so that we can set the other options that are available only to a gateway.

Interfaces Tab

Just as we did earlier in this chapter when we configured the host, we need to define an interface for the gateway. To add an interface, follow these steps:

1. Click the Add button.

2. Type the name of the interface. In this example, we use the name *external.*

3. Type the IP address of the interface.

4. Type the subnet mask for the IP address.

5. Click the Security tab. The Security tab is used to define parameters relating to anti-spoofing. The Security tab contains two sections—Valid Addresses and Spoof Tracking. The choices in the Valid Addresses section are:

➤ *Any*—No spoof tracking.

➤ *This Net*—Only packets that originate from the network connected to the interface are allowed.

➤ *No Security Policy!*—Basically, don't use this. It is used when a security policy is used on a different interface.

➤ *Others*—Packets are allowed from networks other than those on the interface.

➤ *Others+*—Same as the Others option, except you can specify the addresses that you want to grant access to.

➤ *Specific*—Packets are allowed from the specified addresses only.

The Spoof Tracking section determines how you will handle the logging of spoofed traffic. All spoofed traffic is dropped by default, but you can determine how it is recorded by choosing one of the following options:

➤ *None*—No logging.

➤ *Log*—Logged to the FireWall-1 log.

➤ *Alert*—An alert is sent, based on properties in the Log And Alert portion of the Properties Setup screen.

For now, we can leave the Valid Addresses option set to Any.

6. Repeat Steps 1 through 5 to create the record for the internal interface. Use *internal* as the device name, *10.0.0.1* as the IP address, and *255.0.0.0* as the subnet mask.

The next tab that becomes available as a gateway is the Certificates tab. Let's take a quick look at the Certificates tab.

Certificates Tab

The Certificates tab allows you to apply certificates from a CA (certificate authority) to your firewall. In our example, we have not defined any certificate servers yet, so we cannot add any certificates to the list. Regardless, this is the tab that would be used for applying certificates.

Authentication Tab

The Authentication tab specifies the authentication schemes that are enforced on the firewall. If a user tries to authenticate with another scheme than what is selected, they will be refused access through the firewall. The available schemes are:

➤ S/Key

➤ SecurID

➤ OS Password

➤ VPN-1 & FireWall-1 Password

➤ RADIUS (Remote Authentication Dial-In User Service protocol)

➤ AXENT Pathways Defender

➤ TACACS (Terminal Access Controller Access Control System)

Configure the Authentication tab as follows:

1. For this example setup, leave the authentication options set to the default choices. The options are discussed further in Chapter 10.

2. Click OK to save the firewall object.

Both the firewall and the workstation defined earlier in this chapter should now appear in your Network Objects list, as shown in Figure 4.5.

Creating Network and Domain Objects

Inside of the Network Objects tool, you have the ability to create network and domain objects just as you did with workstations. Networks and domains are a collection, or group, of objects that are managed as a single entity. This allows you

Figure 4.5 Network Objects tool with defined objects.

to perform management tasks on a very high level, whereas creating workstations allows administration on a granular level.

Network Objects

A network can be internal or external. A network is considered *internal* if it is protected by the firewall and *external* if it is not. Let's jump right in and create an internal network:

1. Click Manage on the menu in the Policy Editor.

2. Click Network Objects on the Manage menu.

3. Click the New button on the Network Object menu.

4. Select Network on the drop-down menu.

The Network Properties dialog box contains two tabs (see Figure 4.6)—*General* and *NAT*. The General tab is similar to the General tab in the Workstation Properties dialog box. In the Network Properties dialog box, the General tab is used to store the basic information about the network.

General Tab

The General tab of a network object is similar to that of a workstation object. To configure the General tab in the Network Properties dialog box, follow these steps:

1. In the Name field, insert the name of your internal network. In this example, we'll call ours *Phoenix*.

2. Enter an IP address for the network. In our example, we will use *10.0.0.0*, the network address we assigned as internal to our firewall.

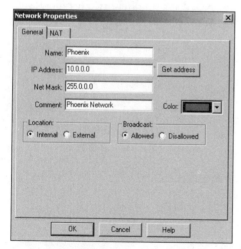

Figure 4.6 The Network Properties dialog box.

3. Enter a description in the Comment field. We will use *Phoenix Network*.

Note: Make sure you enter the network address, and not an actual IP address.

4. Because the network is protected by the firewall, we will leave the Internal option selected in the Location area.

5. Mark the device as a green object, because it is internal.

6. The last option on this tab is the Broadcast option. This option allows you to specify the network's broadcast IP address as being a part of the network. Leave the Broadcast option set to Allowed, so that you can allow broadcast traffic to pass within the network.

The next tab that we want to look at handles how this object will handle network address translation; it is the NAT tab.

NAT Tab

NAT (network address translation) is covered at length in Chapter 9. At this point, just know that this tab is used for selecting if and how a network will handle NAT. At this point, you only need to complete a couple final setup steps:

1. Click OK to save the network object and return to the Network Objects tool.

2. Create a second network called *Boston*. Insert an IP address of *172.16.10.0*, a subnet mask of *255.255.255.0*, and a description of *Boston Network*. Further, this network will be a blue object, because it will be external.

Network objects allow us to specify networks and subnets that we want to specify as a particular entity within our firewall. However, what if we didn't want to specify an IP range, but instead wanted to use a fully qualified domain name? In this case, we would want to create a domain object.

Domain Objects

When a domain object is used in a rule, the IP address of the source is resolved using the reverse-lookup method to determine if the packet is allowed to pass. This allows some additional flexibility when specifying a particular network so that we are not locked down to a particular address range, especially if we are referring to an external, Internet-valid IP range that could potentially change.

 Rules containing domain objects should be placed at the lower end of the rule base.

Defining a domain object is pretty easy, as described here:

1. In the Domain Properties dialog box in the Network Objects tool, enter a fully qualified domain name in the Name field. In our example, we will use *www.mynetwork.com*.

2. In the Comment field, type "My Internal FQDN" as the description.

3. This domain will be internal to the firewall, so make the color green.

4. Click OK to save the domain object and return to the Network Objects tool. Notice that the new objects display in the Network Objects tool, as shown in Figure 4.7.

Part of what makes a network is the fact that all of the machines have the ability to communicate with one another. To facilitate those communications, we need communication devices such as switches and routers in order to control the flow of traffic. That said, it only makes sense that we would want our firewall to be aware of these devices inside of its database. For this purpose, FireWall-1 gives us the ability to create Communication Device objects.

Managing Communication Devices

FireWall-1 has the ability to manage some aspects of routers and switches. Defining these devices serves two purposes. First, defining routers and switches enables you to add them to your rule base to control traffic to and from them. Second, defining routers and switches enables you to manage ACLs (access control lists) for Cisco, Nortel / Bay Networks, 3Com, and Microsoft Steelhead routers as well as switches. In addition to the two main reasons for defining routers and switches, a third purpose exists for a router that is a little less impacting: Namely,

Figure 4.7   The Network Objects tool with new objects.

defining a router grants you the ability to list a router as a FireWall-1 Enforcement Module.

Note: The FireWall-1 option is available only on Bay Networks routers.

Defining a Router

For practice, let's define a Cisco router. The five tabs in the Router Properties dialog box for a Cisco Router are:

➤ General

➤ Interfaces

➤ NAT

➤ SNMP

➤ Setup

To create a router object, follow these steps:

1. Click Manage on the menu bar in the Policy Editor.

2. Click Network Objects on the Manage menu.

3. Click the New button on the Network Object menu.

4. Select Router on the drop-down menu.

We need to enter the basic information for our router, so the first tab that we will work with is the General tab.

General Tab

The General tab (see Figure 4.8) in the Router Properties dialog box is where you define the basic properties for the router. To configure the General tab in the Router Properties dialog box, follow these steps:

1. In the Name field, insert a name of a fictitious router that is external to your network. In this chapter's example, we'll call the router *Arizona_Router*.

2. Enter an IP address for the router. In our example, we will use 192.168.1.3.

3. Enter a description for the router. For instance, you could indicate that the router connects to your ISP. For our example, we will type "Router to ISP".

4. Like the workstations and networks, the location of the router is in reference to your firewall. This device sits outside of the firewall; therefore, it is an external device.

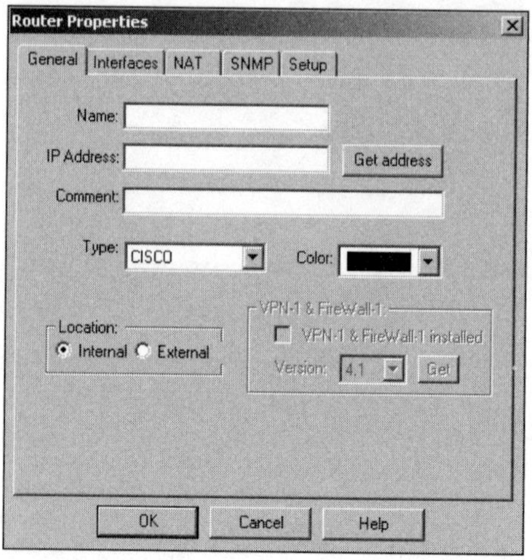

Figure 4.8 General tab in the Router Properties dialog box.

5. Based on the Check Point recommendations, you should mark this device as a blue object because it is external.

6. The Type field is a drop-down menu in which you select the manufacturer of the router. Notice that if you select Bay Networks, the VPN-1 & FireWall-1 section on the General tab in the Router Properties dialog box becomes enabled. For our example, we will select Cisco.

Routers have interfaces, just as workstations do. Therefore, we need to specify the names and IP addresses of these objects so that we are aware of how they fit into our network scheme. For this purpose, we have the Interfaces tab.

Interfaces Tab

The Interfaces tab is used for listing the name of the router's NIC, the IP address, and the subnet mask. To configure an interface, follow these steps:

1. Click the Add button.

2. Type the name of the interface, which is *Arizona_Router* in our example.

3. Type the IP address of the interface.

4. Type the subnet mask for the IP address.

5. Click OK.

6. The Security tab is used to define parameters relating to anti-spoofing. Please refer back to the Securirity tab information in the "Defining a Workstation as a Gateway" section.

7. Repeat Steps 1 through 5 to create the record for the router's other interface. Use *ISP* as the device name, *38.187.128.10* as the IP address, and *255.255.0.0* as the subnet mask.

NAT Tab

Network address translation is covered at length in Chapter 9. At this point, just know that this tab is used for selecting if and how a router will handle NAT.

SNMP Tab

The SNMP tab is used to configure the router with the ability to retrieve or set SNMP information. Although we will not be configuring, let's take a brief look at the settings:

➤ *sysName*—The name of the object

➤ *sysLocation*—The location of the object

➤ *sysContact*—The name of the contact person

➤ *Read Community*—The community that has read permissions to this object

➤ *Write Community*—The community that has write permissions to this object

All routers have a specific set of security requirements. If we want a firewall to manage our routers, we need to inform it of the security attributes used to access the router. The Setup tab contains the security information for the router object.

Setup Tab

The Setup tab allows you to enter the information for managing the router, such as username and password. The Setup tab varies based on which router you define on the General tab.

Defining a Switch

Defining a switch, like a router, has two main purposes. Namely, when you define a switch, you can add it to your rule base to control traffic, and you can use a defined switch to manage a Xylan switch that has run the FireWall-1 software.

For the test, you don't need to know how to configure a Xylan switch; you just need to know that FireWall-1 can run on a Xylan.

To create a switch object, follow these steps:

1. Click Manage on the menu in the Policy Editor.

2. Click Network Objects on the Manage menu.

3. Click the New button on the Network Object menu.

4. Select Switch on the drop-down menu.

Now, let's define a generic switch for our rule base. The Switch Properties dialog box contains the following six tabs:

➤ General

➤ Interfaces

➤ NAT

➤ SNMP

➤ VLAN

➤ Setup (Xylan only)

Setting up the General, Interfaces, NAT, and SNMP tabs for a switch is the same as it would be for a router. In this example, we will name the switch *First_Floor*, set the IP address to *10.0.0.10*, and type "1st Floor Switch" in the Comment field. In addition, we will set the type for *Other*, make it an *internal* device, and change the color to *green*. After you've made those configurations, click the VLAN tab.

VLAN Tab

Most switches allow for configuration of a virtual local area network (VLAN). A virtual LAN is a local area network with a definition that maps workstations on some basis other than geographic location. The virtual LAN controller can change or add workstations more easily than with a physical LAN.

To add a VLAN to the switch configuration, follow these steps:

1. Click the Add button.

2. Enter the VLAN number.

3. Enter the name of the VLAN that is defined on the switch.

4. Enter the protocol that is defined on the switch.

5. Click OK.

After you configure the VLAN tab, click OK in the Switch Properties dialog box to add the switch to your Network Objects list. Take a look at the list—it's getting longer and longer! See the need for the color scheme now?

Creating Firewall Objects

When you create a firewall object, the object enables you to manage third-party firewalls, such as CES, Timestep, and Cisco. These firewalls can be integrated with FireWall-1 to allow for the configuration of alternative security implementations. In this section, we will go through the steps required to add a Cisco PIX object to our Network Objects.

To create an integrated firewall object, follow these steps:

1. Click Manage on the menu in the Policy Editor.

2. Click Network Objects on the Manage menu.

3. Click the New button on the Network Object menu.

4. Select Integrated Firewall on the drop-down menu.

Initially, there are four tabs in the Integrated Firewall Properties dialog box. This will vary depending on the model you select. The four initial tabs are:

➤ General

➤ Interfaces

➤ SNMP

➤ NAT

I'll skip the Interfaces, SNMP, and NAT tabs in our example, because these tabs have been already been covered at length earlier in this chapter.

General Tab

Like the General tabs in the other properties dialog boxes presented in this chapter, this tab is used to store the most basic information about an object. In this instance, the information pertains to a firewall object. To configure this tab for a firewall object, follow these steps:

1. In the Name field, enter in a name for the integrated firewall. In our example, we will name our integrated firewall *Boston_PIX*.

2. Enter an IP address into the IP Address field. In our example, we will use *172.16.10.1*.

3. Enter a description into the comment field. In this example, we will use *Boston office PIX firewall*.

4. We're going to break from the Check Point standard on this object and use yellow as the color, because this is both external and a firewall.

5. This object is obviously not in our internal network, so set this as an external device.

6. In the Type drop-down list, select Cisco. You will now see two additional tabs:

   ➤ Setup-A

   ➤ Setup-B

Let's configure the new tabs, starting with the Setup-A tab, and then look at the Setup-B tab. These setup tabs are specific to a Cisco PIX firewall. Other types of firewalls have different tabs, so I would suggest looking at each type of firewall's tabs individually.

Setup-A Tab

The Setup-A tab shows the properties specifically relating to a Cisco PIX firewall (see Figure 4.9). There are several sections to this tab:

➤ *Inside Addresses*—Where the PIX firewall controls address translation.

➤ *Enable Password*—Password used to access the PIX firewall.

➤ *PIX Password*—Password required to enable communications to the PIX firewall. The default password is *cisco*.

➤ *Version*—Version of the PIX firewall.

➤ *Xlate Timeout*—Amount of time before a PIX translation slot time will expire.

➤ *Conn Timeout*—Connection slot timeout.

➤ *Server*—A previously defined authentication server.

➤ *Shared Secret*—Public key to encrypt communications.

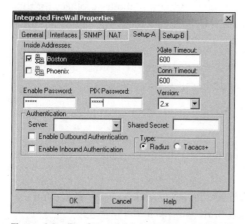

Figure 4.9   The Setup-A tab in the Integrated Firewall Properties dialog box.

➤ *Enable Outbound/Inbound Authentication*—Request authentication for inbound or outbound communications.

➤ *Type*—Chooses an authentication scheme, Radius or Tacacs+.

Note: Chapter 10 discusses authentication issues in more detail.

To configure the Setup-A tab, follow these steps:

1. Click the checkbox next to Boston to select it as the network where the PIX firewall handles address translation.

2. Leave the Xlate Timeout, Comm Timeout, and Version set to their default values.

3. Enter an enable and PIX password. For this example, we'll use *cisco*.

4. Don't do anything in the Authentication area, and then click the Setup-B tab to continue.

We'll now configure the Setup-B tab.

Setup-B Tab

The Setup-B tab offers additional information relating to the PIX firewall, including:

➤ *RIP Inside*—Defines internal RIP settings.

➤ *Rip Outside*—Defines external RIP settings.

➤ *Failover*—Determines if a secondary (backup) PIX firewall is active for failover.

➤ *Private Link Key Duration*—Time, in minutes, until a private PIX key is changed.

➤ *Private Link Connections*—Lists the PIX units that you have created a private link connection to the Management Server.

To configure the Setup-B tab, follow these steps:

1. Check the Default checkboxes for both of the RIP sections.

2. Click OK. You will be returned to the Network Objects tool.

Now we have a bunch of objects in our Network Objects tool. Of course, this is a fairly small amount compared to what you may encounter in a real-world environment. As an administrator, having the ability to place objects into similar groups makes your job much easier. For this purpose, FireWall-1 gives you the ability to create group objects.

Creating Group Objects

A group object is a quick-and-easy object to create. Groups are important in the creation of your rule base. Groups make management much easier because they allow you to take objects and group them, rather than adding them one at a time into your rule base. Let's say that you had a dozen Web servers that you wanted to apply the same rules to. Wouldn't it be much easier if we put them all under one "label" and created a single rule, rather than twelve separate rules? Let's create a group object to place the network we created into a single entity.

To create a group object, follow these steps:

1. Click Manage on the menu in the Policy Editor.

2. Click Network Objects on the Manage menu.

3. Click the New button on the Network Object menu.

4. Select Group on the drop-down menu.

There is only one tab in the Group Properties dialog box. In the example setup, we're going to group the Phoenix and Boston networks together, and call the group *Known Networks*. We'll also add a description of *Networks that we know and trust*, and we'll make all of our group objects *orange* in our color scheme.

Adding an object is pretty straightforward. There are two columns on the screen:

➤ Not In Group

➤ In Group

It can't get much clearer than that! To add an object, click the object and then click the Add button. The object will be moved from one column to the other. After you have added both the Phoenix and Boston networks, click OK to save the object.

Groups do not have to be of the same type. However, use good judgment when creating groups. Objects should have some similarities or related purposes to warrant being combined into a group. An example of a homogenous group could be a workstation working as a non-firewalled gateway and a router. Both objects are working as gateways and may need to have the same rules applied.

Configuring Logical Servers

A logical server is a group of machines that offer the same type of service and are used in a load-balanced environment. Logical servers are not tested on the CCSA exam, but you should know the properties you can configure for them, because you might run across this while administering a FireWall-1 server in the real world. The property fields for the Logical Servers dialog box are:

➤ *Name*—Name of the logical server.

➤ *IP Address*—Address of a single host.

➤ *Comment*—Description of the logical server.

➤ *Color*—Color scheme.

➤ *Server's Type*—Either HTTP or Other.

➤ *Persistent Server Mode*—If checked, a user would remain connected to the same physical server for the length of the session.

➤ *Servers*—List of predefined servers.

➤ *Balance Method*—Way in which the servers in the group will be balanced.

When developing a network scheme, many administrators choose to set aside ranges of IP addresses for different types of networked objects. Rather than creating objects for each individual object within a range, an administrator may find it advantageous to create a single address range object. In the next section, we will create an address range object for some Microsoft Terminal Servers.

Creating Address Range Objects

An address range is a group of continuous IP addresses that serve a particular function. An example of an address range might be domain controllers, terminal servers, Citrix servers, Web servers, and so on. The key to setting up an address range is that the addresses must be in sequence. In other words, you cannot have gaps in an address range. The minimum amount of IP addresses for an address range is two, because it would be pointless to make an address range for one IP address.

To create an address range object, follow these steps:

1. Click Manage on the menu in the Policy Editor.

2. Click Network Objects on the Manage menu.

3. Click the New button on the Network Object menu.

4. Select Address Range on the drop-down menu.

Let's say that we have three servers running as terminal servers in our internal network that we want to define as an address range. To perform this setup, we would need to configure the two tabs in the Address Range Properties dialog box for a Cisco Router. The tabs are:

➤ General

➤ NAT

Let's configure an address range.

General Tab

The General tab in the Address Range Properties dialog box is used for almost all of the information used in reference to an address range, as you can see in Figure 4.10. To configure the General tab, follow these steps:

1. In the Name field, enter a name for the address range. In our example, we will name our address range *Internal_TS_Servers*.

2. Enter the first IP address in the First IP Address text box. We will use *10.0.0.20* for our first IP address.

3. Insert the last IP address in the range into the Last IP Address text box. In our example, the last IP address will be *10.0.0.23*.

4. Change the color of the range to green for an internal object.

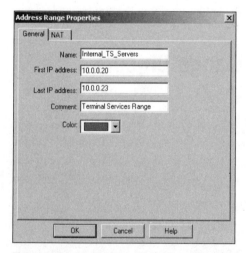

Figure 4.10 General tab in the Address Range Properties dialog box.

NAT Tab

Network address translation is covered at length in Chapter 9. At this point, just know that the NAT tab is used for selecting if and how an address range will handle NAT.

Practice Questions

Question 1

> Creating a color scheme is not important; it just makes the rule base look pretty.
>
> ○ a. True
>
> ○ b. False

Answer b is correct because the statement is false. A color scheme is absolutely important to a firewall configuration. Color schemes make it easier to identify objects and to differentiate among various locations of objects.

Question 2

> Which brand of switches can have the FireWall-1 software installed?
>
> ○ a. Cisco
>
> ○ b. Bay Networks
>
> ○ c. Allcatel
>
> ○ d. Xylan

Answer d is correct. Only the Xylan brand of switches can be configured to use the FireWall-1 software. Answers a, b, and c are incorrect because none of those brands can have FireWall-1 installed onto them.

Question 3

What objects can you create using the Network Objects tool? [Check all correct answers]

❑ a. Networks

❑ b. Web sites

❑ c. Switches

❑ d. Integrated firewalls

❑ e. Groups

❑ f. Workstations

❑ g. Address ranges

❑ h. Routers

❑ i. Users

❑ j. Domains

❑ k. Logical servers

Answers a, c, d, e, f, g, h, j, and k are correct. You can use the Network Objects tool to create objects for networks, switches, integrated firewalls, groups, workstations, address ranges, routers, domains, and logical servers. Answer b is incorrect because there is no Web site object in the Network Objects tool. Answer i is incorrect because users are defined in the Users tool.

Question 4

When will the Management Server see a workstation as a FireWall-1 Enforcement Module?

○ a. When you change the color to red

○ b. When you enter the IP address of the firewall

○ c. When you change the location to external

○ d. When you click the VPN-1 & FireWall-1 checkbox

Answer d is correct. The Management Server will not recognize a workstation as being a FireWall-1 Enforcement Module until you check the VPN-1 & FireWall-1 checkbox. Answer a is incorrect because changing the color does not change how the Management Server views an object. Answer b is incorrect because the Management Server does not know the role of a workstation based on the IP address. Answer c is incorrect because a workstation can be an Enforcement Module regardless of its location.

Question 5

> What makes an object an internal object?
>
> ○ a. Your Management Server controls it and your firewall protects it.
>
> ○ b. It is at your physical location.
>
> ○ c. It is part of your domain.
>
> ○ d. None of the above.

Answer a is correct. The rule of thumb for objects is that if the object is either controlled by you as an administrator or is protected by your firewall, it's an internal object. Answer b is incorrect because an internal object does not have to reside at the same physical location as you. Answer c is incorrect because domains have no effect on your objects.

Question 6

> Which brands of routers have special configuration tabs in the Router Properties dialog box? [Check all correct answers]
>
> ❑ a. 3Com
>
> ❑ b. Bay Networks
>
> ❑ c. Cabletron
>
> ❑ d. Cisco
>
> ❑ e. Nokia
>
> ❑ f. Steelhead

Answers a, b, d, and f are all correct. 3Com, Bay Networks, Cisco, and Steelhead routers include special configuration tabs in the Router Properties dialog box. Answers c and e are incorrect because the Router Properties dialog box does not have a setup tab for Cabletron or Nokia. Other router brands can be listed under the Type listing of *Other*, but do not have special configuration options.

Question 7

On the Security tab of the Interfaces tab, what does spoof tracking do?

- ○ a. Chases "ghost" packets through your network.
- ○ b. Provides a cool way to hide an IP address.
- ○ c. Determines which action is taken when a spoofed packet is detected.
- ○ d. Traces the MAC address of a spoofed packet.
- ○ e. None of the above.

Answer c is correct. The Spoof Tracking section on the Security tab determines the action that will be taken if a spoofed packet is detected. The options are None (no action taken), Log (spoofing attempt is logged), and Alert (an alert is sent). Answer a is incorrect because IP spoofing does not chase packets. Answer b is incorrect because Spoof Tracking does not hide IP addresses. Answer d is incorrect because Spoof Tracking does not attempt to trace the IP address back to a MAC address.

Question 8

What is not needed to start the Policy Editor?

- ○ a. Username
- ○ b. Key from a certificate authority
- ○ c. Password
- ○ d. Address (or hostname)

Answer b is correct. CAs are not used for connection to the Policy Editor. Answers a, c, and d are incorrect because all three options—username, password, and hostname—are necessary when starting the Policy Editor.

Question 9

In an address range object, the IP addresses must be sequential.

- ○ a. True
- ○ b. False

Answer a is correct because the statement is true. The IP addresses used in an address range object must be sequential in order to create the object.

Question 10

How many additional tabs does a Cisco PIX firewall create in an integrated firewall object?

○ a. One

○ b. Two

○ c. Three

○ d. Five

○ e. None

Answer b is correct. When you define an integrated firewall object as a Cisco PIX firewall, two additional tabs are created: Setup-A and Setup-B. These tabs are specific to the Cisco PIX configuration.

Need to Know More?

 Check Point Security Software: Introduction to FireWall-1. Official Check Point courseware.

 Goncalves, Marcus and Steven Brown. *Check Point FireWall-1 Administration Guide.* McGraw-Hill, New York, NY, 1999. ISBN 0-07-134229-X. This book serves as a good bookshelf reference for FireWall-1.

 Waters, Jason, Matthew Rees, and Jeffrey Coe. *CCNA Routing and Switching Exam Cram, Second Edition.* The Coriolis Group, Scottsdale, AZ, 2000. ISBN 1-57-610628-4. This is a great book for administrators who want to know more about Cisco routers and switches.

 Wenstrom, Mike. *Managing Cisco Network Security.* Cisco Systems, Inc., San Francisco, CA, 2001. ISBN 1-57-870103-1. This book is considered to be the definitive book for managing Cisco network security.

 www.checkpoint.com, the Check Point Web site, offers some basic installation information regarding the various types of installations and OS platforms.

Other Management Objects

Terms you'll need to understand:

- ✓ User Datagram Protocol (UDP)
- ✓ Remote procedure call (RPC)
- ✓ Internet Control Message Protocol (ICMP)
- ✓ Transmission Control Protocol (TCP)
- ✓ Uniform Resource Identifier (URI)
- ✓ URL Filtering Protocol (UFP)
- ✓ Uniform Resource Locator (URL)
- ✓ Remote Authentication Dial-In User Service (RADIUS)
- ✓ Terminal Access Controller Access Control System (TACACS)

Techniques you'll need to master:

- ✓ Implementing group objects
- ✓ Grouping users
- ✓ Differentiating among various types of resource objects
- ✓ Implementing time objects
- ✓ Implementing service objects
- ✓ Implementing resource objects
- ✓ Implementing server objects
- ✓ Implementing user objects
- ✓ Implementing user templates
- ✓ Choosing a URI match type

Chapter 4 focused on creating and managing the various types of network objects; in this chapter, I focus on the other management objects. Network objects are the heart and soul of the Check Point firewall object tools; however, the firewall can't function without the support of the additional management objects. The other management objects allow you to manage objects such as TCP ports, UDP ports, RPC ports, ICMP, users, time, and other areas that can and most likely will affect your firewall. The following management tools are covered in this chapter:

➤ Services Manager

➤ Resources Manager

➤ Server Manager

➤ User Manager

➤ Users On Account Unit

➤ Time Manager

➤ Key Manager

Note: In our current software implementation, the Users On Account Unit service is unavailable. This option is used to manage users on an LDAP account unit. Managing LDAP users is not covered by the CCSA exam, and it does not need to be activated.

The first management object I discuss in this chapter is the Services Manager. Let's take a look at the Services Manager and how it works.

Services Manager

If you look at your current rule base after opening the Policy Editor (which should still be blank), you will notice that *Services* is the header for the third column (not counting the rule number). This should tell you something—namely, that services are pretty important. FireWall-1 uses the services in conjunction with the network objects to determine exactly what type of traffic is blocked. A firewall rule can specify that only certain services be allowed (or denied) or that all services can be allowed (or denied). The types of services you can manage are:

➤ TCP

➤ UDP

➤ RPC

➤ ICMP

➤ Other

➤ Group

➤ Port Range

The next few sections take a look at each of the preceding types of services individually. Each service has specific details in their configuration that make configuring each unique. Let's start out with TCP services.

TCP Services

Transmission Control Protocol (TCP) is built on top of the Internet Protocol (IP) and is almost always seen in the combination TCP/IP (TCP over IP). TCP adds reliable communication, flow-control, multiplexing, and connection-oriented communication. It also provides full-duplex, process-to-process connections. TCP is used to send and receive data, guaranteeing transmission from the source to the destination.

The TCP object allows you to specify the ports that are used to support a particular service you are defining. Different software packages use different ports to deliver their service. For example, Citrix MetaFrame uses port 1494 to establish communications. If you were allowing communications to an internal Citrix server, you would need to allow 1494 to pass through your firewall; otherwise, the end user and server would not be able to communicate.

To illustrate the TCP service, let's create a TCP object using the following steps:

1. In the Policy Editor, click Manage (which is the same way you start when you create a network object).

2. On the Manage menu, click Services to display to the Services menu.

Note: Notice that Check Point provides several predefined services. These services cover the majority of services you'll need, but several are missing.

3. On the Services menu, click New.

4. Click the TCP button. You will now see the TCP Service Properties dialog box, as shown in Figure 5.1. At this point, a TCP service does not exist, so we're going to create a service for Citrix MetaFrame in this example.

5. In the Name field, enter a name for your service. It would make the most sense to name the service after the application you are using, but the choice is yours. In this example, I entered the name "Citrix_Metaframe".

6. In the Comment field, enter a description for the service. For this example, I entered "For Access to Citrix".

7. In the Color drop-down list, choose a color; I chose black as our color of choice for this service.

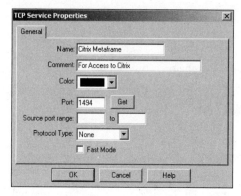

Figure 5.1   The TCP Service Properties dialog box.

8. In the Port text box, enter a port number. The port number is the number chosen by the service developer (such as Citrix) to handle the software's communications. For Citrix MetaFrame, the port number is 1494.

 If you do not enter a port number, FireWall-1 will attempt to resolve it for you.

9. Next, you need to address the Source Port Range settings. Source ports can be a bit confusing. A source port is the range of ports that a client uses for a service. When you specify a source port, you are telling FireWall-1 that you want only clients using the specified ports to be allowed to pass traffic using the service. For this example's service, I won't specify a source port range.

10. The Protocol Type drop-down list box is used to determine the type of service that works with the particular service. Although I won't be using this, the four choices are:

> ➤ None

> ➤ FTP

> ➤ URI

> ➤ SMTP

11. Next, you need to address the Fast Mode option. Fast Mode is used to speed the communications for the service. When the Fast Mode checkbox is checked, FireWall-1 bypasses the inspection of future packets using the service after the initial packet is analyzed.

12. Click OK to save the object.

TCP services is probably the most commonly used service, but there are others that you will run into from time to time. Probably the next most likely to encounter will be UDP services.

UDP Services

UDP (User Datagram Protocol) can be defined as the Internet standard Network layer, Transport layer, and Session layer protocols, which provide simple but unreliable datagram services. UDP adds a checksum and additional process-to-process addressing information. UDP is a connectionless protocol that is layered on top of IP. Unlike TCP, UDP neither guarantees delivery nor requires a connection. Because it does not guarantee delivery, it has a higher performance level than TCP.

Like the TCP object, the UDP object is used to create a UDP service that is specific to an application or service. Creating a UDP object is similar to creating a TCP object, as you can see in the following steps:

1. In the Policy Editor, click Manage.

2. On the Manage menu, click Services.

3. On the Services menu, click New.

4. Click the UDP button. You will now see the UDP Service Properties dialog box, as shown in Figure 5.2. In this example, we'll create a generic UDP service.

5. In the Name field, type the name of the service. For this example, I entered "Unreal_Audio" as the object name.

6. In the Comment field, type a description of the object. The description for this example is New Streaming Audio Service.

7. In the Color list box, select a color. In this example, I selected black.

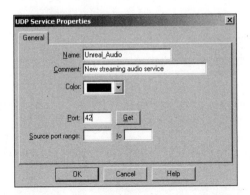

Figure 5.2 The UDP Service Properties dialog box.

8. Next, enter a port in the Port text box. For our example, the setup uses port number 42.

9. Leave the Source Port Range text boxes blank; this option serves the same purpose as the Source Port Range option in the TCP Service Properties dialog box.

10. Click OK to save the object.

Another protocol that can be defined using the Services Manager is RPC. Let's take a look at how RPC services are defined.

RPC Services

RPC (remote procedure call) is a protocol that allows a program running on a source host to cause code to be executed on another host without the need to have the code written for the function. RPC is often found in the client/server model of distributed computing. An RPC is initiated by a client sending a request message to a server to execute a certain procedure using specific codes. A message is then sent back to the client with the results of the request. Creating an RCP object is similar to creating a TCP object, as you can see in the following steps:

1. In the Policy Editor, click Manage.

2. On the Manage menu, click Services.

3. On the Services menu, click New.

4. Click RPC. As with the TCP and UDP Service Properties dialog boxes, the RPC Service Properties dialog box contains only one tab to configure—the General tab—which is shown in Figure 5.3. In this example, we'll create a generic RPC object.

5. In the Name field, type the name of the service. I entered "Generic_RPC" as our object name.

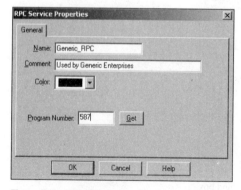

Figure 5.3   The RPC Service Properties dialog box.

6. In the Comment field, type a description for the object. In this example, the description is Used By Generic Enterprises.

7. In the Color drop-down list, select a color. I selected black.

8. In the Program Number text box, enter a program number. A program number is RPC's version of a port. If you don't enter a program number, the firewall will try to resolve it. For this example, I entered program number 587.

9. Click OK to save the object.

The next type of service we can define is ICMP services. Let's define ICMP and see how we configure it in FireWall-1.

ICMP Services

ICMP (Internet Control Message Protocol) is a protocol that is used between a host and a destination for message control and error reporting. The purpose of control messages is to provide feedback about problems in the communication environment. ICMP messages typically report errors in the processing of datagrams. The **PING** command is a good example of an ICMP message. **PING** sends a small packet to a destination address and records how many times the packet is sent and returned, the bytes, the time of roundtrip transfer, and the *time to live (TTL)*. Let's create a generic ICMP object:

1. In the Policy Editor, click Manage.

2. On the Manage menu, click Services.

3. On the Services menu, click New.

4. Click ICMP. The ICMP Service Properties dialog box opens. Notice that there is only one tab to configure—the General tab—which is shown in Figure 5.4. In this example, we'll create a generic ICMP object.

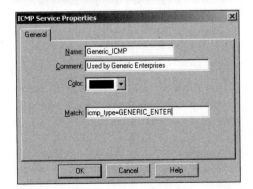

Figure 5.4   The ICMP Service Properties dialog box.

5. In the Name field, type the name of the service. I entered "Generic_ICMP" as our object name.

6. In the Comment field, type a description for the object. The description used in this example is Used By Generic Enterprises.

7. In the Color drop-down list box, select a color. I selected black.

8. Next, enter a match number in the Match text box. A match number is a string that allows an Inspection Engine to determine if a packet belongs to the new service. For this example, enter *icmp_type=GENERIC_ENTER*.

Note: For an example of an ICMP service, see the predefined "mask-reply" ICMP service.

9. Click OK to save the object.

This covers the most common services that can be defined in FireWall-1. However, what about services that do not fit into these categories? Let's look at how other service objects are created.

Other Services

The *other services* or *other objects* classification is Check Point's catchall service. This classifications contains services that do not fall into any of the aforementioned areas. Instead of creating a service object under this category, let's take a look at an existing one, as follows:

1. In the Policy Editor, click Manage.

2. On the Manage menu, click Services.

3. On the Services menu, click in the list of predefined services, and type "MS". This will open MSExchange.

4. Verify that the MSExchange service is highlighted, and click Edit. Notice that the name of the properties box is actually User Defined Service Properties, as shown in Figure 5.5.

5. In the Name field, you can see the name of the service, which is MSExchange.

6. Take a look at the description. See how detailed it is? The more detailed you can be in your descriptions, the easier you make administration for yourself.

7. Now, look at the Match text box. The text box is the same as with the ICMP service; it's a string that tells the Inspection Engine what to do with a packet and if the packet relates to this service. The Pre-Match text box is for code to be executed prior to the rule base, and the Prologue text box is used to place a code string before the Properties macros in the rule base.

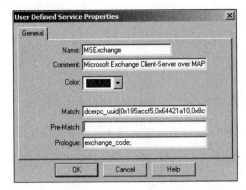

Figure 5.5   The User Defined Service Properties dialog box.

8. Click Cancel to exit the object.

Like network objects, we can group together services by creating a group object. In the next section, you will learn how to group together individual services.

Group Services

A group object for services is a quick-and-easy object to create. Groups are important in the creation of your rule base. Groups make management easier because they allow you to take objects and group them, rather than add them one at a time into your rule base.

To create a group object for services, follow these steps:

1. In the Policy Editor, click Manage.

2. On the Manage menu, click Services.

3. On the Services menu, click New.

4. Select Group. As you can see in Figure 5.6, the Group Properties dialog box contains only one page. For this example, let's say we want to block certain services from being able to hit our firewall. Specifically, we want to group bootp, nbdatagram, nbname, and nbsession and call our group *Silent_Services*.

5. In the Name and Comment text boxes, enter a name and description. For this exercise, I entered *Silent Services* and *Silent Services we want dropped*, respectively.

6. Choose a color in the Color drop-down list box. I selected orange for the group objects.

7. At this point, adding a service is pretty straightforward. Notice the Group Properties dialog box contains two columns:

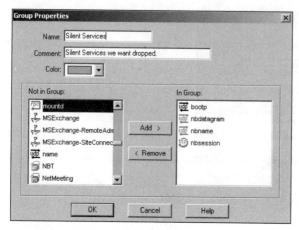

Figure 5.6 The Group Properties dialog box.

> ➤ Not In Group

> ➤ In Group

To add a service, scroll down the list of services in the Not In Group list, and click a service you want to include in the group. Then, click the Add button. The service will be moved from one column to the other. Add the other services in the same way.

8. After you have added all the services to your group (which are bootp, nbdatagram, nbname, and nbsession for this example), click OK to save the object.

The last type of service that I will discuss is port range services. Port range objects allow you to create an object that can include a great deal of services under one object. Let's take a look at how a port range service is defined.

Groups do not have to be of the same type. However, use good judgment when creating groups. Services should have some similarities or related purposes to warrant being combined into a group.

Port Range Services

Port range objects are very similar to address range objects found in the Network Objects tool. Port ranges allow the TCP and UDP protocols to specify a starting and ending port range. If a range of ports is specified, a firewall will allow action (accept, reject, or drop) to be taken only when inspecting packets using the services that fall within the port range.

Creating a port range object is simple, as you can see here:

1. First, choose a name for the port range using the Policy Editor.

2. Next, enter the first port for the range.

3. Then, enter the last port in the range.

4. Enter a description in the Comment field, and select a color for the object in the Color drop-down list.

5. Choose the protocol type, either TCP or UDP.

6. Click OK to save your object.

The next management tool to discuss is the Resources Manager. Let's take a look at how the Resources Manager is used on FireWall-1.

Resources Manager

In a Check Point firewall, resources are used in much the same way as services. A resource is used to match packets and perform actions on those packets when they pass through the firewall. One difference between resources and services is that resources can be used only with FTP, HTTP, and SMTP. Although I will not be creating the resources in this book, you need to know the basics about this topic. Resources can be created in the following four categories:

➤ URI (used for HTTP)

➤ SMTP

➤ FTP

➤ Group

In the next few sections, I'll cover each these categories except for the group object (a group object in resources is the same as creating one for network objects and services). Let's start by looking at the URI resource.

URI Resources

In order for a Uniform Resource Identifier (URI) to work, an HTTP security server must be installed and defined. The purpose of a URI resource is to bring security to the next level by giving more details about the service itself. You'll find three tabs in a URI Definition dialog box—General, Match, and Action.

General Tab

The General tab, shown in Figure 5.7, contains several options that you can use to define the following:

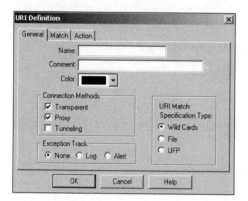

Figure 5.7 The General tab in the URI Definition dialog box.

➤ *Name*—Name of the URI definition

➤ *Comment*—Description of the URI

➤ *Color*—Color scheme

➤ *Connection Methods*—Option to select one, two, or all three connection methods

➤ *URI Match Specification Type*—The match specification method that will be used by this object: either Wild Cards, File, or UFP

➤ *Exception Track*—How the firewall will track usage (None, Log, or Alert)

Of particular note are the URI Match Specification types. As you can see in Figure 5.7, there are three URI Match Specification Type options to choose among—Wild Cards, File, and UFP. Wild card matching is used to match similar sites; think of it like using wildcards in DOS. File matching uses a separate file, which contains multiple URIs for the firewall to match against. UFP matching uses categories to determine the fate of a packet.

Match Tab

The Match tab's options vary based on the type of matching you specify on the General tab. If you choose the Wild Cards option, the following are available for configuration on the Match tab:

➤ *Schemes*—The type of traffic to which the resource applies. The choices are http, mailto, ftp, news, gopher, wais, and other. Multiple selections can be made. For others, you can place an asterisk in the box as a wildcard.

➤ *Methods*—The method of transfer for the traffic. The options are GET, POST, HEAD, PUT, and Other. Again, multiple selections can be made and an asterisk can be placed in the Other field for a wildcard.

➤ *Host*—Either a hostname or an asterisk as a wildcard.

➤ *Path*—A subdirectory or a wildcard.

➤ *Query*—Any text following a question mark in a link, or an asterisk for a wildcard.

If you specify File Match on the General tab, the following options are available on the Match tab:

➤ *Import*—Import a file containing a list of URIs to be matched.

➤ *Export*—Export a list of URIs that were previously imported.

A URI file must be formatted by typing the URL (Uniform Resource Locator) and the IP address of the URI, separated by a tab. Only one URI per line is allowed.

If you specify UFP Match on the General tab, the Match tab will include the following options:

➤ *UFP Server*—A predefined UFP server.

➤ *Categories*—This is where you would select categories that you previously defined for the UFP server selected.

As with our other objects, you can see that the General tab is used to define the basic properties of the object. On the Action tab, I will define exactly how the packets are handled by this object.

Action Tab

The Action tab determines how a packet will be handled by the resource. The Action tab is the same for each of the three matching types, and it offers the following options:

➤ *Replacement URI*—Identifies the IP address or host that will be returned to the requestor in place of the requested URI.

➤ *HTML Weeding*—Allows the firewall to strip scripts, applets, and ActiveX components.

➤ *CVP*—Allows you to specify a separate CVP (Content Vectoring Protocol) server and how it will handle the packet, if at all.

➤ *Response Scanning*—Allows you to block Java code.

The next resource type is an SMTP resource. SMTP should be familiar to you already because it is the most common method of transferring email between servers. Let's see how we can use an SMTP resource on our firewall.

SMTP Resources

The SMTP (Simple Mail Transfer Protocol) protocol is used to transfer email between mail servers. An SMTP resource allows you to redirect mail, drop mail, strip attachments, set a maximum message size, and hide internal addresses. The SMTP Definition dialog box contains four tabs—General, Match, Action1, and Action2.

General Tab

The General tab contains basic information about the SMTP resource, including:

➤ *Name*—Resource name.

➤ *Comment*—Description of the resource.

➤ *Color*—Color scheme.

➤ *Mail Server*—Where the mail is forwarded to.

➤ *Error Handling Server*—Where error notifications are sent.

➤ *Exception Track*—How the firewall will track usage. The choices are None, Log, and Alert.

➤ *Notify Sender On Error*—Whether to notify the sender when a message could not be sent.

Next, we need to tell the firewall how to determine which packets to manage. We do this by using the next three tabs: Match, Action1, and Action2.

Match Tab

The Match tab can be used to match a sender or receiver name in a packet to determine how the packet will be handled. You can specify the sender, receiver, both, or an asterisk for a wildcard.

Action1 Tab

The Action1 tab is used to manipulate the information in a field. The left side of the dialog box is the text to be matched, and the right side displays what the text will be changed to.

Action2 Tab

The Action2 tab allows further handling of an SMTP packet. Here, you can define the following:

➤ *Strip MIME Of Type*—MIME (Multipurpose Internet Mail Extensions) attachments of the specified type will be stripped.

➤ *Don't Accept Mail Larger Than*—Maximum size of a message that will be allowed.

➤ *CVP*— Content Vectoring Protocol server selection.

➤ *Allowed Characters*—Either 8-bit ASCII or 7-bit ASCII.

SMTP resources can be very handy for purposes such as mail scanning to prevent virus intrusion. In a corporate network, we also want to protect ourselves from files that may be transferred to and from our network via the Internet. For this purpose, we have the ability to create FTP resources. Let's see how an FTP resource can be used to protect our network from unwanted files.

FTP Resources

An FTP resource is simply an FTP security server. An FTP security server allows you to authenticate content based on the **PUT** and **GET** commands. It also allows you to check files being transferred for viruses for an added layer of protection. The FTP Definition dialog box contains three tabs: General, Match, and Action.

General Tab

The General tab is small and simple. The only configurations you need to make here are the name, comment, color, and tracking settings.

Match Tab

The Match is used to match a particular path. You can type in a full path or enter an asterisk for a wildcard. You can also select the direction in which you will be examining packets, by specifying **PUT**, **GET**, or both.

Action Tab

The Action tab allows you to name a CVP server and specify how the CVP server will handle the file. The CVP server can pass on it, inspect it, or inspect and correct any issues with the file.

Server Manager

The types of Server Manager objects available are:

➤ *UFP*—A URL Filtering Protocol server, used to define a URI resource.

➤ *CVP*—A Content Vectoring Protocol server, used to examine packets and files.

➤ *RADIUS*—Remote Authentication Dial-In User Service, used for authentication.

➤ *RADIUS Group*—A group of defined RADIUS servers.

➤ *TACACS*—Terminal Access Controller Access Control System, used for authentication.

➤ *DEFENDER*—Axent Defender, another option for authentication.

➤ *LDAP Account Unit*—Allows LDAP databases to work with the firewall for authentication.

➤ *CA*—Certificate authority server.

➤ *Policy Server*—An additional feature for security. Part of the SecuRemote package.

 Knowing the details of Server Manager objects is not necessary to pass the CCSA exam, but you should know the types of Server Manager objects available.

Although you don't have to know much about Server Manager for the CCSA exam, you may want to navigate around it a bit if you have the software at your disposal. The next management tool is the User Manager. The User Manager allows us to get very granular on how we allow access through the firewall to individual users.

User Manager

The User Manager tool is used for authentication of users and groups. You can allow and restrict user access through a firewall in a number of ways. Managing users is a great way to keep track of which users in your internal network have access to the Internet, remote sites, and anywhere that your firewall is connecting to. Inside of the User Manager tool, you can create three separate objects—Groups, External Users, and Templates. After you have created your templates, you can create your users from them. Let's create a new template (then, we'll look at creating users and groups).

Creating a User Template

To create a user template, follow these steps:

1. In the Policy Editor window, click Manage.

2. On the Manage menu, click Users.

3. Click New on the Users dialog box.

4. Select Template on the drop-down list which appears after clicking on New.

Note: You probably noticed that there is a default template already in place. When you set up your firewall, the default template is created automatically. You can either modify the default template or create a new one.

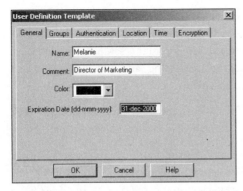

Figure 5.8   The General tab in the User Definition Template dialog box.

At this point, you should see a User Definition Template dialog box on your screen, as shown in Figure 5.8. When you define users in FireWall-1, you have a great number of configuration options that you can use to control firewall usage at a very granular level. In the User Definition Template dialog box, you'll find the following tabs that can be configured:

➤ *General*—The General tab contains the basic information about a user. Here, you enter the name of the user, comment, color, and account expiration date. For our example, let's create a template named *Marketing*. In the Comment field, type a description of *Marketing Users*. I will use black for my color scheme, and set an expiration date of *31-Dec-2001*.

   Dates must be entered in this format: "dd-mmm-yyyy".

➤ *Groups*—We have not created any groups yet, but when groups are available, you can select a group and make the user a member of the group by clicking the Add button.

➤ *Authentication*—Chapter 10 discusses authentication in detail. However, know that the Authentication tab is where you can determine how a user is authenticated against the firewall.

➤ *Location*—The Location tab has three sections: Source, Destination, and Network Objects. The Source box determines where the user will be allowed access *from*. The Destination box determines where the user will have access *to*. You can place objects in the Source and Destination fields by highlighting a predefined network object and clicking the Add button in the appropriate field (Destination or Source). Let's say you want the Marketing department to be able to access the Boston and Phoenix networks only, but they can access these networks from any source. To configure this setup, you would leave the Source field set to the default (Any) setting, and add the Boston and Phoenix networks to the Destination field.

➤ *Time*—Pretty straightforward here; you simply select the days of the week and time of day when users are allowed access to through the firewall.

➤ *Encryption*—Chapter 10 covers encryption in more detail. However, know that the Encryption tab is used to select and configure IKE and FWZ encryption. Also, note that the same encryption scheme must be in place on the VPN tab for the workstation that the user is working on. The Encryption tab also offers the tracking options of None, Log, and Alert.

After you configure the tabs in the User Definition Template dialog box to create a template, you're ready to create new users, as described in the next section.

Creating Users

Now that the template is complete, let's create a few new users, as described here:

1. In the Users tool of the Policy Editor, click the New button.

2. Click the Marketing option on the drop-down list which appears after clicking on the New button. You should see a User Properties dialog box that contains all of the information you preconfigured for your template earlier.

3. Enter a name into the Name text box and a description for the user in the User Properties text box, and then click OK. Your user is created!

4. To create another user, follow Steps 1 through 3. Enter a name. For the example setup, I entered *Kaitlyn* as the user's name and *Marketing Intern* as the description text. Because this person is an intern, we only want her to be able to access the network from one workstation. Therefore, display the Location tab and move the *Workstation1* object to the Source field, and then click OK.

After you've created a couple of users, you can move on to create a group, as described next. Groups, as with network objects, services, and resources, are a great way to put several user objects under one object.

Creating a Group

Creating a user group is similar to creating other groups. To create a new group, follow these steps:

1. After opening the User Manager in the Policy Editor, click the New button.

2. Click the Group option on the drop-down list that appears after clicking on the New button.

3. Select a name for your group. I named the example group Marketing_Dept.

4. Enter a description for the group, and then move the users who you want to be part of this group to the *In Group* box.

5. Click OK to save your group.

As you become more familiar with FireWall-1, you will discover how important user objects are to your firewall. Try creating several user objects with different properties—you can use them later after I discuss implementing the rule base.

Time Manager

Certain companies may be interested in stopping casual Web surfing during business hours. For this purpose, creating a time object is very useful. Time objects give us the ability to define when a rule is in effect, therefore controlling when specific traffic is allowed to pass through the firewall. To create a time object, follow these steps:

1. In the Policy Editor, click on Manage and then Time.

2. Create a name, description, and color for your time object.

3. Select the times of the day that the object is responsible for. For this example, let's say you don't want people to browse the Internet at lunch. In that case, you could enter "08:30" in the From field and "11:59" in the To field. As you can see in Figure 5.9, there are three different time ranges that you can define.

4. Because you want people to be able to access the Internet again after lunch, you would need to create another pair of times in the Time Of Day box.

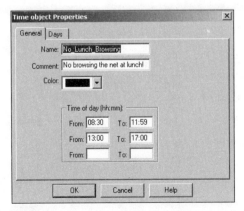

Figure 5.9   General tab in the Time Object Properties dialog box.

Below your first time restriction, type "13:00" in the From field and type "17:00" in the To field. See Figure 5.9 for an example.

5. Click OK.

 When you configure a time object, ensure that you use military time.

Notice in Figure 5.9 that the Time Object Properties dialog box also includes a Days tab. You can use the Days tab to specify the days of the week or month that the time object is in effect.

Key Manager

The Key Manager tool is not covered on the CCSA exam, but you should know that this tool is used create new Manual IPSec keys. Keys are used for the encryption of data that will be passed through the firewall.

Practice Questions

Question 1

> URI definitions can be used to redirect URIs to a defined location.
>
> ○ a. True
>
> ○ b. False

Answer a is correct because the statement is true. The Action tab of the URI definition is used to determine what will be done if a packet meets the URI criteria. You can enter a replacement URI in the Action tab.

Question 2

> Which of the following is not a type of service object definable in the Services Manager tool?
>
> ○ a. TCP
>
> ○ b. UDP
>
> ○ c. ICMP
>
> ○ d. IPX

Answer d is correct. IPX is not a definable object in the Services Manager tool. Answers a, b, and c are incorrect because they all present valid options for creating a service object.

Question 3

> What actions can a CVP take in regards to an SMTP definition? [Check all correct answers]
>
> ❑ a. None
>
> ❑ b. Strip
>
> ❑ c. Quarantine
>
> ❑ d. Read/Write
>
> ❑ e. Read
>
> ❑ f. Alert

Answers a, d, and e are correct. A CVP can either be set to not inspect a message (None), reject the message (Read), or accept and correct it (Read/Write). Answers b, c, and f are incorrect because a CVP server does not strip, quarantine, or send an alert.

Question 4

Which of the following is not a tab in the User Definition Template dialog box?

○ a. General

○ b. Interface

○ c. Authentication

○ d. Location

Answer b is correct. There is no Interface tab in the User Definition Template dialog box. The only tabs available on the User Definition Template dialog box are General, Groups, Authentication, Location, Time, and Encryption. Answers a, c, and d are incorrect because the General, Authentication, and Location tabs are among the tabs available in the User Objects Properties dialog box.

Question 5

What is the benefit of selecting a source location for a user?

○ a. It allows you to restrict where the user can be allowed access from.

○ b. It allows you to restrict where the user can be allowed access to.

○ c. Location, location, location!

○ d. It helps with knowing where a person is sitting.

Answer a is correct. Selecting a source destination for a user allows you to restrict the user to a particular network object, such as a workstation or network. Answer b is incorrect because selecting the source location does not restrict where the user is allowed access to. Answer c is a nonsense answer and is therefore incorrect. Answer d is incorrect because selecting a source location for a user does not define where they might sit in an office.

Question 6

Which of the following server objects can perform authentication? [Check all correct answers]

❑ a. TACACS

❑ b. RADIUS

❑ c. CVP

❑ d. NT RAS

❑ e. Policy Server

❑ f. Axent Defender

Answers a, b, and f are correct. TACACS, RADIUS, and Axent are valid options for server objects that provide for authentication. Answer c is incorrect because CVP stands for Content Vectoring Protocol. Answer d is incorrect because NT RAS is not used as a server object. Answer e is incorrect because no such server object exists.

Question 7

What benefit is gained by adding an FTP resource?

○ a. An FTP resource allows you to configure the FTP service in your network.

○ b. An FTP resource creates a secure tunnel to the FTP server.

○ c. An FTP resource allows you to specify inspection for connections and files transferred.

○ d. None of the above.

Answer c is correct. An FTP resource is used to inspect both the connection and the data being transferred to and from an FTP server. Answer a is incorrect because creating an FTP resource does not affect the configuration of the FTP service on the network. Answer b is incorrect because an FTP resource does not create any tunnels.

Question 8

> What is not an option for exception tracking in an SMTP resource?
>
> ○ a. None
>
> ○ b. Page
>
> ○ c. Alert
>
> ○ d. Log

Answer b is correct. Page is not an option for exception tracking. Answers a, c, and d are incorrect because they list the three options for tracking for an SMTP resource, which are None, Log, and Alert.

Question 9

> What is the maximum amount of time restrictions can you create in a single time object?
>
> ○ a. One
>
> ○ b. Two
>
> ○ c. Three
>
> ○ d. Four

Answer c is correct. You can create up to three time restrictions for a time object.

Question 10

> In a TCP service, what does the Protocol Type field define?
>
> ○ a. If this service will be TCP or IP.
>
> ○ b. The protocol type (None, FTP, SMTP, or URI) that is associated with the service.
>
> ○ c. The proper handshaking method between the source and destination.
>
> ○ d. There is no Protocol Type field.

Answer b is correct. The Protocol Type field allows you to associate a service with a type of protocol and, therefore, a type of security server to enforce it. Answers a, c, and d are incorrect because none of these answers defines the Protocol Type field.

Need to Know More?

 Goncalves, Marcus and Steven Brown. *Check Point FireWall-1 Administration Guide*. McGraw-Hill, New York, NY, 1999. ISBN 0-07-134229-X. This book serves as a good bookshelf reference for FireWall-1.

 Wenstrom, Mike. *Managing Cisco Network Security*. Cisco Systems, Inc., San Francisco, CA, 2001. ISBN 1-57-870103-1. This book is considered to be the definitive book for managing Cisco network security.

 www.checkpoint.com, the Check Point Web site, offers some basic installation information regarding the various types of installations and OS platforms.

Designing a Rule Base

. . . .

Terms you'll need to understand:

✓ Security policy

✓ Rule base

✓ Drop (action)

✓ Reject (action)

✓ Explicit rule

✓ Implicit rule

✓ Pseudo rule

✓ Implicit drop rule

Techniques you'll need to master:

✓ Creating a rule base

✓ Using the Rule Base Wizard

✓ Defining rule base elements

✓ Adding rules

✓ Identifying the elements of a rule

✓ Differentiating between implicit and explicit rules

✓ Ordering rules

✓ Setting rule base properties

✓ Differentiating between drop and reject actions

✓ Verifying a rule base

✓ Installing a rule base

✓ Uninstalling a rule base

Up to now, we have worked on installing and configuring our firewall and adding objects to it. Everything that we have done to this point was necessary to move on to the next step: creating a security policy, where all of the objects that we have defined can be put to use. The security policy is the piece of the firewall that defines the actions that will be taken. Let's begin by creating our first security policy.

Creating a Security Policy

The preceding chapters in this book discuss how to create all of the objects you need to create a security policy. In this chapter, you'll learn how to begin developing a security policy. A security policy enables you to tell a firewall how to handle the traffic to the network objects you created. In addition, the security policy dictates the manner in which the objects will handle the traffic that is sent to and from the firewall. Some of the determinations a security policy makes include:

➤ Where traffic is originating from

➤ Where traffic is destined for

➤ What services will be allowed to and from an object

➤ How the traffic to and from an object will be tracked

➤ On which objects to install a rule

➤ The time of day to enforce a rule

To create your security policy, you must use the Policy Editor to create a rule base. Figure 6.1 shows an example of an empty rule base.

You can create a rule base in three ways. The first method is to use the Rule Base Wizard. The wizard allows a novice security administrator to easily create a rule base without having to add rules individually. The wizard is also useful for setting up a quick firewall configuration that doesn't require much tweaking. Once the wizard creates a rule base, you can still go in and change whatever you think is necessary. The greatest asset of the wizard is that it gives you a starting ground for your rule base, and it creates many of the initial objects for you.

The second method you can use to create a rule base is to use Check Point's predefined templates. Check Point provides four templates that you can choose from:

➤ *Starter Network template*—Single network with a mail server

➤ *Publisher Network template*—Single network with published (WWW, FTP, and so forth) servers

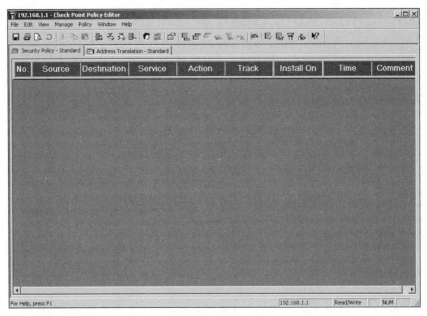

Figure 6.1   A blank rule base.

➤ *Web and DMZ Network template*—Mail and Web servers in a DMZ network as well as a single internal network

➤ *FTP and DMZ Network template*—Same as the Web and DMZ template, except an FTP server replaces the Web server

The template server is a great starter rule base for a novice administrator. The template server gives you an outline that illustrates how Check Point would set up and define a rule base. In this book, I will not be going into detail about the templates, but you should know that the Check Point templates exist when and if you need them.

The last method you can use to create a rule base is to manually define each rule individually. Manually defining a rule base can be a little bit tricky, but you'll find that it becomes easier with experience. When you define your rule base manually, you'll need to define the network address translation (NAT) rules as well. The advantage of creating a rule base manually is that you build your policy from scratch, so you are not dependent on predefined rules. Of course, there are disadvantages to creating a rule base manually, as well. The most glaring disadvantage is the possibility of creating an error in your rule base. Because you are creating all the rules yourself in this type of setup, it is very easy to slip up and make an error. For this reason, you should plan your rule base ahead of time and then verify the rule base after it has been installed.

Using the Rule Base Wizard

The Rule Base Wizard in FireWall-1 is very similar to a wizard you might see in a Microsoft product, such as Word or Excel. The Rule Base Wizard guides you through the steps of choosing a template, defining your firewall, and defining network objects, services, resources, and other objects that you created in the previous chapters. This chapter shows you how to create new objects using the wizard, but the new objects will not delete the ones you've already created. To work through the Rule Base Wizard, follow these steps:

1. Open the Policy Editor, if it is not already open.

2. After you have logged into the firewall, click File, and then click New. You will see the three options for creating a firewall.

3. Click the Rule Base Wizard option, and then click OK.

4. Next, you have to choose the type of rule base you want to create. You can choose from among six types of rule bases (see Figure 6.2):

   ➤ *Starter Network template*—Single network with a mail server.

   ➤ *Publisher Network template*—Single network with published (WWW, FTP, and so forth) servers.

   ➤ *Web and DMZ Network template*—Mail and Web servers in a DMZ network as well as a single internal network.

   ➤ *FTP and DMZ Network template*—Same as the Web and DMZ template, except an FTP server replaces the Web server.

   ➤ *DMZ Network template*—A combination of the FTP, Web, and DMZ networks, plus the internal network.

   ➤ *Secure Mail*—Mail server that also has SecuRemote POP3 access.

   For this example, choose the Starter Network template.

5. After you select the Starter Network template, click OK.

6. Click Next to move past the First Step screen.

7. Next, you need to define your gateway as an object. Enter a name for the firewall, and click Next (see Figure 6.3).

Note: The name you assign here will be a different name than you assigned in Chapter 4.

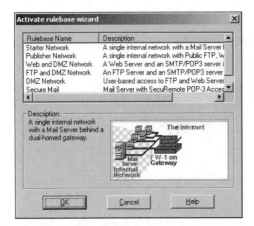

Figure 6.2   Predefined templates in the Rule Base Wizard.

Figure 6.3   Naming the gateway.

8. The next screen prompts you to enter the gateway's IP address. You can use the same IP address that you used in Chapter 4. Click Next after you have entered the IP address into the field.

9. Next, you need to define the interfaces for the gateway. You have two options for this step. The first option is to click the Get button to have FireWall-1 search for the IP addresses of the gateway. The second option is to click Next and skip to the next step. Then, you can go back later and enter in the addresses of the interfaces by using the management tools.

Note: If you click Next in Step 9 without defining interfaces for your gateway, you will see a warning screen. Click Yes to continue.

10. At this point, you need to configure the internal network and where you want services you will be allowing the users to access. When the Next Step screen appears, click Next.

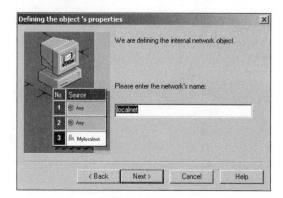

Figure 6.4 The internal network name.

11. You now need to define the internal network object (see Figure 6.4). Enter a name for the internal network or leave the default of *localnet*. Click Next to proceed.

12. Next, you need to assign the network IP address and subnet mask to the network object. In this example setup, we'll use 10.0.0.0 and 255.0.0.0. After you have entered the IP and subnet information, click Next to continue.

13. The next screen asks if the IP range you just entered is a valid Internet range. Because it is not (in our example), click No, and then click Next.

14. The next step involves configuring network address translation. The Policy Editor prompts you to decide how you want to hide the internal addresses and translate them to the outside world. You can hide the internal network behind the IP address of the firewall or choose another, valid IP address. In this example, we will use the firewall address to keep the setup simple. Click the radio button for The External IP Address Of The Gateway option, and click Next.

15. Now, you need to decide what traffic, if any, you want to allow the internal network to pass to the Internet. You can choose from among three choices:

    ➤ All

    ➤ Selected

    ➤ None

    The All and None options are self explanatory. The Selected option allows you to determine which services you want to allow the internal users to pass. Selecting services can be a bit tricky for a novice security administrator, because a novice might not know which services are dependent on other services. For this example, click the Selected option so you can run through the steps.

16. FireWall-1 wants to group the services that you will be selecting for the internal users. Creating a group for the services is similar to the procedure you completed in Chapter 5 when you grouped the services together. First, you need to select a name for your group. The default name is *InternetServices*. You can keep the default or change it, and then click Next.

17. Now, you need to select the services to add to the group. The Policy Editor will give you a short list of common services (see Figure 6.5). Select the services that you want to make available, or, optionally, you can click the All Of The Above checkbox to select all of the services. After you have selected your services, click Next.

18. The third section of the wizard enables you to define how FireWall-1 will handle mail traffic. When the Next Step screen appears, click Next. You will be asked if you have a mail server. If you do not have a mail server, FireWall-1 will skip this section and move on. In this example, we want to configure the firewall to handle mail for practice, so you should click Yes, and then click Next.

19. Enter a name for the mail server, or use the default name, which is *mailer*. Here, you are simply defining a workstation object as a mail server. After you have entered the name of the mail server, click Next to continue.

20. You will now be asked to enter the IP address of the mail server. Choose an internal (invalid) IP address, and enter it here. Click Next to continue.

21. Once again, you need to choose a valid address to assign for network address translation. This address needs to be a *valid* Internet address, and it must be different from the address of the firewall. FireWall-1 will use the address within its NAT table to determine the internal location of the mail server so that it can allow mail traffic to pass. Enter in a valid Internet address; we will use the same scheme of 192.168.1.x for the example setup. Click Next to continue.

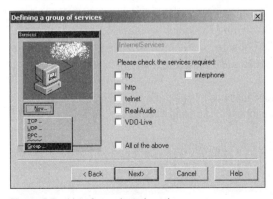

Figure 6.5   List of preselected services.

22. The next section of the Rule Base Wizard requests information about how you want the firewall to handle bootp, nbname, nbdatagram, and nbsession services. There are many reasons for blocking this type of traffic; some are for security issues, and others are to simply block unnecessary traffic from passing through the firewall. Check Point recommends that these services be dropped without any type of alert to avoid excessive logging. Click Drop, and then click Next to continue.

23. You've arrived at the final step of the Rule Base Wizard! Click Finish to install the policy. If you want, you can also go back and make changes to the information you have entered before you click on Finish. From here, you can continue on with the example.

Your security policy will now have several lines of information on the Security Policy tab in the Policy Editor (which is the main screen). We won't be working with this configuration, so feel free to move around inside of the objects; click them, click the Address Translation tab, look at the comments on each of the rules, and try to get an idea of what the rules mean. While you're looking around, though, keep the following in mind:

➤ Don't save the rule base.

➤ Don't install the policy (that is, don't click the icon that looks like a tower).

After you have moved around the screens a little bit, close the Policy Editor. Don't worry, we'll be looking at everything a little more closely in a moment. Click No when asked if you want to save your changes.

Manually Configuring a Rule Base

Creating a rule base manually takes a little more effort than creating a rule base using the Rule Base Wizard, but working manually gives you a better feel for the Policy Editor interface and what goes into creating a rule base. As an administrator, you will be spending a lot of time working with the Policy Editor, so the best way to get comfortable with developing the rule base is through trial and error. Because I have already discussed how to create objects in previous chapters, the only task we need to complete now is to create the rules.

> FireWall-1 examines rules one by one, from top to bottom. Properly ordering rules is important to installing a firewall properly.

First, reopen the Policy Editor. You will once again be presented with a blank security policy. Maximize the Policy Editor window so you can see everything on the screen.

Before we start creating rules, let's quickly review the columns at the top of the policy (see Figure 6.6):

➤ *No.*—The rule number.

➤ *Source*—The source of the traffic.

➤ *Destination*—The destination of the traffic.

➤ *Service*—The service that will be allowed or denied from the source or to the destination.

➤ *Action*—The action that will be taken by the rule.

➤ *Track*—The setting that indicates if and how traffic meeting the criteria of the rule will be tracked.

➤ *Install On*—The gateway(s) the rule will be enforced on and in which direction it will be enforced.

➤ *Time*—The time object to add to the rule.

➤ *Comment*—Brief explanation of the rule.

Now, you're ready to create a rule, as follows:

1. Click Edit on the top of the Policy Editor menu.

2. Click Add Rule, and then click Top.

A blank rule will be added to the rule base. This rule is known as the *default rule*, as shown in Figure 6.7. Let's begin by creating the firewall stealth rule.

The Stealth Rule

The stealth rule is used to stop access directly to a firewall. This rule is extremely important in protecting your firewall from the outside world. Because your firewall is the gateway to and from your internal network, you'll want to prevent as much

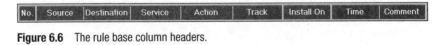

No.	Source	Destination	Service	Action	Track	Install On	Time	Comment

Figure 6.6   The rule base column headers.

2	⊜ Any	⊜ Any	⊜ Any	drop		Gateways	⊜ Any	

Figure 6.7   The default rule.

"Internet presence" to the outside world as possible. Fundamentally, this rule makes the firewall transparent to anyone who might try to contact it. Let's go through the column setup for the stealth rule:

1. The first step is to configure the source of the traffic. In this example, you want to block all traffic to the firewall, so leave the Source field set to Any.

2. The destination is going to be your firewall (in our example, we named our firewall *Arizona*). Right-click the Destination field in the first rule, and then click Add. Select Arizona from the list of objects, and click OK. The Arizona firewall object is added to the Destination field.

3. The Service field will remain set to Any. You don't want any services to be allowed to hit your firewall! Optionally, you could choose certain services to drop by right-clicking in the Service field and selecting the services.

   Let's stop for a moment and talk about actions. As mentioned, actions determine how a firewall will handle a packet. Common available actions can be summarized as follows:

   ➤ *Accepting* a packet mans the firewall will allow the packets to pass through the firewall.

   ➤ *Dropping* a packet means the firewall refuses and drops a packet without notifying the requestor.

   ➤ *Rejecting* a packet means the firewall refuses the packet but notifies the requestor that the packet has been rejected.

   ➤ *User Authentication*, *Client Authentication*, and *Session Authentication* all refer to types of authentication that are discussed in Chapter 10.

   ➤ *Encryption* and *Client Encryption* refer to encryption methods that will be briefly discussed in Chapter 10.

   For now, we will focus on Drop, Reject, and Accept. Sticking with our philosophy that we want the firewall to remain as invisible to the outside world as possible, dropping is the method of choice. Now, let's return to creating the stealth rule.

4. The action for this rule will be to drop the traffic. You can right-click the Action field to see the other options. We've already stated that we want the firewall to be invisible, so leave the Action field set to Drop.

   It's time for another break in the action. At this point, we need to discuss *tracking*. Tracking is used to report occurrences in which traffic meets the conditions of the rule. Leaving the Track field blank will cause a firewall to not track the traffic. Not using tracking is a good idea for rules that you expect to have a lot of usage, such as rules allowing an internal network out to the Internet. The other settings include:

➤ *Short*—Offers a brief amount of information in the Log Viewer.

➤ *Long*—Offers a more lengthy description of the traffic being logged.

➤ *Accounting*—Logs the traffic in more of an accounting format; this setting is not used very frequently.

➤ *Alert*—Allows an alert to be sent.

➤ *Mail*—Sends an email message to a defined recipient.

➤ *SNMP Trap*—Issues an SNMP trap.

➤ *UserDefined*—Tracks the packets based on predefined user criteria.

Different administrators will handle tracking of a stealth rule different ways, depending on how much information he or she will want to track on traffic sent directly to a firewall.

5. Select how you want traffic that meets the criteria of this rule to be logged in the Traffic field. For this rule, you might want to track using the Long option. That way, you'll have detailed information about anyone who attempts to access your firewall.

Now, I need to talk a little about the Install On field. You use the Install On field to determine on which firewall and in which direction you want the rule to be installed. For this field, you can choose from the following options:

➤ *Gateways* means that you will be enforcing the rule on all gateways in the direction specified.

➤ *Destination* means that you will only be enforcing the rule coming inbound.

➤ *Source* is the reverse of Destination; it means you will only enforce the rule going outbound.

➤ *Routers* and *Integrated Firewalls* imply that the rule will be enforced on predefined routers and integrated firewalls, respectively.

➤ *Target* lets you select the predefined gateway, router, or integrated firewall that you have defined.

You may want to install a stealth rule using any of the above options, but the most common choice is to install on Gateways.

6. Select where you want to install the rule. Commonly, the Install On field is left on Gateways rather then set to a firewall or other object. For this example, leave the Install On field set to Gateways.

7. Leave the Time field set to Any. You do not need to specify a time, because you want this rule to run 24/7/365. If you were to apply a time restriction to this rule, you would have to predefine a time object in your Object Manager.

8. In the Comment field, double-click in the box, and then type "Stealth Rule". Comments are as important when you're creating rules as when you're creating objects. The larger a rule base gets, the more difficult it can become to remember exactly why a rule was implemented. Make it easier on yourself and add as many comments in as possible!

Compare your rule to the rule shown in Figure 6.8. Your rule should look similar to, if not exactly like, the rule in the figure. After you have compared the rules, use the information in Table 6.1 to create some additional rules. Click Edit in the Policy Editor menu, click Add Rule, and then click Bottom to create a new rule below all of the existing rules. After you add the rules in Table 6.1, make sure that you save your rule base!

The Cleanup Rule

The cleanup rule is used to catch the remaining traffic that is not handled by the preceding rules. The cleanup rule is usually configured to drop any remaining packets that do not fit the criteria you have determined. Because this rule catches

Table 6.1   Additional rules.

Source	Destination	Service	Action	Track	Install On	Time	Comment
Phoenix	Any	Any	Accept	None	Gateways	Any	Network Outbound
Boston	Phoenix	Any	Accept	None	Gateways	Any	Traffic from Boston
Any	Any	Silent_Services	Drop	None	Gateways	Any	Drop Broadcasts

No.	Source	Destination	Service	Action	Track	Install On	Time	Comment
1	Any	Arizona	Any	drop	Long	Gateways	Any	Stealth Rule
2	Phoenix	Any	Any	accept		Gateways	Any	Network Outbound
3	Boston	Phoenix	Any	accept		Gateways	Any	Traffic from Boston
4	Any	Any	Silent_Services	drop		Gateways	Any	Drop Broadcasts

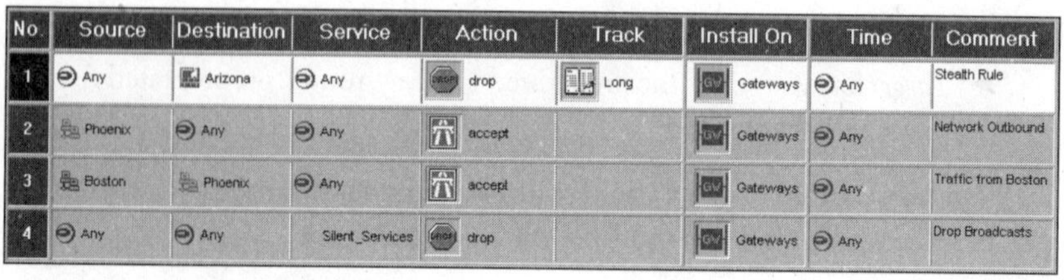

Figure 6.8 The completed stealth rule.

whatever is not handled earlier, the cleanup rule must obviously sit at the bottom of the rule base. Logging on the cleanup rule is optional, but it can be useful when troubleshooting issues regarding communications through a firewall. To create a cleanup rule, follow these steps:

1. Click Edit, click Add Rule, and then click Bottom.

2. Set the Source, Destination, and Service fields to Any.

3. Set the Action field to Drop, unless you want to notify the requestor that the traffic has been refused (in that case, set the Action field to Refuse).

4. Set the Track field to Short.

5. Set the Install On field to Gateways.

6. In the Time field, retain the default Any setting.

7. In the Comment field, type "Cleanup Rule".

Figure 6.9 shows the completed table of rules; compare it to your table. You'll be able to add and tweak rules in the next few chapters, so don't be discouraged if you think this rule base is too simple.

Implicit Rules

Implicit rules (also called *implied rules* or *pseudo rules*) are rules that are created automatically by FireWall-1 from information taken from the security properties as well as the explicit rules you created in your rule base. One type of implicit rule is the *implicit drop rule*. An implicit drop rule functions in the same manner as a cleanup rule, except that it does not allow for tracking of the rule, because it is not *explicitly* defined in the rule base. The concept behind the implicit drop rule is the same as the cleanup rule—if a particular type of traffic is not in the rule base, drop it!

To view the implicit rules, click View in the Policy Editor and then click Implied Rules.

No.	Source	Destination	Service	Action	Track	Install On	Time	Comment
1	Any	Arizona	Any	drop	Long	Gateways	Any	Stealth Rule.
2	Phoenix	Any	Any	accept		Gateways	Any	
3	Boston	Phoenix	Any	accept		Gateways	Any	
4	Any	Any	Silent_Services	drop		Gateways	Any	Drop Broadcasts

Figure 6.9 The completed rule base.

Verifying a Rule Base

Installing the rule base is the last step in configuring your security policy. However, before you install the rule base, you should verify it to make sure that there are no conflicts or errors in your configuration. To verify a rule base, follow these steps:

1. Click Policy.

2. Click Verify.

3. You will be asked which policies you want to verify. Check Security and Address Translation, and click OK.

 You can also check a rule base by clicking the Verify button in the Policy Editor toolbar.

FireWall-1 will verify whether the rule base and address translations are properly configured. If they are correct, you will see a message that the rules verified correctly. If the rules are not properly configured, you will receive a message that states where errors have occurred. After you verify that your rule base is properly configured, you're ready to install it.

Installing a Rule Base

Now that you know that your rule base is configured correctly, you need to install it to the Management Module. Installing the rule base is fairly simple. To install the rule base, follow these steps:

1. In the Menu bar of the Policy Editor, click Policy.

2. Click Install.

3. Select the object that you want to install on; for the example setup, choose to install on the Arizona firewall.

4. Click OK.

 You can also install a rule base by clicking the Install button (which resembles a tower) in the Policy Editor toolbar.

FireWall-1 will begin to compile the rule base into code that the Enforcement Module can understand. Once the rule base is compiled, the compiled security policy will be downloaded to the Enforcement Module, and your firewall will be ready to protect your network from the outside world! Of course, you do have some more administrative changes to make on your Enforcement Module, but, at this point, you have a live, functioning firewall!

Uninstalling a Rule Base

In some situations, you might need to uninstall a rule base. Uninstalling a rule base is just as easy as installing it. To uninstall a rule base, follow these steps:

1. In the Menu bar of the Policy Editor, click Policy.

2. Click Uninstall.

3. Select the object that you want to uninstall from; in this example, we would uninstall from the Arizona firewall.

4. Click OK.

 You can also uninstall a rule base by clicking the Uninstall button (which resembles a fallen tower) in the Policy Editor toolbar.

Uninstalling a rule base could come into play for several reasons. One reason could be that you chose the wrong Enforcement Module to install a policy on and you need to remove the rule base quickly to resume communications. Whatever the reason, it's important to note that the Security Module can be removed with the click of a button.

Practice Questions

Question 1

> In the Rule Base Wizard, you can assign the valid IP address of the firewall to a mail server.
>
> ○ a. True
> ○ b. False

Answer b is correct. When defining a mail server in the Rule Base Wizard, the valid IP address of the mail server must be different than the firewall's IP address.

Question 2

> _____ rules are derived from the rules you create in the rule base as well as the firewall properties.
>
> ○ a. Explicit
> ○ b. Stealth
> ○ c. Cleanup
> ○ d. Implicit

Answer d is correct. Implicit rules are rules that are created without any action from the administrator. Answer a is incorrect because explicit rules are rules that you create yourself in the rule base. Answers b and c are incorrect because stealth rules and cleanup rules are explicit rules created in the rule base.

Question 3

> The _____ is like the implicit drop rule, except that the implicit drop rule does not log information.
>
> ○ a. Implicit rule
> ○ b. Explicit rule
> ○ c. Cleanup rule
> ○ d. Stealth rule
> ○ e. Pseudo rule

Answer c is correct. The cleanup rule is the same as the implicit drop rule except for the fact that you can log traffic information using the cleanup rule. Answers a, b, d, and e are incorrect because none of these answers are similar to the implicit drop rule.

Question 4

Where should the stealth rule be placed in a rule base?

- ○ a. At the bottom
- ○ b. In the middle
- ○ c. At the top
- ○ d. It doesn't matter.
- ○ e. There is no such thing as a stealth rule.

Answer c is correct. The stealth rule should always be placed at the top of a rule base, unless there are authentication and encryption rules in the rule base (in which case, the stealth rule should come immediately after those rules). Answers a, b, and d are incorrect because the placement of the stealth rule should always be at the top. Answer e is incorrect because the stealth rule does exist and is an important part of the security policy.

Question 5

Which of the following is not a valid action for a rule?

- ○ a. Drop
- ○ b. Refuse
- ○ c. Accept
- ○ d. Reject
- ○ e. User Auth
- ○ f. Client Auth
- ○ g. Session Auth
- ○ h. Encrypt
- ○ i. Client Encrypt

Answer b is correct. There is no action named Refuse. Answers a, c, d, e, f, g, h, and i are incorrect because Drop, Accept, Reject, User Auth, Client Auth, Session Auth, Encrypt, and Client Encrypt are all valid actions that a rule can take.

Question 6

Which of the following are elements of a rule base? [Check all correct answers]

❑ a. No.

❑ b. Source

❑ c. Destination

❑ d. Services

❑ e. Action

❑ f. Track

❑ g. Install On

❑ h. Time

❑ i. Comment

Answers a, b, c, d, e, f, g, h, and i are all correct. All of the choices are valid elements in a rule base. Elements of a rule base refer to the options that are available for configuration on each rule.

Question 7

Which of the following is not a valid method that you can use to create a new security policy?

○ a. Rule Base Wizard

○ b. Rule Base template

○ c. Empty Database (Manual)

○ d. Network Discovery

Answer d is correct. FireWall-1 cannot auto-discover your network to create a rule base. Answers a, b, and c are incorrect because you can create a rule base by using the wizard, using predefined templates, or using an empty database to create a rule base manually.

Question 8

What is another name for a new, blank rule?

○ a. Empty rule

○ b. Unverified rule

○ c. Rule-in-progress

○ d. Default rule

Answer d is correct. The name for a newly created, unedited rule is *default rule*. This simply means that the rule has not had any modifications made to it after adding it to the rule base.

Question 9

In a rule base, what is the Install On element responsible for determining?

○ a. Which firewall to enforce a rule on.

○ b. The network a rule will be installed on.

○ c. Which users to block with a rule.

○ d. The Install On element is not a valid element.

Answer a is correct. The Install On element is used to determine which firewall object to install a rule on. Answer b is incorrect because the Install On element does not determine the network a rule will be installed on. Answer c is incorrect because the Install On element does not determine which uses to block. Answer d is incorrect because the Install On element is a valid element.

Question 10

You can determine the order in which FireWall-1 reads the rules in a rule base.

○ a. True

○ b. False

Answer a is correct. Yes! You can determine the order that FireWall-1 reads the rules by moving the rules around in the rule base. However, FireWall-1 will still read the rules from top to bottom. One of the main reasons to verify a rule base is to make sure that your rules are ordered correctly and do not conflict with one another.

Need to Know More?

 Goncalves, Marcus and Steven Brown. *Check Point FireWall-1 Administration Guide.* McGraw-Hill, New York, NY, 1999. ISBN 0-07-134229-X. This book serves as a good bookshelf reference for FireWall-1.

 www.checkpoint.com, the Check Point Web site, offers some basic installation information regarding the various types of installations and OS platforms.

Administering the
Rule Base

Terms you'll need to understand:

✓ Security servers
✓ SYNDefender
✓ Interface direction
✓ Routing Information Protocol (RIP)
✓ Spoofing
✓ Anti-spoofing
✓ SYN gateway
✓ Passive SYN gateway
✓ Lightweight Directory Access Protocol (LDAP)

Techniques you'll need to master:

✓ Configuring SYNDefender
✓ Determining the direction in which to apply rules
✓ Setting up log and alert properties
✓ Configuring security server properties
✓ Configuring LDAP properties
✓ Configuring Connect Control
✓ Disabling a rule
✓ Enabling anti-spoofing
✓ Hiding a rule

Properly securing your network with a firewall requires more than just creating and installing a security policy. As with any application package or operating system, little pieces of information must be modified to provide the maximum capabilities of the product. FireWall-1 is no exception; it requires some additional work to offer top performance. In this chapter, I discuss how to make these modifications and how they affect firewall performance.

Configuring Firewall Properties

Creating the rule base and installing it is only the tip of the iceberg when you are installing FireWall-1. After you design and implement rules in your rule base, you need to take the next step and configure some of the properties of FireWall-1, which will help you to create a more secure gateway as well as give you some other helpful administrative options. Therefore, the next step in tuning the firewall is to modify the firewall properties. Like the rule base, the firewall properties are modified inside of the Policy Editor. To open the Properties Setup dialog box in the Policy Editor, follow these steps:

1. Click the Policy option on the menu bar of the Policy Editor.

2. Click Properties.

The Properties Setup dialog box contains several tabs. In this chapter, we will be looking at the following tabs:

➤ Security Policy

➤ Log And Alert

➤ Security Servers

➤ SYNDefender

➤ LDAP

➤ Connect Control

The Security Policy Tab

The first tab in the Properties Setup box is the Security Policy tab, as shown in Figure 7.1. The Security Policy tab has several options available for configuration. Let's take a look at the options you can configure using this tab.

Apply Gateway Rules To Inteface Direction

The Apply Gateway Rules To Interface Direction drop-down list enables you to determine which direction rules will be implemented by default. Chapter 2 discusses the various directions that data can flow in a FireWall-1 gateway. In a

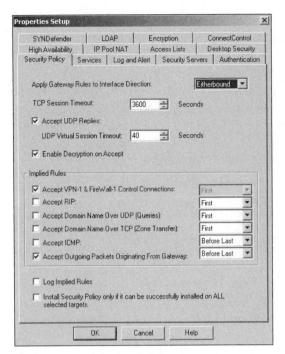

Figure 7.1   The Security Policy tab.

nutshell, inbound traffic is traffic that will have the security policy enforced on it as the traffic enters the firewall. Outbound traffic is traffic that will have the security policy enforced on it as the packet leaves the firewall. And eitherbound traffic enforces the security policy on traffic, regardless of whether it's entering or exiting the firewall. Eitherbound inspection gives you the most security on your firewall, although there is some performance decrease because of the added analysis.

TCP Session Timeout

The TCP Session Timeout option allows you to set the amount of time allowed before a TCP session is closed. A TCP session is created after the initial packet from a source is verified against the firewall security policy and is allowed to pass. After the packet is allowed to pass, the session is started. If after the timeout period the same source attempts to pass traffic again, another session must be created. The default setting for this option is 3,600 seconds.

Accept UDP Replies

The Accept UDP Replies checkbox is used to allow the firewall to accept UDP packets in use by an established UDP service. The UDP service attempts to create a two-way communication between two parties (source and destination). Only packet replies that are sent from the second party (destination) are allowed to communicate back to the first party (source). By default, this option is checked.

UDP Virtual Session Timeout

The UDP Virtual Session Timeout setting is similar to the TCP session timeout. The UDP replies that are sent from the destination host must keep up communications before this timeout counter expires. If the counter expires, the hosts must establish a new reply channel and have the first packet analyzed by the firewall again. The default setting for this option is 40 seconds.

Enable Decryption On Accept

Checking the Enable Decryption On Accept checkbox allows the Enforcement Module to decrypt incoming packets even if a rule is not specifically set to include any type of encryption. By default, this option is checked.

Implied Rules

The options in the Implied Rules section of the Security Policy tab enable you to define settings that pertain to rules that are created automatically by the firewall. Chapter 6 defines implied rules (also known as *implicit rules* or *pseudo rules*); basically, *implied rules* are rules that are created automatically by the firewall. However, implied rules can be configured using the Security Policy tab to fit the needs of the administrator and the environment. The options you can configure are:

➤ *Accept VPN-1 & FireWall-1 Control Connections*—This rule is used to control other firewalls as well as authentication servers. If checked, the only option for placement in the firewall is first. This option is enabled by default.

➤ *Accept RIP*—Enabling this option allows RIP (Routing Information Protocol) traffic to be passed and used by the firewall. This is not enabled by default. This rule can be placed first, last, or before the last explicit rule.

➤ *Accept Domain Name Over UDP (Queries)*—This rule allows domain name queries to be accepted by *named. Named* is used to resolve hostnames of machines to their IP addresses. By default, this rule is not enabled. This rule can be placed first, last, or before the last explicit rule.

➤ *Accept Domain Name Over TCP (Zone Transfer)*—This rule is used to control the transfer of DNS zone information between DNS servers. By default, this rule is not enabled. This rule can be placed first, last, or before the last explicit rule.

➤ *Accept ICMP*—This rule is used to determine if ICMP (Internet Control Message Protocol) traffic will be accepted by the firewall. By default, this rule is not enabled. This rule can be placed first, last, or before the last explicit rule.

➤ *Accept Outgoing Packets Originating From Gateway*—This rule handles traffic generated from an Enforcement Module. By default, this rule is enabled. This rule can be placed first, last, or before the last explicit rule.

Once you determine what you will accept or deny for traffic, you may want to determine how implied rules are handled. This option can be set using the Log Implied Rules checkbox.

Log Implied Rules

The Log Implied Rules checkbox enables you to set your implied rules to be logged by the firewall. If checked, packets that are enforced by the implied rules will be logged in the log records. This can create extra, unnecessary logging on your firewall. It is recommended to use this only for troubleshooting purposes and remove it after it is no longer necessary.

Install Security Policy Only If It Can Be Successfully Installed On ALL Selected Targets

The Install Security Policy Only If It Can Be Successfully Installed On ALL Selected Targets option's name pretty much describes the purpose of the option. If the policy can't be installed on all the targets selected, then it will not be installed at all. This is not enabled by default.

The Log And Alert Tab

On the Log And Alert tab, you'll find the log and alert properties, as shown in Figure 7.2. This tab is used to control how the firewall will log traffic and send alerts. As you can see in the figure, this tab is divided into two sections—alerts and tracking. Let's take a look at each section.

Alerts

The top section in the Log And Alert tab provides options that apply mostly to how alerts will be handled when they occur. The first two options, however, apply to the log file in general. The options available in this area are:

➤ *Excessive Log Grace Period*—Enables you to set the amount of time between logging of similar packets. The default setting is 62 seconds.

➤ *Log Viewer Resolver Page Timeout*—Specifies the amount of time before the firewall displays the log page without resolving hostnames in the Log Viewer GUI. The default setting is 20 seconds. I discuss the Log Viewer GUI in Chapter 11.

➤ *Popup Alert Command*—Indicates the command that is executed when an alert is generated. By default, the command is **fwalert**.

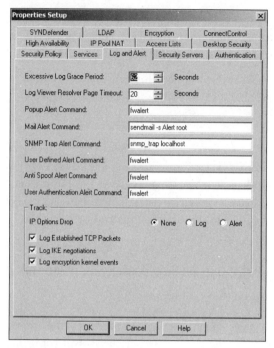

Figure 7.2 The Log And Alert tab.

➤ *Mail Alert Command*—Indicates the command that is executed if mail to be sent is defined as the tracking type in a rule. By default, this option is set to **sendmail –s Alert root**.

➤ *SNMP Trap Alert Command*—Specifies the command that is executed when SNMP (Simple Network Management Protocol) trap is defined as the tracking type in a rule. By default, this option is set to **snmp_trap localhost**.

➤ *User Defined Alert Command*—Specifies the command that is executed when user-defined is defined as the tracking type in a rule. By default, this option is set to **fwalert**.

➤ *Anti Spoof Alert Command*—Refers to the Interface tab of the firewall, which is found in the properties of the workstation object. If anti-spoofing is set to Alert, this command will be executed. By default, this is set to **fwalert**.

➤ *User Authentication Alert Command*—Indicates the command that is executed when user authentication criteria are met. By default, this option is set to **fwalert**.

Setting alerts properties allows you the flexibility to determine how you want to handle any situation that may need immediate attention. For those situations that do not require immediate attention, but still need to be recorded, you'll need to set tracking options, which are covered next.

Track

The bottom section of the Log And Alert tab in the Properties Setup dialog box applies to various logging options for special packets. The available options are:

➤ *IP Options Drop*—Determines how and if IP options will be tracked. The available options are None, Log, and Alert. None is selected by default.

➤ *Log Established TCP Packets*—Specifies whether to log packets for connections that have arrived after the TCP timeout period.

➤ *Log IKE Negotiations*—Refers to logging Internet Key Exchange (IKE) encryption. IKE is discussed in some detail in Chapter 10.

➤ *Log Encryption Kernel Events*—Logs kernel encryption events.

Next, I discuss the properties for security servers. Security servers play a specific role in a FireWall-1 configuration, and as such, they require their own individual configuration settings to be set.

The Security Servers Tab

A security server is responsible for handling authentication based on particular services or protocols. The security server is where the decision-making process is controlled for HTTP (Hypertext Transfer Protocol), FTP (File Transfer Protocol), and other like services. Chapter 2 discusses security servers in more depth. The Security Servers tab (shown in Figure 7.3) provides options that you can use to configure security servers. This tab is divided into two sections, so you can configure welcome message files and your HTTP setup.

Welcome Message Files

The top portion of the Security Servers tab is used to define the location of the welcome message files for specific services. By default, all of the welcome message text boxes are empty. You can define welcome message files for the following services:

➤ Telnet

➤ FTP

➤ Rlogin

➤ Client Authentication

➤ SMTP

Welcome messages are not a critical part of a network, and in some cases you may want to avoid them. For example, in a government network, welcome messages should be avoided to reduce the curiosity of would-be hackers.

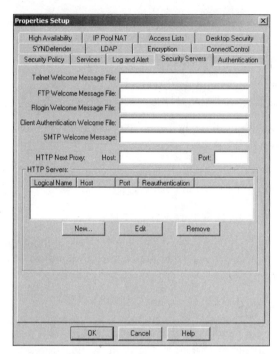

Figure 7.3   Security Servers tab.

HTTP Setup

The HTTP setup portion of the Security Servers tab in the Properties Setup dialog box is divided into two parts. The first part consists of the HTTP Next Proxy setting, which allows you to set the hostname and port number of an HTTP proxy that is in use behind the firewall. The second section—the HTTP Servers area—is used to configure the names and port numbers of HTTP servers behind the firewall. Clicking New allows you to define a new HTTP server, where you would specify the logical name, hostname, and port number of the HTTP server.

The SYNDefender Tab

The SYNDefender tab is used to define settings for protecting the firewall from denial of service (DoS) attacks. A *SYN* is a packet that is used for initiating communication between a source and a destination host. The SYN is sent from the source to the destination, and the destination returns a SYN/ACK to the client acknowledging its existence. When the source receives the SYN/ACK from the destination, the source returns its own ACK to let the destination confirm the source's existence.

In a SYN attack, a source host spoofs an IP address of an unreachable host and begins sending SYN packets to a would-be destination server. When the destination server receives the SYN packet, it attempts to return a SYN/ACK to the source of the first packet. Unfortunately, the host is not reachable because the source is not a functioning IP address. Because the destination host does not receive the ACK from the source, it continues to send the SYN/ACK until a timeout period is reached. The SYN attack occurs when the attacker begins sending multiple SYNs to the server, which will eventually overload the server. Check Point has developed SYNDefender to protect servers from such an attack.

Before we look at the configuration options on the SYNDefender tab, let's look at the two types of SYNDefender configurations. Check Point's SYNDefender can be applied in two ways:

➤ SYN gateway

➤ Passive SYN gateway

Each SYN gateway option handles SYN traffic differently. Let's look at each type.

SYN Gateway

The main purpose behind the SYN gateway is to clear SYN requests from a server's queue. In the gateway configuration, SYNDefender takes over the role of the client. When a SYN request is issued to a server from a client, the firewall passes the packet to the server. When the server sends the SYN/ACK packet back to the client, the firewall passes the SYN/ACK to the client but also sends an ACK to the server. This method ensures that the queue does not get overloaded by SYN floods but still allows for free communications. If the client is a valid IP host, the ACK from the client will be passed to the server as well, but it will ultimately be dropped because the handshake is complete.

Passive SYN Gateway

In the passive configuration, SYNDefender sits as a proxy between a client and a server. When a SYN request is issued from the client to the server, SYNDefender verifies that the three-way handshake can be completed with the host before passing the SYN request to the server. If the request is valid (in other words, not an attack), the relay will forward the request and open the communication.

SYNDefender Settings

The properties tab for SYNDefender is pretty sparse and doesn't require much configuration (see Figure 7.4). You can choose among the following three methods for deploying SYNDefender using this tab:

➤ None (the default)

➤ SYN Gateway

➤ Passive SYN Gateway (SYNDefender Relay)

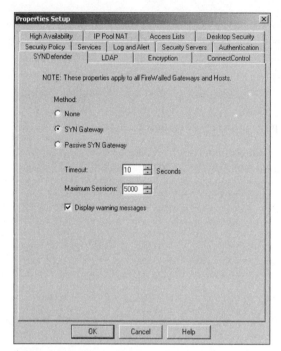

Figure 7.4   SYNDefender tab.

If a gateway method is chosen, the Timeout and Maximum Sessions fields become available. The Timeout field enables you to specify the amount of time to wait for a connection before dropping the connection attempts from the host. The Maximum Sessions field allows you to specify the number of connections that can be allowed between the firewall and the server. If this threshold is reached, the firewall will not allow new connections to be created.

The LDAP Tab

Before I review the LDAP tab, I want to tell you a little about LDAP (Lightweight Directory Access Protocol) itself. LDAP is a software protocol used to enable anyone to locate organizations, individuals, and other resources, such as files and devices in a network, whether on the Internet or on a corporate intranet. LDAP is part of X.500, a standard for directory services in a network. LDAP is lighter because, in its initial version, it did not include security features. Microsoft includes LDAP in Windows 2000 as the foundation of Active Directory. Novell, Netscape, and Cisco are also large backers of LDAP technologies.

In a network, a directory tells you where in the network an object is located. For example, LDAP allows you to search for an object without knowing where that object is located (although additional information will help with the search). Knowing pieces of information about an individual can help facilitate a search of the LDAP directory for that person.

An LDAP directory is organized in a simple tree hierarchy consisting of the following levels:

➤ The root directory (the starting place, or the source of the tree)

➤ Countries

➤ Organizations

➤ Organizational units

➤ Individuals

Now that you have a general idea about LDAP's capabilities, let's look at how Check Point implements it into FireWall-1. On the LDAP tab, there are several options for configuration. However, many of the options are disabled. To enable the LDAP features, click the Use LDAP Account Management checkbox to enable the following fields for configuration:

➤ *Time-Out On LDAP Requests*—This field is used to set the time, in seconds, before an LDAP request times out. The default setting in this field is 20 seconds.

➤ *Time-Out On Cached Used*—This field is used to set the time before a user who is cached is no longer valid and must be searched for again in the LDAP database. The default setting for this field is 900 seconds.

➤ *Cache Size*—This field is referring to the maximum number of users that you want the firewall to cache at one time. The default cache size for this field is 1,000 users.

➤ *Password Expires After*—This field is disabled by default; however, it can be enabled so that you can set the number of days before the LDAP password expires. The default setting (when enabled) is 90 days.

➤ *Allow Account Unit To Return*—This field is used to set the maximum number of hits (records matching the search criteria) that can be returned. The default setting for this field is 10,000 entries.

➤ *Display User's DN At Login*—This is a checkbox to display a user's DN (Distinguishing Name) when he or she logs in. This can be useful for troubleshooting purposes, such as when users with the same name are in the same account record.

Connect Control Tab

Controlling the flow of traffic to a server is important for maintaining server response time. *Load balancing* is the term commonly associated with distributing traffic among servers. Load balancing is the act of distributing traffic evenly across a set of computers so that no single device is overloaded. Load balancing is especially important for networks where it's difficult to predict the number of requests that will be issued to a server. Busy Web sites typically employ two or more Web servers in a load balancing scheme. If one server starts to get swamped, requests are forwarded to another server with more capacity. Load balancing can also refer to the communications channels themselves.

In FireWall-1, the Connect Control tab is used to configure the setting for load balancing servers inside of a firewalled network. FireWall-1 can direct traffic to servers in a load-balanced environment so that no one server is overloaded. The Connect Control tab contains the following two fields for configuration:

➤ *Load Agents Port*—Specifies the port that the load measuring agent communicates through. The load measuring agent is a service that receives data about a server's workload.

➤ *Load Measurement Interval*—Sets the time that the load measuring agent waits before measuring the load.

Load balancing is a great way to offer your users higher network "up-time."

The Remaining Properties Setup Tabs

All of the tabs in the Properties Setup dialog box play an important role in properly configuring a firewall. When you have the opportunity, take a look at each of the tabs to get an idea of what each one does. I cover the Authentication and Encryption tabs in Chapter 10; those tabs are also important when you're administering your firewall.

In addition to configuring your firewall properties, you need to complete some other administrative tasks to get the maximum potential out of your configuration. Therefore, let's close the Properties Setup dialog box and take a look at some other key configuration tasks. Namely, I spend the remainder of this chapter talking about IP spoofing as well as disabling and hiding rules. Guarding your network from IP spoofing is an important security measure, and hiding and disabling rules makes administration of a security policy much easier. Let's take a look at how to use each of these features.

IP Spoofing

IP spoofing can best be described as "identity theft." With IP spoofing, a host sitting somewhere on the Internet takes the IP address of another host as its own for a variety of reasons. As discussed earlier in this chapter, IP spoofing is a popular way to generate DoS attacks by generating packets from a nonexistent IP address and fooling a server into generating a SYN/ACK.

Companies have developed improved technologies to prevent IP spoofing attacks on a network. Routers and firewalls have become much more aware of IP spoofing and better at determining if packets have originated from the network they claim to have been. Check Point in particular has developed an anti-spoofing feature that guarantees that packets that are being passed through the firewall are coming from a valid host. Anti-spoofing rules are enforced before any of the rules in the rule base, which reduces firewall overhead.

In Chapter 4, we briefly looked at anti-spoofing when we defined interfaces for network objects. When applying anti-spoofing, it is important to make sure that you are applying it to the correct interface. Applying it on the wrong interface can cause your firewall to function improperly. Let's take another look at the anti-spoofing options available on a firewall. For this discussion, let's open up the firewall, named *Arizona* (which we created in Chapter 4), and go to the Interface tab. Click the Internal interface, and then click the Edit button. Let's recap the settings on the Security tab. There are two separate sections in the Security tab—Valid Addresses and Spoof Tracking. The choices for the Valid Addresses section are:

➤ *Any*—No spoof tracking. This means that the firewall will allow packets from any network to pass without examining them to see if they meet anti-spoofing criteria.

➤ *This Net*—Only packets that originate from the network connected to the interface are allowed. This Net is generally used for internal interfaces for a network; it means that only packets from hosts that fall within the network range of the interface are allowed.

➤ *No Security Policy!*—Basically, don't use this. Choose this option only when a security policy is used on a different interface.

➤ *Others*—Packets are allowed from networks except from those listed in the Valid Addresses section of the object's other interfaces.

➤ *Others+*—Same as the Others option, except that you can specify IP addresses that you to allow access to.

➤ *Specific*—Packets are allowed from the specified addresses only.

The Spoof Tracking section determines how you will handle the logging of spoofed traffic. All spoofed traffic is dropped by default, but you can determine how it is recorded by using one of the following settings:

➤ *None*—No logging.

➤ *Log*—Logged to the FireWall-1 log.

➤ *Alert*—An alert is sent, based on properties in the Log And Alert portion of the Properties Setup dialog box.

To configure anti-spoofing for your firewall, follow these steps:

1. On the internal interface for the Arizona router, set the anti-spoofing option to This Net. This setting allows only packets that have originated from the network to enter through the interface.

2. For the external interface, set the anti-spoofing option to Other. By choosing Other, you indicate that packets are allowed to enter through the interface only if they originate from an IP address other than those on the internal interface.

3. Set tracking to Log.

Anti-spoofing can be a bit confusing, but the important point to remember here is that you are setting this interface by interface. In this example, we use Other on the external interface because we know that traffic generated from 10.0.0.0 can only be coming from the internal interface. If traffic with a 10.0.0.x host was coming from the external interface, it is obvious that someone is spoofing the traffic.

Disabling Rules

Disabling a rule in a rule base might seem like a strange action to take. However, it can be a useful troubleshooting tool. You might want to disable rules for a number of reasons. For example, you might want to disable a rule to grant temporary access to an object which would otherwise be denied access because of a particular rule. Disabling rules is also a great way to keep from causing additional headaches down the road. Let's say that you are making several changes to your rule base. Imagine that you deleted several rules during your changes and found out later that several of the rules needed to be reinstated. It would be much easier if you could just enable the rules instead of having to find documentation about the rules or try to re-create them from memory.

Disabling a rule is rather easy. Figure 7.5 shows an example of a disabled rule. To disable a rule in the rule base, follow these steps:

Figure 7.5   A disabled rule.

1. Select a rule.

2. Right-click the rule number.

3. Select Disable Rule on the drop-down list.

 The steps described in this section disable a rule in the rule base only. For the change to take place on your firewall, you must reinstall the security policy.

Hiding Rules

Hiding rules (also known as *masking*) is an easy way to clean up your rule base. For example, let's say you have a bunch of disabled rules that you don't plan to use, and you do not want to see them every time you open up the Policy Editor to make changes. You can hide those rules from the rule base but still have them remain a functioning (or in this case, disabled) rule. For illustrative purposes, let's hide the rule that we disabled in the preceding section:

1. Select the disabled rule (or any rule, if you prefer).

2. Right-click the rule number.

3. Select Hide Rule on the drop-down list.

Now that the rule is hidden, there's one procedure left to look at—getting the rule back! To restore a hidden rule, click View on the Policy Editor menu, and then select Show Hidden on the View menu.

Note: If you hid a rule that was between other rules, you would notice that the rule numbers skip the hidden rule's number. This is a good way to tell if you are masking rules in your policy.

As you can begin to see in this chapter, the Check Point FireWall-1 puzzle consists of many pieces. Each piece plays an important role in the configuration and administration of the firewall. Installing a firewall properly requires completing many more tasks than just creating a rule base and plugging it onto an Enforcement Module. Tasks such as applying the policy settings, disabling rules, hiding rules, and configuring the firewall for IP spoofing are all just as important as the rules themselves.

Practice Questions

Question 1

Hiding a rule stops a rule from being installed on an Enforcement Module.

○ a. True

○ b. False

Answer b is correct. Hiding a rule only removes the rule from being seen in the rule base. To stop a rule from being installed, you must either disable or completely remove the rule.

Question 2

The Connect Contol tab is used to configure properties relating to which of the following?

○ a. Connection speed

○ b. User access

○ c. Access timeout

○ d. Load balancing

○ e. All of the above

○ f. None of the above

Answer d is correct. The Connect Control tab is used to control the load agents port and load measurement interval used for load balancing traffic between servers in a network. Answer a is incorrect because there is not a tab that controls connection speed. Answer b is incorrect because the Authentication tab controls user access. Answer c is incorrect because the Authentication tab also controls amount of time before access timeout.

Question 3

> How many steps are required to complete a SYN handshake?
>
> ○ a. One
>
> ○ b. Two
>
> ○ c. Three
>
> ○ d. Four
>
> ○ e. This number varies

Answer c is correct. Three steps are required to complete a SYN handshake. The first step is the SYN being sent to the destination host. The second step is the destination host responding with a SYN/ACK. When the source receives the SYN/ACK, it sends its own ACK back to the destination to confirm receipt of the SYN/ACK—the third step.

Question 4

> Which of the following is not a configuration option for SYNDefender?
>
> ○ a. None
>
> ○ b. SYN Gateway
>
> ○ c. Passive SYN Gateway
>
> ○ d. None of the above

Answer d is correct because all of the listed options are available when you configure SYNDefender. You have three options for configuring SYNDefender. None does not install SYNDefender; this is the default. SYN Gateway and Passive SYN Gateway are the two options for activation of the SYNDefender.

Question 5

> Which tab in the Properties Setup dialog box allows you to set the names of welcome message files?
>
> ○ a. Services
>
> ○ b. Security Policy
>
> ○ c. Authentication
>
> ○ d. LDAP
>
> ○ e. Log And Alert
>
> ○ f. Security Servers
>
> ○ g. None of the above

Answer f is correct. The Security Servers tab in the firewall properties screen is used to select the welcome messages used for Telnet, FTP, rlogin, Client Authentication, and SMTP services.

Question 6

> What does LDAP stand for?
>
> ○ a. Low Density Access Platform
>
> ○ b. Light Distribution Access Protocol
>
> ○ c. Lightweight Directory Access Protocol
>
> ○ d. Lightweight Department Access Protocol
>
> ○ e. LDAP doesn't stand for anything.

Answer c is correct. LDAP stands for Lightweight Directory Access Protocol. LDAP is used to access information directories that contain searchable information on many different topics.

Question 7

With regard to the Connect Control feature, which of the following options is used to set the time that the load measuring agent waits before measuring the load?

○ a. Load Agents Port

○ b. Load Measurement Interval

○ c. Load Agents Timeout

○ d. None of the above

Answer b is correct. The Load Measurement Interval setting is used to set the time that the load measuring agent waits before measuring the load. Answer a is incorrect because the Load Agents Port option specifies the port that the load measuring agent communicates through. Answer c is incorrect because Load Agents Timeout is not a configuration option for Connect Control.

Question 8

What are the directions in which you can apply gateway rules to an interface in the Security Policy tab? [Check all correct answers]

❏ a. Inbound

❏ b. Eitherbound

❏ c. Internetbound

❏ d. Outbound

❏ e. Entering

❏ f. Exiting

Answers a, b, and d are correct. You can apply the gateway rules in three directions: inbound, eitherbound, and outbound. Inbound is set by default. Answers c, e, and f are incorrect because they are not valid traffic directions options in FireWall-1.

Question 9

Kaitlyn is setting up a firewall for the first time. She is trying to decide how she wants to apply anti-spoofing to her firewall. She sets the external interface anti-spoofing properties to This Network. When users on the Internet try to get access to her Web site, they cannot gain access. All of her rules appear to be correct. What happened?

○ a. The network allows only machines with IP addresses on the same network as the one connected to the interface.

○ b. She has not properly set her HTTP settings in the firewall properties.

○ c. The users are using the wrong URL to access the Web site.

○ d. Nothing. Check with the ISP to make sure its service is running properly.

Answer a is correct. The This Network setting is typically used for internal interfaces. Kaitlyn should have used Others, Others+, or Specific. Using This Network allows only packets that originate from the network that is the same as the one connected to the interface. Answer b is incorrect because the problem does not tie into the HTTP settings of the firewall. Answers c and d are incorrect because the problem relates to the anti-spoofing settings, not the URL or ISP.

Question 10

It is a good idea to reinstall the security policy after disabling a rule.

○ a. True

○ b. False

Answer a is correct. For the most part, you should reinstall your security policy after making any changes. A disabled rule is disabled only in the rule base unless the security policy is reinstalled.

Need to Know More?

 Goncalves, Marcus and Steven Brown. *Check Point FireWall-1 Administration Guide*. McGraw-Hill, New York, NY, 1999. ISBN 0-07-134229-X. This book serves as a good bookshelf reference for FireWall-1.

 Scambray, Joel, Stuart McClure, and George Kurtz. *Hacking Exposed: Second Edition*. McGraw-Hill Professional Publishing, New York, NY, 1992. ISBN 0-07-212748-1. Scambray, McClure, and Kurtz do a great job of looking at network security from a hacker's perspective.

 http://ciac.llnl.gov/ciac/bulletins/f-08.shtml presents an article stored on the Computer Incident Advisory Center Web site for the U.S. Department of Energy. This article contains some great information about IP spoofing.

 www.checkpoint.com, the Check Point Web site, offers some basic installation information regarding the various types of installations and OS platforms.

Remote Administration and Firewall Synchronization

Terms you'll need to understand:

✓ Management Module

✓ Firewall Module

✓ Access control rights

✓ Redundant remote management

✓ Remote communications

✓ Route costing

✓ High availability

✓ Firewall synchronization

Techniques you'll need to master:

✓ Identifying the components of the remote management architecture

✓ Configuring a firewall to be managed remotely

✓ Managing a security policy remotely

✓ Removing remote management

✓ Identifying the ports used between the Management Module and FireWall-1

✓ Configuring synchronization

Remote administration should not be a new concept to anyone in the networking arena. Software packages that serve the sole purpose of administering a machine from a remote location have been on the market for years. In the past few years, this technology has grown exponentially as the need for advanced remote administration has risen. Early on, Check Point realized the need for remote administration and developed features built into the software to fill this need.

For many companies, the need for remote managers has risen for several reasons. For some companies, remote administration is necessary because smaller, satellite offices do not have their own network staff or anyone who can support their firewalls and networking components on a day-to-day basis. Because of this, a central office or headquarters where the MIS (Management Information Services) or IT (Information Technology) staff resides must be able to administer and configure firewalls, switches, servers, and any other equipment that might reside at the remote locations.

For other companies, limited resources might be the reason a firewall is managed remotely. For instance, an organization might have slightly larger remote offices, but each office might have only one technician on site. Let's say that there are 100 satellite offices nationwide, and each has its own firewall in a public frame relay network. Instead of having to get the technicians up to speed or having a firewall administrator at each site, the home office could have one firewall "expert" who manages all of the equipment.

Whatever the reason behind using remote administration, security is always a key issue when important information is passed over any type of unsecured line. When referring to unsecured lines, I'm not only talking about the Internet but also high-speed lines, dial-up access lines, and any other forms of communications that must travel over any measurable amount of distance. In this chapter, I discuss remote administration and how FireWall-1 secures data that's transferred between the Management Module and the Firewall Modules.

Understanding How Remote Management Works

In a Check Point FireWall-1 distributed architecture, remote management can be configured so that a single Management Server can be used to manage multiple Firewall Modules. The Management Server for this type of environment would be used to store the log files of the Enforcement Modules and the databases of the Enforcement Modules, and it would be used for compiling the security policies for each of the Enforcement Modules. A Check Point FireWall-1 Management Server can be configured to control up to 50 firewalled devices. The architecture for remote management is configured in a three-tier environment, as described here:

➤ *GUI clients*—The GUI (graphical user interface) clients are used for the visual representation of the information on the Management Modules. You can use the GUIs (Policy Editor, Log Viewer, and System Status) to view and manipulate the data that is stored on the Management Modules.

➤ *Management Modules*—Although the modifications of rules are completed using the GUI clients, the actual firewall manipulation and management are handled on the Management Module. All of the network objects, services, resources, servers, users, times, and keys are stored and managed from this piece of the firewall components. Logs and system status information are also stored here instead of on the Firewall Modules.

➤ *Firewall Modules*—As discussed in Chapter 2, the Firewall Module handles the passing of packets between two nodes, network address translation, authentication, and other key functions. In a distributed environment, the Firewall Module is used to enforce the security policy developed by the Management Module and to pass along the status of the firewall and any data that has been logged to the Management Module.

Each of these pieces plays a role in remotely managing a firewall. All three pieces must be in place to manage a remote firewall (or a local firewall, for that matter). In the case of a remote firewall, you need to make sure that communication and administration between the GUI, Management Module, and Firewall Module are secure. In the next section, we will look at how Check Point goes about securing remote management.

Securing Remote Management

As stated earlier in this chapter, securing remote management communications is important when administering a firewall over any distance. Remote management is secured by encrypting the data that is being transmitted from a Management Module to a Firewall Module. However, this only covers you from the Management Module to the Firewall Module. How about authentication of administrators to the Management Modules?

Obviously, an administrator needs to make sure that only authorized users are allowed to connect to Management Servers. In Chapter 3, we configured GUI clients and administrator accounts for this purpose. For remote management, administrators are authenticated using *access control rights*. Access control rights are established in a three-step process, as follows:

1. The GUI client transmits the username, password, and IP address of the client machine to the Management Server specified in the logon screen (see Figure 8.1).

Figure 8.1   Logon screen for the Policy Editor.

2. If the IP address of the client machine is a valid IP address as specified in the Management Server's configuration, the Management Server will validate the username and password supplied.

3. After the username and password are verified, the Firewall Module passes the security policy, objects, and log database for the client to manipulate.

This method of handshaking is important to prevent unwanted changes to a firewall, which in turn may compromise the network's security. Next, I'll cover the ports that FireWall-1 uses to communicate between the different modules.

Remote Management Ports

Like any application, FireWall-1 must be able to communicate between its different modules. Because the information being transferred must conform to standards for communications, FireWall-1 must use TCP ports for communications between the Management Module and the Firewall Module. FireWall-1 has a standard group of ports that are part of the service group *FireWall-1* in the Services database. In order for the Management Module to control the Firewall Module, these ports must be opened to allow data to pass between the two modules. Table 8.1 shows each service's name, port, and function.

Redundant Remote Management

Preventing system downtime is one of the largest obstacles that network administrators and engineers have to face in the networking arena. Redundant power supplies, redundant processors, redundant NICs (network interface cards), redundant

Table 8.1	The components of FireWall-1.	
Service	Port	Function
FW1	256	Used for exchanging license keys.
FW1_log	257	Used for transferring log information.
FW1_mgmt	258	Used for loading or retrieving a security policy.

high-speed connections and so on—all of these fault-prevention methodologies have become commonplace in today's environment.

In a FireWall-1 environment, multiple Management Servers can be configured to manage various firewalls. The catch here is that for redundant remote management to work, you must have the same exact security policy installed on the Firewall Modules. There is no automatic synchronization between the Management Modules; however, it is possible to synchronize Firewall Module, as described in the section "Synchronizing Firewall Modules" later in this chapter.

Creating a Remote Security Policy

You can create a remote security policy in two ways. The first way is to create the rules for the remote firewalls in the same rule base as the local firewall. If you recall from Chapter 6, you can use the Install On field of a rule to determine the gateway that a particular rule will be installed on. This method has its pros and cons. The main advantage is that you can see all of the rules on the screen at one time, making it easier to see all of the rules in your enterprise. The main drawback is that as the rule base on a Management Server grows, maintaining a large rule base and keeping all of the rules on a maintainable order can become increasingly difficult.

To make management of a remote rule base easier, you can create a number of rule bases and save them to your Management Servers. In most cases, this solution is a much more useful and manageable solution than adding rules into a predefined rule base. Let's take a look at both methods.

Adding Remote Rules to a Security Policy

To illustrate the process of adding remote rules to an existing security policy, let's open up the rule base that we have been working with up to this point in the book. To get started, start the Policy Editor tool and log into the Management Server. This will bring up the rule base that you created previously in Chapter 6.

Now, you're going to need to create another Check Point Firewall Module that is going to represent your remote firewall. Let's assume that you are opening a remote office in Los Angeles. To do this, follow these steps:

1. Click Manage in the Policy Editor.

2. Click Network Objects on the Manage menu.

3. Click the New button on the Network Object menu.

4. Select Workstation from the drop-down menu. On the Workstation menu, enter the following information:

➤ *Name*—Los_Angeles

➤ *IP Address*—90.0.0.1

➤ *Comment*—Los Angeles Firewall

➤ *Location*—Internal (because it is managed by this Management Server)

➤ *Type*—Gateway

➤ *VPN-1 & FireWall-1*—Enabled

➤ *Color*—Red

Next, you need to define the Los Angeles network.

5. Click Manage in the Policy Editor.

6. Click Network Objects on the Manage menu.

7. Click the New button on the Network Object menu.

8. Select Network on the drop-down menu.

9. In the Network Object dialog box, enter in the following information:

➤ *Name*—Los_Angeles_Net

➤ *IP Address*—172.18.10.0

➤ *Net Mask*—255.255.254.0

➤ *Comment*—Los Angeles Network

➤ *Location*—Internal (because it is managed by this Management Server)

➤ *Color*—Green

Now, you are ready to create a few rules using the Los_Angeles network and the Los_Angeles firewall. Make sure to create a stealth rule for the Los_Angeles firewall. When creating these rules, make sure to change the Install On option by right-clicking in the Install On field, selecting Add, and then clicking Targets. You will want to select the Los_Angeles firewall from the drop-down list. After the rules have been added, you can install the security policy to the firewalls (assuming you have an actual firewall named Los_Angeles; if you do not have one, do not attempt this, because it will fail).

 If you do not want the rest of the rules in the rule base applied to the Los_Angeles firewall, you must change the Install On option for the other rules to specify the Arizona router.

Creating a New Rule Base

You can save multiple rule bases to hard media for the purpose of backing up your rule base as well as adding the ability to create multiple rule bases. If you created the rules for the Los_Angeles router in the preceding section, delete the Los_Angeles rules. Then, save your rule base. This is a pretty simple step. To save your rule base, click File|Save As. Enter a policy name in the Save Rule Base As dialog box; in this example, we will save ours as *Arizona*. Notice that the name in the Security Policy and Address Translation tabs changes.

Next, you could take one of two actions. First, you could create a whole new rule base by clicking File|New. Or, you could delete the existing rules from the rule base to save yourself some time. For this example, we will simply create a new rule base, as described here:

1. Click File|New and then create a stealth rule for the Los_Angeles firewall, a rule that will allow traffic from the Los_Angeles network to any destination, and a cleanup rule. You can also create some additional rules if you choose. Make sure to select the Los_Angeles firewall in the Install On field, like you did in the previous section.

2. To save this rule base, click File|Save As.

3. Now that the Los Angeles rule base is saved, reopen your Arizona rule base, because you will continue to work with this in future chapters. To reopen the Arizona rule base, click File|Open. In the Open Security Policy dialog box that appears (see Figure 8.2), highlight the Arizona policy on the menu and click Open.

Whether to create multiple rule bases—one for each Firewall Module—or a single rule base that covers all of the firewalls in a wide area network is at the discretion of the administrator. However, for new administrators, it may be less overwhelming

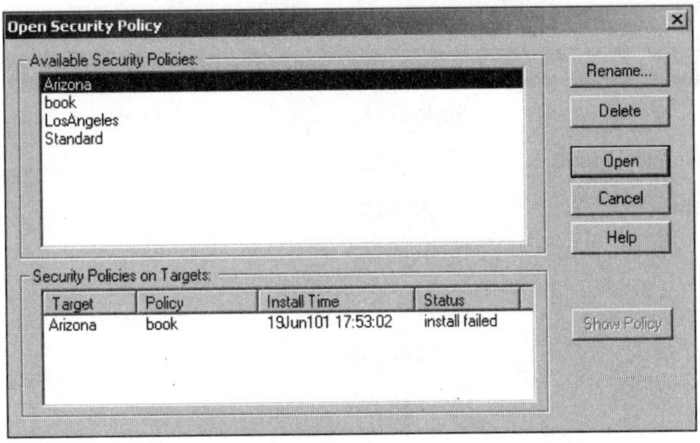

Figure 8.2   Opening a security policy.

if you create multiple rule bases until you feel comfortable with combining them into a single rule base.

Synchronizing Firewall Modules

FireWall-1 offers the ability to configure multiple firewalls in a redundant set. If one Firewall Module fails, the other module will take over communications automatically and allow connections that have already been established. Table 8.2 shows the connection types that are maintained and those that are lost when failover occurs. Synchronized firewalls provide the ability to route packets, and they add fault tolerance by providing high availability to network communications.

Routing

As routing has evolved over the years, the need for *costing* has developed. The general concept behind costing is to determine what routed path gives the most return. In terms of routing, costing is determined by certain metrics so that certain routes are given preference to particular destinations.

The Open Shortest Path First (OSPF) routing protocol uses costing metrics to determine paths. Instead of just counting the number of hops, OSPF determines its paths by using *link states* that take into account additional network information. OSPF allows a user to assign cost metrics to a router, so certain paths are given preference. That said, the next statement might seem a little bit strange. FireWall-1 has the benefit of foregoing the costed routes and allowing either firewall in a synchronized cluster to handle the traffic. Synchronization is configured in this manner so that the connection remains transparent to end users at all times.

High Availability

The concept of high availability is that a particular function—be it a firewall, server, router, or even a simple phone line—has certain cost consequences based on the

Table 8.2 FireWall-1 features that failover.	
Communication	**Status**
Basic protocols (HTTP, FTP, and so forth)	Maintained
NAT (network address translation)	Maintained
Authentication	Dropped/lost
Security servers	Dropped/lost
Encryption	Dropped/lost
SecureRemote	Dropped/lost

amount of downtime that it incurs. Compaq corporation uses the following statistics (on its Web site at **www.compaq.com/services/promotions/advantage/ cod.html**) to illustrate the effect that downtime can have on a corporation:

➤ *1 hour of downtime*—Cost a telecom company nearly $500,000 (U.S.).

➤ *.1 percent system downtime*—Cost a utility company 25,000 staff hours.

➤ *4 hours of cargo operation downtime*—Cost an airline $2 million (U.S.).

➤ *Downtime (in general)*—Cost a defense contractor 8 percent of its total annual staff hours.

Let's roll this concept back into your environment. Let's say that your corporation is an investment company. Imagine that you have only one firewall, and a hardware failure occurs. If the brokers in your investment company are using the Internet for the purposes of tracking and trading stocks, they would be unable to perform their basic job function.

With the high availability provided by firewall synchronization and assuming that you have two firewalls configured in a cluster, if one of your firewalls crashes, the remaining firewall will be able to handle the requests from the downed firewall.

Setting Up Synchronization in a Unix Environment

Setting up synchronization is fairly simple. To configure synchronization between two firewalls in a Unix environment, follow these steps:

1. Create a file named sync.conf in the $FWDIR/conf directory on both of the machines hosting the Firewall Module. The only item this file should contain is the hostname or IP address of the other Firewall Module. So, if you had Phoenix-A and Phoenix-B firewalls, you would enter "Phoenix-B" in the sync.conf file on Phoenix-A and "Phoenix-A" in the sync.conf file on Phoenix-B.

2. At the command prompt, stop both of the firewalls by using the **fwstop** command.

3. At the command prompt, enter "fw putkey -n <local ip address> <remote ip address>" on both of the firewalls. This command is used to establish a control path between the firewalls.

4. At the command prompt, restart both of the firewalls by using the **fwstart** command.

Setting Up Synchronization in a Windows NT Environment

There is not much difference between configuring a Windows NT firewall for synchronization and a Unix firewall. However, you should still know the differences between the two. To set up synchronization in a Windows NT environment, follow these steps:

1. In Windows NT, create a file named sync.conf in the %systemroot%\ FW1\4.1\conf directory on both of the machines hosting the Firewall Module. The only item that this file should contain is the hostname or IP address of the other Firewall Module. So, if you had a Phoenix-A and Phoenix-B firewall, you would enter "Phoenix-B" in the sync.conf file on Phoenix-A and "Phoenix-A" in the sync.conf file on Phoenix-B. The key difference here compared to a Unix installation is to make sure that you are creating the file in the correct directory, because you need to tunnel down into the directories a little more when you are using Windows NT.

2. In the %systemroot%\FW1\4.1\bin directory, find the fwstop executable file. Optionally, you can just stop the firewall services using the Services option in the Control Panel.

3. Go to the %systemroot%\FW1\4.1\bin directory if you have not already, and type "fw putkey -n <local ip address> <remote ip address>" on both of the firewalls. This command is used to establish a control path between the firewalls.

4. At the command prompt, restart both of the firewalls by typing the **fwstart** command, or you can restart the firewall services using the Services option in the Control Panel.

Configuring Multiple Synchronized Connections

Now, let's take synchronization to the next level. You can set up more than one synchronized connection between two firewalls to create even more redundancy. To do this, follow these steps:

1. Open sync.conf in the $FWDIR/conf directory on both of the machines hosting the Firewall Module. Enter the additional IP addresses of the remote firewall.

2. At the command prompt, stop both of the firewalls by using the **fwstop** command.

3. At the command prompt, restart both of the firewalls by using the **fwstart** command.

The control path between the two firewalls has already been established; therefore, you should not perform another **putkey**.

Synchronization between both of the firewalls is transmitted between both of the connections now. However, the Firewall Module that is receiving the information will make only one change to its state tables.

Synchronization Limitations

Although synchronizing firewalls for redundancy is a great feature provided by Check Point, you should be aware of several restrictions that come with synchronization:

➤ The Firewall Modules must be managed by the same Management Module.

➤ The Firewall Modules must have the same security policy installed.

➤ The Firewall Modules must be using the same OS version. In other words, an NT Firewall Module cannot be synchronized with a Solaris Firewall Module.

➤ The Firewall Modules must be using the same software version. FireWall-1 synchronization is not backward or forward compatible. Version 4.1 will synchronize only with other 4.1 modules, and the same is true for version 4.

➤ User authentication will be lost if the original connection is dropped.

➤ Encrypted connections do not work correctly between synchronized Firewall Modules.

➤ Accounting data for a Firewall Module will not function properly if two firewalls are synchronized.

➤ SecureRemote (VPN) connections cannot be synchronized.

➤ NAT will work, but a lot of advanced planning and detailing must be made if synchronization of address translation is to work properly.

➤ Clock synchronization is very important. Synchronization of system clocks must be within one second of each other. Clock synchronization is important because if the timing is more than a second off, the connection will timeout.

Remote management and synchronization may not play into every person's environment; however, both concepts are important to understand for both the exam and to have a full understanding of FireWall-1. Each of these features has its limitations, but each also offers expanded management capabilities for administrators and can make your workload much lighter. If you have access to two or more firewalls, trying remote management and synchronization is the best way to get a good understanding of how each works.

Practice Questions

Question 1

> Different versions of the Firewall Module can be used with synchronization.
>
> ○ a. True
>
> ○ b. False

Answer b is correct. Synchronization can be implemented only if both of the Firewall Modules are running the same version of FireWall-1.

Question 2

> To install a rule onto a particular firewall, you must change the _____ field.
>
> ○ a. Log
>
> ○ b. Firewall
>
> ○ c. Install On
>
> ○ d. Destination
>
> ○ e. Action
>
> ○ f. None of the above

Answer c is correct. To enforce a rule on a particular Firewall Module, you must specify the firewall in the Install On field. Answers a, b, d, e, and f are incorrect because these options do not produce the required result. Answer a is incorrect because the Log field provides only tracking of data, not where to install a particular rule. Answer b is incorrect because no such field as Firewall exists. Answer d is incorrect because the Destination field represents the location where the data in question is being transferred to. Answer e is incorrect because the Action field determines how the traffic will be handled.

Question 3

What ports are used for managing a Firewall Module remotely?

○ a. 256, 257, 258

○ b. 257, 258, 259

○ c. 255, 256, 257

○ d. 254, 255, 256

○ e. 21, 23, 80

Answer a is correct. Port 256 is used for the exchange of license keys. Port 257 is used for transferring log information, and port 258 is used for loading and retrieving a security policy. Answers b, c, d, and e are incorrect because port 21 is used for FTP, 23 is used for Telnet, 80 is used for HTTP, and 254 and 255 are undefined.

Question 4

The concept of _____ is that a particular item has a cost consequence based on the amount of downtime it incurs.

○ a. Synchronization

○ b. High costing

○ c. High availability

○ d. Costing

○ e. None of the above

Answer c is correct. High availability is a measurement of the amount of time a particular function is up versus the time that it is down. The more time that a server, for example, can be kept up and running, the higher its availability is thought to be. Answer a is incorrect because synchronization is the act of matching two or more firewall rule bases. Answer b is incorrect because high costing is a fictitious term. Answer d is incorrect because costing is the act of measuring the cost consequence of any action.

Question 5

> Which of the following are the tiers of remote management? [Check all correct answers]
>
> ❏ a. Services
>
> ❏ b. Remote administration
>
> ❏ c. GUI clients
>
> ❏ d. Management Module
>
> ❏ e. Network Module
>
> ❏ f. Firewall Module
>
> ❏ g. INSPECT Module

Answers c, d, and f are correct. The three tiers of remote management are GUI clients, Management Module, and Firewall Module. All three of these pieces are necessary in order to manage a firewall remotely. Answer a is incorrect because services are part of the rule base. Answer b is incorrect because remote administration is the act of remotely managing a Firewall Module. Answer e is incorrect because the Network Module is a fictitious module type. Answer g is incorrect because the INSPECT Module is responsible for providing authentication, auditing of the firewall, performing network address translation, and controlling the transfer of traffic in and out of the firewall.

Question 6

> What file must you create to set up firewall synchronization?
>
> ○ a. synch.conf
>
> ○ b. sync.conf
>
> ○ c. sync.cfg
>
> ○ d. synch.cfg
>
> ○ e. You don't have to create a file; it is already there.

Answer b is correct. To configure FireWall-1 to synchronize between two files, you must create a file named sync.conf. Answer a is incorrect because "sync" should not be spelled with an "h". Answers c and d are incorrect because they are invalid file names.

Question 7

What information must be put into the sync.conf file?

○ a. The IP address/hostname of this firewall

○ b. The IP address/hostname of the other firewall

○ c. The IP address/hostname of both firewalls

○ d. A common password

Answer b is correct. In the sync.conf file, you must enter the IP address of the Firewall Module that you will be synchronizing with. On the second firewall, you must enter the IP address of the first firewall. Answer a is incorrect because the IP address or hostname of the local firewall does not need to be entered into the file. Answer c is incorrect because only the remote firewall's IP address needs to be entered. Answer d is incorrect because a common password is not required.

Question 8

What subfolder must the sync.conf file be placed in?

○ a. bin

○ b. conf

○ c. 4.1

○ d. state

○ e. tmp

○ f. database

Answer b is correct. The sync.conf file must be placed in the %systemroot%/FW1/ 4.1/conf directory in a Windows NT environment. In a Unix environment, the sync.conf file must be placed in the $FWIR/conf directory. The conf directory holds all of the firewall configuration information. The rest of the subdirectories are valid FireWall-1 directories, but they serve different purposes. Answer a is incorrect because the bin folder holds the executable files of FireWall-1. Answer c is incorrect because the 4.1 folder is used as a parent folder to such subfolders such as bin and conf. Answers d, e, and f are incorrect because the state, tmp, and database folders hold firewall state, temporary files, and database files, respectively.

Question 9

> For remote management, administrators are authenticated using _____.
>
> ○ a. Passwords
>
> ○ b. Remote administration
>
> ○ c. Management Modules
>
> ○ d. Access control rights

Answer d is correct. The username, password, and IP address of the GUI client are sent to the Management Module. If all three match up, the access control rights are passed back to the GUI client. Answer a is incorrect because a password is only part of the access control rights. Answer b is incorrect because remote administration is the act of managing the firewall. Answer c is incorrect because Management Modules are pieces of software used by FireWall-1 and are not used to authenticate.

Question 10

> Up to how many firewalls can a Management Module control?
>
> ○ a. 10
>
> ○ b. 20
>
> ○ c. 50
>
> ○ d. 100
>
> ○ e. Unlimited

Answer c is correct. A single Management Module can control up to a total of 50 firewalls.

Need to Know More?

 Goncalves, Marcus and Steven Brown. *Check Point FireWall-1 Administration Guide*. McGraw-Hill, New York, NY, 1999. ISBN 0-07-134229-X. This book serves as a good bookshelf reference for FireWall-1.

 http://ciac.llnl.gov/ciac/bulletins/f-08.shtml is the Computer Incident Advisory Center Web site for the U.S. Department of Energy. This article contains some great information about IP spoofing.

 www.checkpoint.com, the Check Point Web site, offers some basic installation information regarding the various types of installations and OS platforms.

 www.compaq.com/services/promotions/advantage provides information about Compaq's high availability study. (Keep in mind that many other sites on the Internet also discuss high availability.)

Network Address Translation

. . . .

Terms you'll need to understand:

- ✓ Internet Protocol version 6 (IPv6)
- ✓ Network address translation (NAT)
- ✓ Classless InterDomain Routing (CIDR)
- ✓ Address Resolution Protocol (ARP)
- ✓ ARP cache
- ✓ Time to live (TTL)
- ✓ Reverse Address Resolution Protocol (RARP)

- ✓ ARP request
- ✓ ARP reply
- ✓ RARP request
- ✓ RARP reply
- ✓ Static NAT
- ✓ Hide NAT
- ✓ Original packet
- ✓ Translated packet

Techniques you'll need to master:

- ✓ Defining an object as a static NAT object
- ✓ Defining an object as a hide NAT object
- ✓ Configuring ARP on Windows NT

- ✓ Creating a NAT rule
- ✓ Identifying the need for NAT
- ✓ Explaining how an ARP request is sent

187

As the Internet gained popularity during the mid-1990s, network engineers were faced with a pretty big problem—working with a finite number of IP addresses that needed to meet a demand that was growing by leaps and bounds. By 1995, it was obvious that something needed to be done before IP addresses ran out. Three solutions gained immediate popularity throughout the world of technology—Classless InterDomain Routing (CIDR), Internet Protocol version 6 (IPv6), and network address translation (NAT). In this chapter, I cover each of these techniques, with an emphasis on how NAT comes into play with FireWall-1. Understanding how NAT works is not only important for understanding Check Point FireWall-1, but is also an important concept in the world of networking. However, before NAT, there was CIDR, so I'll start the discussion with CIDR and how it came into existence during the growth of the Internet.

Classless InterDomain Routing

Although you will not be specifically tested on Classless InterDomain Routing on the CCSA exam, you need to understand how NAT came into existence. Therefore, let's take a few minutes to discuss CIDR.

Initially, IP addresses were broken down into four address classes:

➤ *Class A*—IP addresses ranging from 1.x.x.x to 127.x.x.x

➤ *Class B*—IP addresses ranging from 128.x.x.x to 191.x.x.x

➤ *Class C*—IP addresses ranging from 192.x.x.x to 223.x.x.x

➤ *Class D*—IP addresses ranging from 224.x.x.x to 247.x.x.x

CIDR was designed to break down these high-level classes (with lots of addresses within the ranges) into smaller subnetworks. As an example of why it became important to break IP addresses into classes, consider a company that needs more than 254 host machines but not quite a full Class B range of 65,533 possible host addresses. In that case, if the company were assigned a Class B range of addresses, the unassigned addresses would sit unused. CIDR takes care of this issue by providing a more robust way of specifying network addresses.

Using CIDR, each IP address has a specific *network prefix* that identifies either a collection of gateways or a single gateway. A destination IP address or route that describes many possible destinations has a shorter prefix and is said to be less specific. A longer prefix describes a destination gateway more specifically. CIDR lets one routing table entry represent a collection of networks that exist on one side of the gateway; these networks do not need to be specified on any specific gateway.

CIDR was a respectable short-term solution to the depleting IP address situation; however, it did not solve the problem—it only prolonged the inevitable. At the time, the long-term solution that was widely agreed on was the implementation of a new Internet protocol—IPv6.

Note: For more information about Classless InterDomain Routing, see Request For Comments (RFC) 1519.

Internet Protocol Version 6

As mentioned, CIDR was a workable solution for temporarily solving the IP address issues and limitations in the 1990s. However, nobody was naïve enough to think that CIDR was going to put the issue to rest. A long-term solution needed to be developed to resolve the coming drought of IP addresses.

The concept of IPv6 (also known as IP Next Generation, or IPng) was developed to take care of the addressing issue as a long-term solution. IPv6, when fully implemented, would offer IP addresses that were four times as many bits as available in IP version 4 (128 bits versus 32 bits). The other advantages offered by IPv6 include:

➤ Options are specified in an extension to the header that is examined only at the destination.

➤ The concept of an *anycast* address provides the ability to send a message to the nearest of several possible gateway hosts so that any of the gateways can handle the passing of the traffic.

➤ The IPv6 header includes extensions that allow a packet to specify a function for authenticating the packet source, providing additional transfer security.

Note: Many RFCs are available on the topic of IPv6; however, a good place to start if you are seeking more information on this topic is RFC 1752. This RFC describes the recommendations made for the IP Next Generation.

At the time this book was written, IPv6 still had no solid date for widespread implementation. However, IPv6 is available and can be implemented in most operating systems for testing purposes. Because IPv6 is still obviously a long way from being fully operational, and given the fact that CIDR did not resolve the IP address issue, something else needed to be done to resolve the address-limitation problem. That "something else" came in the form of NAT—network address translation.

Network Address Translation

At this point, network engineers came full circle in the quest to avoid running out of IP addresses. The Internet community recognized that CIDR was not everything it was cracked up to be and that IPv6 would not come soon enough.

Therefore, everyone put their thinking caps back on and came up with another solution. The solution turned out to be network address translation, or NAT, as it is more commonly referred to.

The initial RFC for NAT is RFC 1631, which describes the basic operation of NAT. To paraphrase RFC 1631, NAT is a method of connecting multiple computers to the Internet (or any other IP network) using one IP address.

Because of this ability, NAT provides several features, including:

➤ NAT can be used to divide a large network into multiple smaller networks. The smaller networks are seen as one IP address to the outside world, which means that changes to the internal networks (additions, deletions, and internal IP changes) do not have an effect on how those networks are viewed from the Internet or other external networks.

➤ Another feature of NAT is the ability to log traffic. Because all the traffic to and from the Internet has to pass through a NAT gateway, it can record all the traffic to a log file.

➤ Because NAT gateways operate on an IP-packet level, most of them have built-in routing capabilities. The networks the gateways serve can be divided into several separate subnets to help simplify administration.

Using NAT allows an administrator to use ranges of IP addresses on an internal network that does not have to be part of the public Internet scheme. To avoid conflict with Internet-valid IP addresses, three ranges are set aside for internal communications. Table 9.1 shows the classes and IP ranges that are available for private use.

NAT also provides one other feature—firewalling. However, this is firewalling in the simplest form. Because NAT basically takes an IP address of a local machine and replaces it with a valid Internet IP address, NAT provides a very low layer of protection from network intrusion. Combining NAT with a stateful-inspection firewall—like FireWall-1—creates a very secure network gateway. The next section covers how NAT has been implemented by Check Point into the FireWall-1 product and the different ways you can use NAT.

Table 9.1   Reserved IP addresses.

Class	Start	End	Number of Available Addresses
A	10.0.0.1	10.255.255.254	16,777,214
B	172.16.0.1	172.31.255.254	65,534
C	192.168.0.1	192.168.255.254	254

How FireWall-1 Handles NAT

A good way to envision how FireWall-1 handles network address translation is to compare it to a translator. When two people who speak different languages try to communicate with each other, the message being passed between the two people is lost if neither can interpret what the other is saying. When that occurs, a third party who understands both people can help clarify the communication. FireWall-1 acts in much the same way.

The firewall translates packet information between a valid IP address on a gateway and an invalid IP address on the gateway. When a packet is directed to a network using a valid Internet IP address that has been assigned to a specific server, the first place the packet must pass through is the firewall (assuming the destination is behind the firewall). The firewall kernel is configured to understand that packets being sent to a particular IP address must be translated to an invalid IP address on the internal network. Conversely, when a packet is sent from the internal network to the outside world, the firewall must take on the reverse role and translate the IP address from the internal scheme to a valid IP address that can be used on the Internet.

Two great aspects of FireWall-1 are that all of the translation is transparent on both sides of the firewall and that translation is done at very high speeds so that transfer time is degraded by only a very small percentage. All of the translation that is being done is recorded on an internal table, which brings us back to the concept of the communication-derived state discussed in Chapter 2.

At this point, you might be wondering how the firewall knows how to handle all of these valid IP addresses. For this purpose, you must use ARP—Address Resolution Protocol.

ARP and RARP

Address Resolution Protocol is used by TCP/IP to map IP network addresses to the hardware addresses used by the data-link protocol. In concept, address resolution refers to the process of finding the address of a computer that's in a network. When an interface requests a mapping for an address not in the cache, ARP queues the message that requires the mapping and broadcasts a message on the associated network requesting the address mapping. If a response is provided, the new mapping is cached, and any pending message is transmitted. At most, ARP will queue one packet while waiting for a response to a mapping request; only the most recently transmitted packet is kept. If the target host does not respond after several requests, the host is considered to be down, which allows an error to be returned to transmission attempts during the time that the host is not responding.

An Ethernet network uses two hardware addresses that identify the source and destination of each frame sent by the Ethernet. The hardware address of a host is known as the Media Access Control (MAC) address. A network interface card is allocated a unique MAC address when the factory manufactures the card. A computer sends the packets it creates with its own MAC address and receives all packets that match its MAC address.

As packets are sent and received, the host begins to create a table of IP addresses and MAC addresses. This table is known as the *ARP cache*. The addresses are stored for a certain time frame, which is determined by a timestamp called time to live (TTL). The cache is periodically cleared, cleaning out the addresses that have reached or exceeded their TTL. The ARP cache is a dynamic table, but it can also have static addresses added to it.

Another important concept is Reverse Address Resolution Protocol (RARP). RARP is used by a host so that it can request its IP address from a gateway server's ARP table. When a host is brought online, the RARP client requests the host's IP address to be sent. If the router is aware of the host's IP address, the RARP server will return the IP address to the host.

Four types of messages can be sent by ARP. They are:

➤ *ARP request*—The host tries to communicate with another host.

➤ *ARP reply*—The target host responds to the initial request.

➤ *RARP request*—The host requests its IP address from a gateway.

➤ *RARP reply*—The host receives a reply from the gateway with the address.

To help clarify how ARP works, let's follow an ARP request as it tries to communicate with another host:

1. The host checks its own ARP cache to see if it is already aware of the destination host's hardware address that correlates to the IP address requested.

2. If the address is not located in the host's cache, a broadcast is sent out to find which host (if any) uses the IP address requested.

3. If the destination host is available on the network and matches the IP address requested, it will return an ARP reply to the host with its hardware address.

When using NAT on FireWall-1, the firewall acts as the valid IP addresses that will be translated to invalid, internal addresses. For this to work properly, ARP must be used to assign the valid IP addresses to the MAC address of the external interface of the firewall. The next few sections look at how using ARP and NAT combine to allow internal, invalid IP addresses to communicate with the outside world.

Using ARP with FireWall-1

FireWall-1 uses ARP to assume the valid IP address of a server that is located on the internal network that is accessible only through an invalid IP address. When a host on the Internet makes an ARP request for a particular server—such as a mail server—the host is sent an ARP reply from the firewall itself. This way, the MAC address of the actual mail server inside of the firewall is still protected. Let's look at an example of how a packet that is destined for an internal server via a valid IP is handled when making a request from a mail server:

1. An Internet host sends an ARP request to the mail server.

2. The firewall, which represents the IP address being sent, responds with its own MAC address.

3. The host begins sending packets to the IP address using the MAC address of the firewall, unaware that it is not the actual MAC address of the firewall.

4. Because the firewall is aware of the MAC address of the server inside of the internal network, it passes the information to the server.

5. The mail server processes the request and sends it back through the firewall.

6. The firewall transmits the data back to the original host as if it were sent from the firewall.

Using ARP can be a little tricky when using FireWall-1 with Windows NT as your operating system. Because ARP takes a few extra steps to configure with Windows NT, let's take a moment to look at what needs to be done.

Considerations with Windows NT

When using ARP with Windows NT, you must perform a few manual steps before ARP will work correctly. First, you must create the file local.arp in the \%localhost\fw\state directory. This file contains the ARP entries for the firewall because NT cannot store permanent ARP entries by itself. The format for this file is as follows:

```
Valid IP address      External MAC address
```

The second task you must complete is to add static routes to the firewall. To do this, you must enter static routes in the following format:

```
route add x.x.x.x(valid IP) y.y.y.y(invalid IP) -p
```

Both of the preceding steps must be completed, or communications will not work correctly.

Now that you have a fundamental understanding of how NAT and ARP work, let's get started implementing it on your firewall.

Implementing NAT on FireWall-1

Not every node behind your firewall will have the same requirements for network address translation. Some nodes will require a valid IP address for themselves, whereas others can share valid IP addresses with other nodes. FireWall-1 provides three address translation modes—hide mode, static source mode, and static destination mode.

Hide Mode

Translating packets using FireWall-1 in hide mode allows an entire network to use a single Internet-valid IP address. When you use NAT's hide mode, you'll see a large gain in IP address conservation, because hundreds of thousands of internal IP addresses can use a single address. Hiding a network behind a single IP address is fairly simple; let's add one to our Phoenix network:

1. Click Manage on the menu bar in the Policy Editor.

2. Click Network Objects on the Manage menu.

3. Scroll down to the Phoenix network object and double-click it.

4. When the Network Properties dialog box appears, click the NAT tab.

5. Here, you need to let FireWall-1 know that the object will use NAT. Therefore, place a checkmark in the Add Automatic Address Translation Rules checkbox.

6. Next, change the Translation Method drop-down list box to Hide so that the firewall knows which NAT mode will be implemented for the object.

7. Enter an IP address for the network object in the Hiding IP Address text box; in this example, we will use 192.168.1.75. This will be the IP address used by all objects that fall into the range of internal IP addresses used within this network object.

8. You can leave the Install On drop-down list box set to All. Your NAT tab for the Phoenix network object should look like the one shown in Figure 9.1.

9. Click OK to save your changes.

Believe it or not, that's all it takes to add a hide mode NAT rule to your firewall. After we create static NAT rules in the next section, we will take a look at the address translation rule base and see how these rules are applied. Let's move on to the static mode address translations.

Figure 9.1   The completed NAT tab in the Network Properties dialog box.

Static Modes

As I just discussed in the previous section, you can use hide mode to funnel multiple internal IP addresses through a single valid IP address. However, how do you assign a single node its own valid IP address? You can do just that by using the static source and destination modes. Using a Web server as an example, let's create a workstation object that will serve as a mail server. For this example, use the following information for the workstation:

➤ *Name*—WWW_Server

➤ *IP address*—10.0.0.100

➤ *Comment*—Web server

➤ *Location*—Internal

➤ *Type*—Host

➤ *Color*—Green

Don't save the object just yet. First, read on to find out how static source mode and static destination mode differ from each other.

Static Source Mode

Static source mode is used to translate packets that are on an internal, invalid IP host and that need to be translated to a valid address. The difference here from a host that's translated in hide mode is that any host configured to use static translation will be the only host that is allowed to be translated to the valid IP address specified. This type of translation needs to occur if you were to use the Web server you are creating as an Internet Web server. If a host on the Internet expects a response from a Web server using its valid static address and it receives a response from the address used in hide mode, communications are lost.

Static Destination Mode

Under most circumstances, hosts that require the use of static source mode are configured to use static destination mode automatically. After reviewing how static source mode works, it should be pretty clear how static destination mode works. When a packet is sent from a host on the Internet, that host can send the packet to only a valid, Internet address. If a host attempts to send an HTTP (Hypertext Transfer Protocol) request to the Web server you are creating using the 10.0.0.100 address, an error would be returned (unless, of course, the host had a server on the local network with the same address).

Because using a 10.x.x.x address is not a valid option, the only other solution is to use the valid address of the host (which I will get to in a moment). However, your server is sitting behind the firewall, not out on the Internet where it can be contacted. Therefore, the firewall must be able to route traffic to the invalid address, and it must be aware of the fact that the valid address correlates to the invalid 10.0.0.100 address. Static destination mode serves this purpose by creating a static mapping of the valid address to the invalid address.

Adding Static NAT

Now that you have a nice foundation regarding how static mode translation works, you're ready to add it to your Web server. To get started, click the NAT tab in the Workstation Properties dialog box for the Web server. At this point, the tab will be blank, just as the Phoenix network object's NAT tab was blank prior to adding the hide mode translation to it earlier in this chapter. To add a static mode translation to the Web server, follow these steps:

1. Place a checkmark in the Add Automatic Address Translation Rules checkbox.

2. Leave the Translation Method drop-down list box set to Static so that the firewall knows that static NAT mode will be implemented for the object.

3. Enter an IP address for the network object in the Valid IP Address text box; in this example, we will use 192.168.1.76. This will be the IP address used exclusively by the Web server for translation.

4. You can leave the Install On drop-down list box set to All. The NAT tab of the WWW_Server workstation object should look like the one shown in Figure 9.2.

5. Click OK to save your changes.

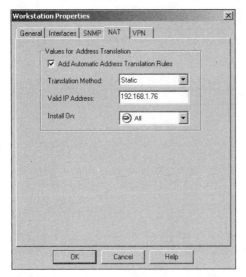

Figure 9.2   The completed NAT tab in the Workstation Properties dialog box.

Now, you will need to create a rule for the new WWW_Server object. For this example, you should create a rule before the cleanup rule, using Any as the source, WWW_Server as the destination, and Accept as the action.

Note: Make sure to save and install your rule base after adding the rule.

Now that you have configured your objects to use NAT, let's see how they look in the NAT rule base.

The NAT Rule Base

When you define NAT on a network object, the address translation information is added to the address translation rule base automatically. You might find it necessary to review the information for troubleshooting purposes, or you might need to create an address translation manually. For these reasons, the NAT rule base exists.

 This book does not describe how to create manual NAT rules because the process is not within the scope of the CCSA exam. However, you will need to know the information listed in the NAT rule base.

Let's open the NAT rule base and take a look. In the Policy Editor, click the Address Translation tab to view the NAT rule base. Your NAT rule base should look similar to the one shown in Figure 9.3. Notice that the NAT rule base is broken into four sections—Original Packet, Translated Packet, Install On, and Comment. Let's take a look at the information that is stored in the Original Packet and Translated Packet sections.

No.	Original Packet			Translated Packet			Install On	Comment
	Source	Destination	Service	Source	Destination	Service		
1	WWW_Server	Any	Any	WWW_Server (Valid Address)	Original	Original	All	Automatic rule (see the network object data).
2	Any	WWW_Server (Valid Address)	Any	Original	WWW_Server	Original	All	Automatic rule (see the network object data).
3	Phoenix	Phoenix	Any	Original	Original	Original	All	Automatic rule (see the network object data).
4	Phoenix	Any	Any	Phoenix (Hiding Address)	Original	Original	All	Automatic rule (see the network object data).

Figure 9.3 The NAT rule base.

Note: The Install On and Comment fields are the same fields that are available in the security policy. Review Chapter 6 if you are unsure of how these options operate.

Original Packet

The Original Packet section provides information about the original, pre-translated packet. This section is broken into three subsections—Source, Destination, and Service. The three pieces of information that you are trying to provide in this section are:

➤ The packet's origin

➤ Where the packet is trying to go

➤ The service being used

Let's look at each of the columns for the Web server object in rule 1 individually:

➤ *Source*—Can be only a single object. This is the origin of the packet that is to be translated. This object is the Web server, using its internal 10.0.0.100 address.

➤ *Destination*—Can be only a single object. This is where the packet is trying to go. This is set to Any.

➤ *Service*—Can be only a single service. This is the service that is being used during the translation. This column is set to Any.

Because there are two sides to the translation (pre-translation and post-translation), it only makes sense that you have to define this information for the translated packet. Let's take a look at the information for a translated packet.

Translated Packet

Explaining the Translated Packet section is a little more difficult than discussing the Original Packet section. The three subsections in the Translated Packet section are the same as the subsections in the Original Packet section—Source, Destination, and Service. However, this time, the sections work a little differently. Let's take a look at the Translated Packet section in the rule that was generated for your network object:

➤ *Source*—Can be only a single object. This is the origin of the packet that is to be translated. This object is the Web server, which is now represented by its valid IP address of 192.168.1.76.

➤ *Destination*—Can be only a single object. This is where the packet is trying to go. This is set to Original, which means that the firewall does not do any translation on the destination.

➤ *Service*—Can be only a single service. This is the service that is being used during the translation. This column is set to Any.

In effect, what this rule is saying is that the host has "changed" IP addresses from 10.0.0.100 to 192.168.1.76, but no other information has been altered. Furthermore, notice in rule 2 that the exact opposite of rule 1 has been implemented. These are the source and destination mode translations, respectively.

The process I just described is network address translation in a FireWall-1 environment. Practice changing objects to use various static and hide modes and test them from internal and external workstations. This is going to be an important concept that you will need to understand for the exam.

Practice Questions

Question 1

> Two address translation modes are available in FireWall-1.
>
> ○ a. True
>
> ○ b. False

Answer b is correct. Three translation modes are available in FireWall-1—static source, static destination, and hide. Although static source mode and static destination mode are often created in pairs, they are still two separate modes.

Question 2

> Which of the following files must you create to ensure that ARP will work correctly on a Windows NT system?
>
> ○ a. local.txt
>
> ○ b. arp.txt
>
> ○ c. arp.sys
>
> ○ d. local.arp

Answer d is correct. The local.arp file must be created in the \%localhost\fw\state directory for ARP to work on Windows NT. Answers a, b, and c are incorrect because they are fictitious files.

Question 3

> Jim is installing a firewall for his corporate network. Jim has a limited amount of valid IP addresses assigned to him by his network provider and must use them carefully. Jim must also provide Internet access to all 100 clients behind the firewall. What translation mode can Jim use and still keep the number of used IP addresses low?
>
> ○ a. Tunnel
>
> ○ b. Static destination
>
> ○ c. Static network
>
> ○ d. Static host
>
> ○ e. Hide

Answer e is correct. Hide mode will allow Jim to use only one IP address for the clients in use behind the firewall. Answer b is incorrect because static destination mode would be used in a one-to-one translation. Answers a, c, and d are incorrect because tunnel, static network, and static host are not translation modes used in FireWall-1.

Question 4

> What does the acronym CIDR stand for?
>
> ○ a. Classless InterDomain Routing
>
> ○ b. Crosslink InterNetwork Routing
>
> ○ c. Classless InterNet Routing
>
> ○ d. Cant InterNetwork Routing
>
> ○ e. None of the above

Answer a is correct. CIDR stands for Classless InterDomain Routing, which was the first attempt to keep IP addresses from running out. CIDR was a short-term fix until IPv6 could be implemented. Answers b, c, and d are incorrect because they are not names of real concepts or objects.

Question 5

Jane needs to add a mail server behind her network. She installs her mail server using the IP address of 10.0.0.105. Jane has assigned a valid IP address to the mail server, created an object for the mail server, and created the MX record in her DNS server. What else must Jane do to begin sending and receiving mail? [Check all correct answers]

❑ a. Nothing

❑ b. Enable NAT on the mail server object

❑ c. Set the NAT mode to hide

❑ d. Set the NAT mode to static

❑ e. Insert the valid IP address into the NAT field of the object

❑ f. Restart the mail server

❑ g. Reinstall the rule base

Answers b, d, e, and g are correct. Before the mail server will be able to communicate with the Internet, Jane must first enable NAT for the object, set the NAT mode to static so that it has its own IP address, type the valid IP address that the object will use, and reinstall the rule base. Answer a is incorrect because there are additional steps that must take place. Answer c is incorrect because using hide mode will not give the mail server a one-to-one (one invalid to one valid) IP address translation. Answer f is incorrect because the mail server does not require a restart.

Question 6

What does the acronym ARP stand for?

○ a. Address Reconfiguration Protocol

○ b. Address Revolution Protocol

○ c. Anonymous Read Protection

○ d. Address Resolution Protocol

○ e. None of the above

Answer d is correct. ARP stands for Address Resolution Protocol. ARP is used to map IP network addresses to the hardware addresses used by the data-link protocol. Answers a, b, and c are incorrect because ARP does not stand for any of these, in terms of networking.

Question 7

What are the types of ARP messages that can be sent by the ARP protocol?
[Check all correct answers]

- ❑ a. ARP request
- ❑ b. ARP response
- ❑ c. ARP reply
- ❑ d. LARP reply
- ❑ e. RARP reply
- ❑ f. LARP request
- ❑ g. RARP request

Answers a, c, e, and g are correct. Answer a is correct because an ARP request occurs when a host tries to communicate with another host. Answer c is correct because an ARP reply occurs when the target host responds to the initial request. Answer g is correct because an RARP request occurs when a host requests its IP address from a gateway, and answer e is correct because an RARP reply occurs when the host receives the reply from a gateway with the address. Answers b, d, and f are incorrect because no such ARP messages exist.

Question 8

What is the location where information about address translation is stored?

- ○ a. NAT folder
- ○ b. NAT GUI
- ○ c. NAT rule base
- ○ d. Log Viewer

Answer c is correct. Information and rules pertaining to address translation are located in the NAT rule base. Regardless of whether address translation is created automatically or manually, the information is ultimately stored in the NAT rule base. Answer a is incorrect because FireWall-1 does not use a NAT folder. Answer b is incorrect because a NAT GUI is not available in FireWall-1. Answer d is incorrect because NAT is not handled by the Log Viewer.

Question 9

What is the next generation of IP addressing known as?

○ a. IPv4

○ b. IPv6

○ c. IPv8

○ d. Currently, there is no name for the next generation of IP addressing.

Answer b is correct. The name that has been decided on for the next generation of IP addressing is IPv6, Internet Protocol version 6. Answer a is incorrect because IPv4 is the name of the current version of IP. Answer c is incorrect because, currently, there is no version of IP named IPv8. Answer d is incorrect because IPv6 is the name for the next generation of IP addressing.

Question 10

What subsections are available in the Original Packet and Translated Packet sections in address translation?

○ a. Source, Target, Service

○ b. Host, Target, Service

○ c. Source, Destination, Protocol

○ d. Source, Destination, Service

○ e. None of the above

Answer d is correct. Source, Destination, and Service are the three subsections found in the Original Packet and Translated Packet sections. Source is the origin of the packet, Destination is the target of the packet, and Service is the services allowed during the translation. Answers a, b, and c are incorrect because they do not show the names of the three subsections.

Need to Know More?

 Goncalves, Marcus and Steven Brown. *Check Point FireWall-1 Admin-istration Guide.* McGraw-Hill, New York, NY, 1999. ISBN 0-07-134229-X. This book serves as a good bookshelf reference for FireWall-1.

 ftp://ftp.isi.edu/in-notes/rfc1631.txt is one of the many locations where you can find RFC 1631, which pertains to the concept of NAT.

 http://ciac.llnl.gov/ciac/bulletins/f-08.shtml is the Computer Incident Advisory Center Web site for the U.S. Department of Energy. This article contains some great information about IP spoofing.

 www.checkpoint.com/products/downloads/fw1-4_1tech.pdf, the Check Point Web site's technical overview document (pages 14 and 15), explains the basic concept of NAT on the FireWall-1 platform.

10

Implementing Authentication and Encryption

Terms you'll need to understand:

✓ User authentication

✓ Transparent user authentication

✓ Client authentication

✓ Session authentication

✓ Implicit client authentication

✓ Session authentication agent

✓ S/Key

✓ Virtual private network (VPN)

Techniques you'll need to master:

✓ Implementing session authentication

✓ Implementing client authentication

✓ Implementing user authentication

✓ Implementing firewall encryption

✓ Identifying authentication schemes

With modern-day security threats such as identification theft, the need for proper identification has risen substantially. Try to write a check, get a credit card balance, pick up voicemail, or sign into your network and you will immediately be asked for identification. These activities each require some sort of identification, or *authentication*, before you can access the services provided. FireWall-1 can be configured to require users to authenticate with the firewall in order to identify the user that is trying to pass through the firewall. FireWall-1 provides three types of authentication—user, client, and session. In this chapter, I discuss how to configure these authentication types as well as configure encryption on the firewall. Let's get started by discussing user authentication.

User Authentication

User authentication is a familiar concept to administrators. Authenticating a user in a FireWall-1 environment is the same as authenticating a user in any operating system, such as Windows NT/2000, Novell, Unix, and so forth. In the case of FireWall-1 user authentication, a user must first authenticate with the firewall before he or she is allowed access to an intended destination. User authentication can be used only for the following services:

➤ FTP (File Transfer Protocol)

➤ Telnet

➤ Rlogin

➤ HTTP (Hypertext Transfer Protocol)

➤ HTTPS (Secure Hypertext Transfer Protocol)

Each time a user tries to initiate communications with a remote server using the preceding services, the communication is redirected to the security server where the user must first identify himself or herself. The default type of user authentication is known as transparent user authentication. By *transparent*, I mean that a user is allowed to connect directly to the destination server; otherwise, the user must first connect to the gateway and then begin communications with the destination server. A typical user authentication communication between the user and firewall looks something like this:

1. A user attempts to begin communications with a remote server.

2. The firewall intercepts the communication and prompts the user for authentication.

3. The user enters a username and password.

4. If the username and password are correct, the connection is allowed to continue to the intended destination. If the username and password are incorrect, the user will not be connected and must reinitiate the communication.

There are two major disadvantages of user authentication on FireWall-1. The first disadvantage to user authentication is that it is limited to the services listed earlier—FTP, Telnet, rlogin, HTTP, and HTTPS. Although these are some of the more commonly used services, thousands of services are not covered. The second disadvantage of user authentication is that authentication must take place each time a new session is requested, which is more of a nuisance to users than a flaw in the method. On the other hand, requiring users to authenticate each time the service is used could be looked at as an advantage, depending on your perspective and security requirements.

The next authentication type is client authentication. Client authentication is not restricted by the limitations of user authentication, but it is a little more difficult to configure. Let's take a look at how client authentication works with FireWall-1.

Client Authentication

Client authentication in FireWall-1 is based on the specific IP address of a source host. This means that access is granted only to IP addresses that are specified on the firewall by you, the administrator. The advantage of client authentication over user authentication is that you are able to use session authentication with any service, and it does not have to be initiated for each service that is used. Client authentication is a three-step process, versus the four-step process of user authentication. Let's take a look at the three steps involved here:

1. The user must begin either an HTTP or a Telnet session with the firewall. If client authentication is configured to use HTTP, the user must access the firewall using port 900. If client authentication is configured to use Telnet, the user must Telnet to the firewall using port 259.

2. When a connection to the firewall is established (either HTTP or Telnet), the firewall will request that the user enter his or her username and password. The firewall will then verify this information.

3. If the firewall recognizes the IP address of the user, it will grant access to the destination.

FireWall-1 can also be configured for *implicit client authentication*. Using implicit client authentication, access is granted to a client without the client having to authenticate with the firewall using HTTP or Telnet. Another key difference between standard and implicit client authentication is that once a user has successfully authenticated with the firewall using user or session authentication, all of the rules in the rule base that are configured to use client authentication are automatically enabled for that user.

Implicit client authentication is not turned on by default. To turn on implicit client authentication, you must make a change to the objects.c file in the FW1\4.1\conf directory. To enable implicit client authentication, search for the line **automatically_open_ca_rules**. Then, change the setting from **false** to **true**.

Now, let's take a look at the third and final authentication option—session authentication.

Session Authentication

Session authentication uses the least amount of resources of the three methods, but it also requires software to be loaded onto users' desktops. The session authentication agent must be loaded onto each workstation that will need access to the Internet. When a connection to a remote machine is requested, the session authentication agent is activated in order to be granted access through the gateway. Let's take a look at the steps involved with session authentication:

1. A user attempts to begin communications with a remote server.

2. When the request to contact the remote server is intercepted by the firewall, the firewall temporarily holds the request and contacts the session authentication agent.

3. The session authentication agent is contacted on the user's desktop. The user is prompted to enter a username and password into the session authentication agent.

4. The agent sends the authentication information back to the firewall, which will either accept or reject the initial communication based on the validity of the login information.

Session authentication offers two advantages. The first advantage is that, as is the case with client authentication, you are able to use session authentication with any service. However, unlike client authentication, you do not have to associate an IP address with the workstation. The obvious disadvantage here is the additional legwork that would be required by you, the administrator. Loading the session authentication agent onto a smaller network is not very difficult, but loading it into an enterprise environment can prove to be very time consuming unless you employ the services of a third-party distribution package.

Moving on, we need to look at how authentication is implemented into the firewall. In the next section, I will show you how to set up the internal authentication schemes available for FireWall-1.

Implementing Authentication

To implement any of the three authentication methods, you need to add new users and set the authentication properties for them in the User Properties dialog box. (Review Chapter 5 if you are unsure of how to complete these tasks.) For the example in this section, create a new user named Drew using the Default template that is provided by Check Point. After you create the account for Drew, click OK in the User Properties dialog box to save the default information. After the User Properties dialog box closes, double-click Drew to reopen the User Properties dialog box.

Note: When creating a user before you save it, verify that the expiration date for the account has not passed.

Next, you want to look at the Authentication tab in the User Properties dialog box. After you click the Authentication tab, you will notice that no authentication setting has been set for the user (or the Default template). You can choose from among the following authentication schemes:

➤ S/Key

➤ SecurID (external)

➤ OS Password

➤ VPN-1 & FireWall-1 Password

➤ RADIUS (external)

➤ AXENT Pathways Defender (external)

➤ TACACS (external)

Because external authentication options aren't available in this example and because setting them up is beyond the scope of this book, I will use only the internal schemes. Let's start by configuring Drew to use the VPN-1 & FireWall-1 Password authentication scheme.

VPN-1 & FireWall-1 Password Authentication Scheme

The VPN-1 & FireWall-1 Password authentication scheme is probably the easiest authentication scheme to implement. To implement the VPN-1 & FireWall-1 Password authentication scheme, follow these steps:

1. Select VPN-1 & FireWall-1 Password in the Authentication Scheme drop-down list on the Authentication tab.

2. In the Settings area, enter a password of up to eight characters. Figure 10.1 shows the Authentication tab using the VPN-1 & FireWall-1 Password authentication scheme.

3. After you enter the password, click OK to save the authentication setting and return to the Policy Editor.

Now, let's create another user and configure the user for OS Password authentication.

OS Password Authentication Scheme

For this discussion, create a new user named Bob using the Default template that is provided by Check Point. After you create the Bob account, click OK in the User Properties dialog box to save the default information. After the User Properties dialog box closes, double-click Bob to reopen the User Properties dialog box.

At this point, you're ready to configure the Bob account to use the OS Password authentication scheme. To do so, click the Authentication tab and select OS Password in the Authentication Scheme drop-down list. You will notice that there are no settings for the OS Password authentication scheme, as shown in Figure 10.2. Although this might seem like the easiest authentication scheme to implement, that is not necessarily true. For the OS Password authentication scheme, a user must have an account on the OS that is running the firewall, and he or she must be able to authenticate against the username and password. Therefore, you must take extra steps to create a network ID to correspond with the FireWall-1 user (or vice versa).

The last internal authentication scheme is the S/Key authentication method. In the next section, you'll create a third user and configure her for S/Key authentication.

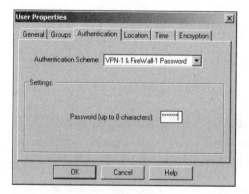

Figure 10.1 User Properties dialog box configured for VPN-1 & FireWall-1 Password authentication.

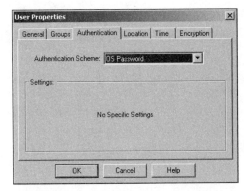

Figure 10.2   User Properties dialog box configured for OS Password authentication.

S/Key Authentication Scheme

For this example, create a new user named Terry using the Default template that is provided by Check Point. After you create the account for Terry, click OK in the User Properties dialog box to save the default information. After the User Properties dialog box closes, double-click Terry to reopen the User Properties dialog box.

After the User Properties dialog box is reopened, click the Authentication tab and select the S/KEY authentication scheme in the Authentication Scheme dropdown list. Notice that the settings box now has the following configuration settings available:

➤ *Seed*—Displays the username (normally).

➤ *Length*—Indicates the cycle of passwords used.

➤ *Password*—Displays a generated, random password.

➤ *Installed On*—Identifies the gateway that will handle authentication.

➤ *Secret Key*—Specifies a secret key, which should be at least 10 characters long.

➤ *Method*—Indicates the hashing method, either MD4 or MD5.

➤ *Generate*—Generates the random password.

➤ *Print Chain*—Prints the password chain.

Note: MD4 and MD5 are algorithms used to verify data integrity and are unique to the specific data. For more information about MD4 and MD5, search the Internet for RFC 1321.

Now, let's enter the S/Key information for Terry as follows:

1. In the Seed text box, enter "Terry".

2. In the Length text box, enter "10".

3. In the Secret Key text box, enter "0123456789".

4. In the Method area, choose the MD5 option.

5. In the Installed On drop-down list, choose Arizona.

6. Click the Generate button to create a random password. Write down the password. Figure 10.3 shows the completed Authentication tab configuration for S/Key authentication.

7. Click OK to save the User Properties dialog box settings.

8. In the User Manager dialog box, click Install. The user database will be installed on the firewall.

 You'll need to perform additional steps to activate the S/Key authentication, but for the purposes of the CCSA exam, you need to understand only how to set up authentication in the User Manager.

We're almost done with authentication; however, you need to complete a few more steps in the Policy Editor to wrap up the process.

Preparing the Rule Base for Authentication

Chapter 4 shows you how to create the Arizona firewall, and it mentions the Authentication tab. For authentication to work, you must tell the firewall which authentication schemes to allow.

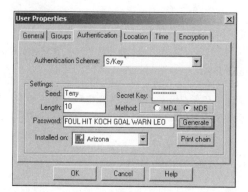

Figure 10.3 User Properties dialog box configured for S/Key authentication.

Setting Allowed Authentication Schemes

To set the authentication schemes allowed, follow these steps:

1. Open the Arizona firewall object and display the Authentication tab. All of the authentication schemes (internal and external) mentioned earlier in this chapter will appear.

2. For the example setup, remove all of the checkmarks except for S/Key, OS Password, and VPN-1 & FireWall-1 Password, as shown in Figure 10.4.

3. Click OK to save the changes.

Next, you need to create rules in your database to reflect the authentication type you decide on. Let's create a rule for user authentication.

Creating a User Authentication Rule

The last step in setting your firewall for authentication is to create a rule in the rule base. To do this, follow these steps:

1. Disable all the rules except for the stealth and cleanup rules. Refer to Chapter 7 for instructions about how to disable rules.

2. Create a new rule below the stealth rule. In the Source field of the rule, right-click and select Add Users Access on the shortcut menu. The User Access dialog box will appear.

3. As shown in Figure 10.5, change the location to Restrict To, and set it to the local network (Phoenix).

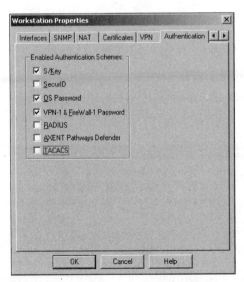

Figure 10.4   Authenticaion tab in the Workstation Properties dialog box for the Arizona firewall.

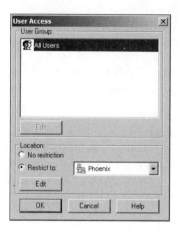

Figure 10.5 User Access dialog box.

4. Click OK to save the settings.

5. Leave the Destination field set to Any and change the Service field to HTTP.

6. Right-click in the Action field and select User Auth on the shortcut menu.

7. You can set the Track and Comment fields if you choose to do so.

The rule you have just created should look similar to rule 2 in Figure 10.6. At this point, you need to verify and install the rule base—this will tell your firewall that any of the defined users on your firewall must use user authentication for HTTP access to any site. To test this setup, use a client in your internal network and try to Telnet to a site outside of your firewall. You should be prompted to enter a username and password.

You can test session authentication and client authentication by changing the action field of the rule, installing the rule base, and trying to connect to a site again. You now have a firewall with the ability to authenticate users!

I am going to switch gears now and briefly discuss encryption. Encryption, like authentication, is used to control who and what is allowed access to and from

No.	Source	Destination	Service	Action	Track	Install On	Time	Comment
1	Any	Arizona	Any	drop	Long	Gateways	Any	Stealth Rule
2	All Users@Any	Any	http	User Auth		Gateways	Any	
	Phoenix	Any	Any	accept		Gateways	Any	Network Outbound
	Boston	Phoenix	Any	accept		Gateways	Any	Traffic from Boston
5	Any	Any	Any	drop		Gateways	Any	Drop Broadcasts

Figure 10.6 Rule base containing a user authentication rule.

your network through the firewall. I'll start out by discussing virtual private networks and how they use encryption.

Virtual Private Networks and Encryption Schemes

A virtual private network (VPN) is a technology that provides the ability to use public networks like the Internet rather than private leased lines for wide area network communications. VPN technologies implement virtual networks that use the same cabling and routers as the public network without compromising security.

The Check Point VPN-1 package is one of the market leaders in VPN implementations because of its easy integration with FireWall-1. The properties for VPN are already installed in the FireWall-1 package and need only the proper licensing for VPN-1 in order to be enabled. It's important for you to understand the encryption schemes and firewall encryption properties.

For a VPN to function properly and securely, it must have the ability to encrypt the data it is passing and create a *tunnel* through a private network. An encryption scheme is an algorithm and key-management protocol used to pass secured keys. These keys are the elements that allow two ends of a VPN tunnel to communicate with one another. If the keys do not match, communications will not be allowed between the two points in the tunnel. Four encryption schemes can be used with FireWall-1/VPN-1:

➤ *IKE*—Internet Key Exchange

➤ *Manual IPSec*—Manual Internet Protocol Security

➤ *SKIP*—Simple Key Management for Internet Protocols

➤ *FWZ*—Proprietary encryption scheme

Each scheme has its own characteristics and methods for encrypting the data being transmitted. On your firewall object, you need to specify which encryption scheme you want to implement by configuring the VPN tab in the Workstation Properties dialog box. Figure 10.7 shows the VPN tab of the Arizona object. As you can see in the figure, two sections are available on the VPN tab:

➤ *Domain*—This area refers to the domain that will be used for encryption. Disabled is the default setting. Setting this field to Valid Addresses is used if you have defined the interfaces for the object. The Other option is used to manually select an encryption domain.

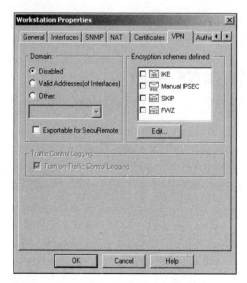

Figure 10.7 VPN tab of the Arizona firewall.

➤ *Encryption Schemes Defined*—This area provides options for the encryption schemes that you can configure for VPN. To edit an encryption scheme, select a scheme's checkbox and click Edit.

You also need to review the settings on the Encryption tab in the Properties Setup dialog box. To open this dialog box, click Policy|Properties. When the dialog box opens, click the Encryption tab. The Encryption tab has configuration options for three of the encryption schemes—SKIP, IPSec, and IKE. Let's take a brief look at the configurable properties for each scheme.

SKIP

You can configure two options in the Encryption tab for SKIP. The configuration options are:

➤ *Enable Exportable SKIP*—Enables the firewall to generate exportable SKIP keys.

➤ *Change SKIP Session Keys*—This is an "either/or" option for SKIP. You can set SKIP to change the key every *x* amount of seconds or every *x* number of bytes. This adds increased security for SKIP encryption.

These options can be left at their defaults and function properly, but the need may arise at some point to change them based on security requirements.

Manual IPSec

There is only one option to set in the Manual IPSec section, and it is for the SPI (Security Parameter Index) allocation range. The SPI range is used to identify traffic using encryption. Specifying an SPI range allocates that range for use by IPSec and will cause IKE to use SPIs outside of the range.

IKE

Before we look at the IKE properties, you should note that IKE is actually an extension of IPSec, and it is used for negotiating security associations between hosts. You can configure two options for IKE in the Properties Setup dialog box. (In actuality, there is a third option you can set; by setting the SPI range for IPSec, you are in effect setting the SPI range for IKE.) The two fields that fall directly into the IKE properties area are:

➤ *Renegotiate IKE Security Associations Every ___ Minutes*—This allows you to set the number of seconds before IKE keys are changed.

➤ *Renegotiate IPSEC Security Associations Every ___ Seconds*—IKE is an extension of IPSec, so you need to let IKE know the number of seconds before the IPSec session keys are changed.

You will not be tested on configuring a VPN or encryption, so you do not need to do any configuration at this time. However, you can open the various encryption schemes to see the additional properties that can be configured for each scheme. Look at how each encryption scheme differs from the other, and open the help file to get more information about each. VPNs and encryption schemes are covered in much more depth on the Check Point Certified Security Engineer (CCSE) exam (Exam 156-305), which is the next exam after the CCSA.

Practice Questions

Question 1

> When using FireWall-1, user authentication will work with any service (FTP, HTTP, RDP, and so forth).
>
> ○ a. True
>
> ○ b. False

Answer b is correct. FireWall-1 will work only with certain services. Those services are FTP, Telnet, rlogin, HTTP, and HTTPS. This is considered a limitation of the user authentication method.

Question 2

> When using client authentication, a client must authenticate using either _____ or _____.
>
> ○ a. FTP or Telnet
>
> ○ b. HTTP or HTTPS
>
> ○ c. HTTP or Telnet
>
> ○ d. Telnet or rlogin

Answer c is correct. For a client to use client authentication, the client must either connect to the firewall using HTTP or Telnet. Answer a is incorrect because a client cannot connect via FTP. Answer b is incorrect because a client cannot connect via HTTPS. Answer d is incorrect because a user cannot connect via rlogin.

Question 3

> Russell, a user on your internal network, is attempting to use client authentication for access to the Internet. Russell attempts to Telnet to the firewall using the IP address of the firewall. Russell has the correct IP address, but he cannot seem to authenticate. You verify that the firewall is running and connected to the local network. What is the most likely problem?
>
> ○ a. Russell does not have the client software loaded on his PC.
>
> ○ b. Russell must Telnet using port 900 to connect to the firewall.
>
> ○ c. Russell does not have an ID and password on the firewall.
>
> ○ d. None of the above.

Answer d is correct. Russell must Telnet to port 259 to begin the authentication session with the firewall. In this configuration, the firewall will not respond for client authentication unless port 259 is used. Answer a is incorrect because no additional software needs to be loaded. Answer b is incorrect because port 900 is not used for client authentication via Telnet; it is used for client authentication via HTTP. Answer c is incorrect because Russell does not need to have a username and password until after the session is established.

Question 4

> Russell decides that using Telnet to authenticate to the firewall is too difficult, and he decides to use HTTP. He attempts to open his Web browser and connect to the firewall, but he does not receive the client authentication screen. Russell has the correct IP address, but he cannot seem to authenticate. You verify that the firewall is running and connected to the local network. What is the most likely problem?
>
> ○ a. Russell does not have the client software loaded on his PC.
>
> ○ b. Russell must use port 900 to connect to the firewall through HTTP.
>
> ○ c. Russell does not have an ID and password on the firewall.
>
> ○ d. None of the above.

Answer b is correct. Russell must open his Web browser and use port 900 to begin the authentication session with the firewall. In this configuration, the firewall will not respond for client authentication unless port 900 is used. Answer a is incorrect because no additional software needs to be loaded. Answer c is incorrect Russell does not need to have a username and password until after the session is established.

Question 5

When a user successfully authenticates to a firewall using _____,
all of the rules using _____ are automatically granted to the user.

- ○ a. Implicit client authentication; client authentication
- ○ b. Client authentication; client authentication
- ○ c. User authentication; user authentication
- ○ d. Implicit client authentication; implicit client authentication
- ○ e. Session authentication; implicit session authentication

Answer a is correct. When a user is successfully authenticated to a firewall using implicit client authentication, all of the rules using client authentication are automatically granted to the user. Answer b is incorrect because the first half of the answer must be implicit client authentication. Answer c is incorrect because the statement does not apply to user authentication. Answer d is incorrect because a rule cannot be defined as being an implicit client authentication rule. Answer e is incorrect because the statement does not apply to session authentication.

Question 6

What does the acronym VPN stand for?

- ○ a. Very private network
- ○ b. Virtual protocol name
- ○ c. Version proprietary network
- ○ d. Virtual private network

Answer d is correct. VPN stands for virtual private network. In a VPN, a private connection is established over a public network (such as the Internet) through the use of a tunneling protocol. Answers a, b, and c are incorrect because they are not the correct definitions of a VPN.

Question 7

> Which of the following are valid encryption schemes for FireWall-1 and VPN-1? [Check all correct answers]
>
> ❑ a. ARP
>
> ❑ b. VPN
>
> ❑ c. IPSec
>
> ❑ d. IKE
>
> ❑ e. IPIke
>
> ❑ f. SKIP
>
> ❑ g. FWZ

Answers c, d, f, and g are correct. IPSec, IKE, SKIP, and FWZ are all valid encryption schemes for FireWall-1 and VPN-1. Answer a is incorrect because ARP stands for Address Resolution Protocol. Answer b is incorrect because a VPN is a virtual private network that uses the encryption schemes. Answer e is a fictitious name and is therefore incorrect.

Question 8

> What is the name of the Check Point proprietary encryption scheme?
>
> ○ a. IKE
>
> ○ b. IPSec
>
> ○ c. FWZ
>
> ○ d. SKIP

Answer c is correct. FWZ is a proprietary encryption scheme developed by the folks at Check Point. Answers a, b, and d are incorrect because they are all industry standard encryption schemes.

Question 9

What is the default setting for the encryption domain on the VPN tab of a firewall object?

- ○ a. Valid Addresses
- ○ b. Other
- ○ c. Disabled

Answer c is correct. The default setting for the encryption domain on the VPN tab of the firewall object is Disabled. Answers a and b are incorrect because you must select Valid Addresses or Other if VPN-1 is to be implemented on the firewall; they are not selected by default.

Question 10

Which of the following authentication types requires software to be loaded on the workstation?

- ○ a. Session authentication.
- ○ b. User authentication.
- ○ c. Client authentication.
- ○ d. None of the authentication types requires software on the workstation.

Answer a is correct. Session authentication requires client software to be loaded on the workstation in order to function. Answers b and c are incorrect because neither of these requires software on the workstation.

Need to Know More?

 Goncalves, Marcus and Steven Brown. *Check Point FireWall-1 Administration Guide*. McGraw-Hill, New York, NY, 1999. ISBN 0-07-134229-X. This book serves as a good bookshelf reference for FireWall-1.

 www.checkpoint.com/products/firewall-1/authentication.html, the Check Point Web site regarding authentication, offers a high-level explanation of how authentication works in FireWall-1.

 www.faqs.org/rfcs/rfcsearch.html is a great site for information about RFCs for VPNs and all of the various encryption schemes.

 www.freesoft.org/CIE/RFC/1321 provides information about RFC 1321, which covers the MD5 algorithm technology.

Monitoring and Performance Tuning

Terms you'll need to understand:

✓ Log Viewer

✓ Security Log

✓ Accounting Entries Log

✓ Active Connections Log

✓ Interface

✓ S_Port

✓ Selection criteria

Techniques you'll need to master:

✓ Identifying the three modes in the Log Viewer GUI (graphical user interface)

✓ Changing modes in the Log Viewer GUI

✓ Identifying the columns in the Log Viewer GUI

✓ Navigating the Log Viewer GUI

✓ Selecting search criteria in the Log Viewer GUI

✓ Applying selection criteria in the Log Viewer GUI

✓ Purging a log file

✓ Creating a new log file

✓ Printing a log file

✓ Saving a log file

✓ Viewing the system status

If you followed along throughout this book, you should now have a fully functional firewall protecting your internal network from the outside world. However, how do you know that your firewall is working properly and performing the tasks that you have configured it to perform? For this purpose, most robust software packages come with tools for monitoring and tuning system performance. Check Point FireWall-1 is no exception, and it provides two very important monitoring tools. FireWall-1 comes with a System Status GUI (graphical user interface) and a Log Viewer GUI to assist administrators in determining if their firewalls are working properly or need any additional maintenance to reach optimal performance. I'll start this chapter by discussing the System Status GUI.

System Status GUI

The System Status GUI gives an administrator a very general view of the statistics for firewalls that are managed from the Management Server. I recommend using the System Status GUI to periodically monitor the stability of a Firewall Module, because it provides a very high level of information that can be accessed quickly. Opening the System Status GUI is easy, as you can see in the following steps:

1. Click Start|Programs|Check Point Management Clients|System Status.

2. Log in to the System Status GUI using an authorized administrator account, password, and the IP address of the Management Server, as shown in Figure 11.1.

3. Click OK to begin.

Note: If the Policy Editor or Log Viewer is open, you can open the System Status GUI by selecting it on the Window drop-down menu.

After the System Status GUI starts, you will see that the window is broken into two subsections—General and VPN-1 & FireWall-1 (as shown in Figure 11.2). Let's look at the two sections separately, starting with the General section.

Figure 11.1   Login dialog box for the System Status GUI.

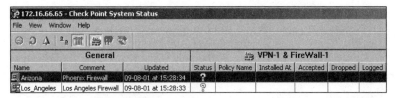

Figure 11.2 The System Status GUI window.

Note: If you have the Check Point High Availability feature enabled, a third section in the System Status GUI will enable you to view the status of the firewall that is associated with the High Availability feature.

General Subsection

The General subsection does not offer any diagnostic information about the firewall; its purpose is to simply itemize the firewalls that you have listed in your Management Server. The General subsection of the System Status GUI, shown in Figure 11.3, consists of three columns:

➤ *Name*—The name of the Firewall Module as it was entered into the Network Objects tool using the Policy Editor.

➤ *Comment*—The comment (if any) for the associated Firewall Module as entered for the object using the Policy Editor.

➤ *Updated*—The last time the status for the Firewall Module was updated. The date is formatted as DD-MM-YY. The time is formatted as HH:MM:SS.

The Name and Comment attributes for objects can be changed by using the Policy Editor and changing the objects themselves. You can refresh the object list by pressing the F5 key on your keyboard, or you can refresh the list by clicking View|Refresh Objects. The toolbar buttons will be discussed later in this chapter.

VPN-1 & FireWall-1 Subsection

This subsection of the System Status GUI contains some helpful statistical information about Firewall Modules. The columns in this subsection sum up the information about packet transfer, firewall status, and installation information. Let's take a look at the columns:

➤ *Status*—Indicates the status of the firewall. If the column contains a checkmark, a security policy is installed. If the column contains an exclamation point, a

General		
Name	Comment	Updated
Arizona	Phoenix Firewall	09-08-01 at 15:28:34
Los_Angeles	Los Angeles Firewall	09-08-01 at 15:28:55

Figure 11.3 The General subsection of the System Status GUI.

security policy is not installed. If the column contains a question mark, the status is currently being updated and is unknown at the moment.

➤ *Policy Name*—Displays the name of the policy that is saved on the Management Server and that is currently installed on the Firewall Module.

➤ *Installed At*—Specifies the date and time that the policy in the Policy Name field was installed onto the Firewall Module. The date is formatted as DD-MMM-YYYY.

➤ *Accepted*—Represents the number of packets that have been accepted by the firewall (in other words, the number of packets that met the criteria of a rule or rules in the rule base and that were allowed to pass through the firewall). This represents packets that pass either to the internal network or to the Internet successfully.

➤ *Dropped*—Represents the number of packets that have been dropped by the firewall. Data packets are explicitly dropped by a rule, by the cleanup rule, or by the implicit drop rule.

➤ *Logged*—Displays any instance of logging if a rule specifies that data should be logged.

As you can see, the System Status GUI is a useful tool for a one-stop look at what is going on with your Firewall Modules. In an enterprise environment, this application can cut down on a lot of administration by enabling you to view the status of all your firewalls on one screen. However, at some point, you might want to view the status of an individual firewall instead of all of the firewalls in an enterprise, and you do this through the Firewall Properties dialog box, discussed next.

Firewall Properties

To open the Firewall Properties dialog box, simply double-click the firewall object that you want to view. After the Firewall Properties dialog box opens (it's represented on screen as *<Firewall Name>* Properties), you will see two tabs. The tabs are the same as the subsections of the firewall list that we have been looking at thus far in this chapter—General and VPN-1 & FireWall-1. The General tab enables you to configure the General properties of the firewall, including:

➤ Name

➤ Comment

➤ Object Status

➤ Updated

➤ VPN-1 & FireWall-1

➤ FloodGate-1

➤ Compression

The VPN-1 & FireWall-1, Floodgate-1, and Compression fields on the General tab can have a value of either Module Installed or Module Not Licensed. If you switch to the VPN-1 & FireWall-1 tab in the Firewall Properties dialog box, you will see the same information as in the VPN-1 & FireWall-1 subsection in the firewall list, including:

➤ Status

➤ Policy Name

➤ Installed At

➤ Accepted

➤ Dropped

➤ Logged

I've now covered the basics of the System Status GUI, but you can also make some configuration changes within the System Status GUI. First, let's take a look at the toolbar buttons, because a lot of work can be done simply by using the toolbar.

Toolbar Buttons

The System Status toolbar (shown in Figure 11.4) has several buttons available, many of which are simply shortcuts for viewing options. However, they make administration much easier because of their easy access. In Figure 11.4, notice that two of the buttons are grayed out (dimmed); this is because the associated modules have not been installed on the firewall. Let's look at the toolbar buttons, from left to right, and their functions:

➤ *Automatic Refresh*—Opens the Refresh Options dialog box, in which you can specify refresh parameters.

➤ *Refresh Objects*—Refreshes the status of the objects.

➤ *Alerts*—Opens the Alerts dialog box.

➤ *Icons*—Changes the screen from list mode to icon mode.

➤ *Details*—Changes the screen from icon mode to list mode.

➤ *VPN-1 & FireWall-1 Details*—Displays (or hides) the VPN-1 & FireWall-1 details subsection.

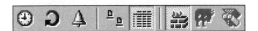

Figure 11.4 The System Status toolbar.

➤ *FloodGate-1 Details*—Displays (or hides) the FloodGate-1 details subsection.

➤ *Compression Details*—Displays (or hides) the compression details subsection.

The last section of the System Status GUI that I need to discuss pertains to alerts.

Alerts

Take a look at the alerts information by clicking the Alerts button in the toolbar. Two separate areas are related to Alerts: the first is the Alerts dialog box you just opened, and the other is the Options dialog box, which we'll look at in a moment.

Alerts Dialog Box

The Alerts dialog box stores actual alerts when they arrive. As you can see in Figure 11.5, the dialog box contains the following two checkboxes, which let you configure how new alerts will be displayed when they arrive:

➤ Play System Default Beep Sound

➤ Show This Window

Each of these options can be enabled and disabled as you choose. Then, you can either close the dialog box or clear all of the alerts by clicking the Clear button at the bottom of the Alerts dialog box.

Options Dialog Box

In addition to selecting options in the Alerts dialog box, you can specify the types of events you want to receive notification about. This information is held in the Options dialog box. To access the Options dialog box, click View|Options.

After the Options dialog box appears, the only two fields that are filled in by default are the ones labeled *Installed*, and both are set to send an alert by default. You can also configure each to issue an alert, send an email message, issue an

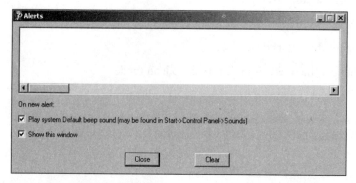

Figure 11.5 The Alerts dialog box.

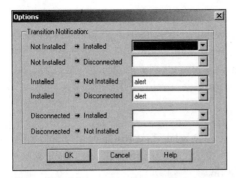

Figure 11.6   The System Status Options dialog box.

SNMP trap, or send a user-defined notification. Let's take a look at what each of the Transition Notification options in Figure 11.6 means:

➤ *Not Installed/Installed*—Firewall has changed status from no security policy installed to security policy installed.

➤ *Not Installed/Disconnected*—Firewall has changed status from no security policy to the firewall being disconnected.

➤ *Installed/Not Installed*—Firewall has changed status from having a security policy installed to not having one installed.

➤ *Installed/Disconnected*—Firewall has changed status from having a security policy installed to being disconnected.

➤ *Disconnected/Installed*—Firewall has changed status from being disconnected to having a security policy installed.

➤ *Disconnected/Not Installed*—Firewall has changed status from being disconnected to not having a security policy installed.

Each of these events can be configured for an alert, email, SNMP trap, or user-defined notification. However, you should try to avoid excess alerts as much as possible.

That's it for the System Status GUI, so let's move on to the Log Viewer GUI.

Log Viewer GUI

Whereas the System Status GUI provides a very high-level view of what is going on with your firewall, the Log Viewer breaks down information to a much more granular level. Using the Log Viewer, you can gather a lot more information about packets that you have chosen to log in the rule base. The key to reading the information in the Log Viewer is to remember that the information stored there is dependent on how you choose to log the rules. Choosing to log a rule in long mode will obviously provide more information than choosing short mode. But, depending on how critical a rule is, it might require only short logging—which allows for a smaller log size. Becoming accustomed to how rules should be logged takes time, but common sense plays an important role.

The Log Viewer has three types of logs:

➤ *Security Log*—This log shows all security-related events that are tracked by the firewall, including rules that are logged, administrative tasks such as installing a rule base, and authentication.

➤ *Accounting Entries Log*—This log shows the information supplied in the Security Log, plus information about elapsed time, bytes, and start date.

➤ *Active Connections Log*—This log shows the same information as the Security Log, plus information about elapsed time, bytes, start date, and connection ID.

Opening the Log Viewer GUI

To open the Log Viewer GUI, follow these steps:

1. Click Start|Programs|Check Point Management Clients|Log Viewer.

2. Log in to the Log Viewer GUI using an authorized administrator account, password, and IP address of the Management Server.

3. Click OK to begin.

The Log Viewer opens with the Security Log as it appears in Figure 11.7. The Security Log might have some entries in it, or it might not. At a minimum, you should have a control log entry from when you installed the firewall (if you have installed the rule base). You will notice that there are several fields in the Security Log, some requiring you to scroll the screen to the right in order to view. Before we look at the various columns and what each means, I'll explain how you can customize your view of the log entries.

Hiding/Unhiding Log Columns

The first point you need to know about the log columns is that you can choose to view or hide any of the columns. Each of the logs has the same column headers, and hiding a column in one log hides it in all of the logs. You might find that one column of information is not very important or useful, so you do not want to view it. In those instances, you can hide the column. To hide a column, follow these steps:

1. Click View on the menu bar.

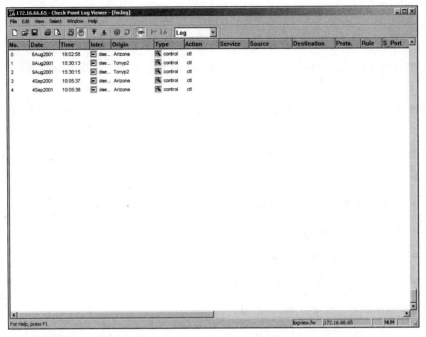

Figure 11.7   The Log Viewer.

2. Click Hide/Unhide on the View menu.

3. Click the column that you want to hide or unhide. Optionally, you could click Unhide All to view all of the columns.

Now that you know how to control column display, let's look at the columns themselves.

Defining the Log Columns

Each column has a purpose in the Security Log, but not every column will have information in it. Whether a column contains information depends on the type of rule and the type of logging selected for the rule. Obviously, the columns concerning encryption will not be used if a firewall is not using encryption. The following list defines the columns from left to right as they appear on screen (note that not all types of logs show all these columns):

➤ *No.*—The number of the log entry

➤ *Date*—The date the log entry was created

➤ *Time*—The time the log entry was created

➤ *Inter.*—The interface the rule was enforced on

➤ *Origin*—The origin (gateway) that enforced the rule

➤ *Type*—The type of action that caused the log entry

➤ *Action*—The action taken on the data packet by the firewall (accept, drop, and so on)

➤ *Service*—The service that was used by the source of the packet (HTTP, FTP, Telnet, and so on)

➤ *Source*—The host that initiated the communication

➤ *Destination*—The intended recipient of the communication

➤ *Proto.*—The communication protocol used (TCP, UDP, and so on)

➤ *Rule*—The rule number that caused the log entry

➤ *Bytes*—The number of bytes transferred

➤ *S_Port*—The source port

➤ *User*—The name of the user (if applicable)

➤ *SrcKeyID*—The KeyID of the source of an encrypted packet (if applicable)

➤ *DstKeyID*—The KeyID of the destination of an encrypted packet (if applicable)

➤ *xlateSrc*—The source address translation information (if applicable)

➤ *xlateDst*—The destination address translation information (if applicable)

➤ *Product*—The product that was in use when the event occurred

➤ *Info*—Additional information (if applicable)

The Accounting Entries and Active Connections logs offer a few more columns than the Security Log does—elapsed time, bytes, and start date; and elapsed time, bytes, start date, and connection ID, respectively.

As you might imagine, a firewall that has been up and running for quite a while can collect a substantial amount of information. Therefore, you should know how to manage log files.

Managing Log Files

At times, you might occasionally need to create a new log file, print a log file, purge a log file, or save a log file to disk. Here's how you can perform each of these tasks:

➤ *Creating a new log file*—Creating a new log file is as easy as clicking File|New. When you do this, you will be prompted to save the current log information to disk and create a new log. Select Yes to continue. The log file will be saved using a name that contains the current date and time.

 | Make sure you know the naming convention for log files!

➤ *Exporting a log file*—You can export a log file to a text file by clicking File|Print. Exporting a log file can be useful for importing it into a database or for manipulating it by other software packages.

➤ *Printing a log file*—To print a log file, click File|Print. Enter your printer configuration as necessary, and your print job will begin spooling. If you have created selection criteria for the log, only the entries that match the criteria will be printed. I discuss creating selection criteria in the next section.

➤ *Purging a log file*—When you purge a log file, you are giving it a clean slate. All of the events in the log are destroyed. To purge a log file, click File|Purge. Make sure you want to remove all the information before you purge it, because once it's gone, it's gone!

➤ *Saving a log file*—Saving a log file can be useful when saving selection criteria or just simply saving your entire log to another file. Unlike creating a new log file, the current data is not purged.

Now that you know how to manage your logs, you're ready to set some selection criteria for the entries you want to view.

Selection Criteria

Using selection criteria is a great way to seek out certain types of information in a log to save it to disk, to print it, or to simply view it on screen. Selection criteria can help you examine problems with your firewalls. For example, if you are unsure if a certain rule is dropping a service that you need, you could view the log entries for the rule that are associated with that particular service.

To illustrate, let's create a new selection criteria to search for any rule that dropped any HTTP traffic that attempted to be passed to the network:

1. Click Select on the menu bar.

2. Select By Columns.

3. Select the Destination column from the drop-down list.

4. When the Destination Selection Criterion dialog box appears, select the Phoenix network and click OK.

5. Click Select|By Columns|Service.

6. When the Service Selection Criterion dialog box appears, select HTTP and click OK.

At this point, only the records that meet the selection will be displayed on screen. If no records match, you will see a pop-up message box stating that there were no records that match the selection.

To remove selection criteria, click Select|By Columns|Current. Highlight the selection criteria and click Delete. Next, click OK; all of the records will reappear on screen.

We've just about reached the end of the road; however, a few other points need to be mentioned regarding monitoring and troubleshooting a Check Point firewall. I'll discuss them now.

Other Monitoring Tips

I could write another book about all the tips and tricks that you could use to monitor and tune your firewall, but for the purposes of the CCSA exam, I need to mention only the following few points:

➤ *Event Viewer*—If you are using Windows NT, the Event Viewer is a very useful tool for troubleshooting many errors on your system. This is a good place to look to see if Check Point has recorded any errors, which can be researched though a Check Point support account.

➤ *Control Panel Services*—Again, speaking in terms of a Windows installation, the Services section of the Control Panel is a helpful tool. Use Services to verify that the Check Point services are started and functioning properly. You might also want to verify that they are set to start automatically, in case your server spontaneously reboots.

➤ *Performance Monitor*—Windows NT provides Performance Monitor to check all of your system functions and determine if everything falls within acceptable ranges. Because FireWall-1 is an application that sits on top of the OS, it's important to monitor the OS itself. Ensure that paging is not excessive, that your system has enough memory, and that the system offers adequate free processing room.

That's it! You now have all the tools that you need to pass the CCSA exam. If you have a firewall that you can use or if you can obtain an evaluation copy, spend some time with the firewall. I can't stress enough how helpful it can be to get comfortable with the firewall hands-on.

Best of luck!

Practice Questions

Question 1

> In the System Status GUI, if you have the _____
> feature enabled, there will be a third section enabled for viewing the status
> of the firewall that is associated with this feature.
>
> ○ a. High Availability
>
> ○ b. RealSecure
>
> ○ c. Firewall
>
> ○ d. None of the above

Answer a is correct. The High Availability feature is available only if the high availability features are installed and configured on the server. Answers b and c are incorrect because neither of these answers produces a third section on the System Status GUI.

Question 2

> On a Windows NT firewall, you can use the _____ section of
> the Control Panel to verify that the Check Point FireWall-1 service is running.
>
> ○ a. Services
>
> ○ b. autoexec.bat
>
> ○ c. Startup
>
> ○ d. Add/Remove Programs

Answer a is correct. Using Services in the Control Panel of Windows NT will enable you to verify that the Check Point FireWall-1 service is running. Answer b is incorrect because Check Point FireWall-1 does not use the autoexec.bat file. Answer c is incorrect because nothing relating to Check Point is placed in Startup. Answer d is incorrect because you cannot verify that the service is running in Add/Remove Programs.

Question 3

> Using _____ is a great option for seeking out certain types of information
> in a log to save it to disk, to print it, or to simply view it on screen.
>
> ○ a. Event Viewer GUI
>
> ○ b. Selection criteria
>
> ○ c. Viewing criteria
>
> ○ d. System Status GUI
>
> ○ e. None of the above

Answer b is correct. Using selection criteria is a great option for seeking out
certain types of information in a log to save it to disk, to print it, or to simply view
it on screen. Answer a is incorrect because the Windows NT Event Viewer GUI
does not provide this type of logging. Answer c is incorrect because no such
option exists. Answer d is incorrect because using the System Status GUI does
not produce the required result.

Question 4

> When a log file is saved, the log file will be saved using a file name that
> contains the current date and time.
>
> ○ a. True
>
> ○ b. False

Answer a is correct. When you save a log file in the Log Viewer GUI, the file is
saved with a file name that contains the current date and time.

Question 5

> You can open the Log Viewer, Policy Editor, and System Status GUIs from
> inside any of the other GUIs.
>
> ○ a. True
>
> ○ b. False

Answers a is correct. After you have opened one of the three GUIs on a GUI
client, you can click Windows on the File menu and open any of the other GUIs
without signing into the Management Server again.

Question 6

> Which of the following is not a viewable column in the Log Viewer?
>
> ○ a. Action
>
> ○ b. Type
>
> ○ c. S_Port
>
> ○ d. Date
>
> ○ e. Service
>
> ○ f. Rule
>
> ○ g. Comment
>
> ○ h. Product

Answer g is correct. The Log Viewer GUI does not include a Comment column. The Comment column is available only in the Policy Editor and System Status GUIs. Answers a, b, c, d, e, f, and h are incorrect because each of these is an available column in the Log Viewer.

Question 7

> The _____ shows the same information as the Security Log, but it also provides information about elapsed time, bytes, start date, and connection ID.
>
> ○ a. Accounting Entries Log
>
> ○ b. Security Log
>
> ○ c. Application Log
>
> ○ d. Event Log
>
> ○ e. Active Connections Log
>
> ○ f. None of the above

Answer e is correct. The Active Connections Log shows the same information as the Security Log, but it also provides information about elapsed time, bytes, start date, and connection ID. Answer a is incorrect because the Accounting Entries Log shows elapsed time, bytes, and start date but not the connection ID. Answer b is incorrect because the Security Log shows the general security information (Date, Time, Origin, and so on). Answers c and d are incorrect because the Application Log and Event Log do not exist in FireWall-1.

Question 8

Which of the following fields appear in the System Status GUI? [Check all correct answers]

❑ a. Accepted

❑ b. Dropped

❑ c. Rejected

❑ d. Refused

❑ e. All of the above

Answers a and b are correct. The Accepted field represents the number of packets that have been accepted by the firewall, and the Dropped field represents the number of packets that have been dropped by the firewall. Answers c and d are incorrect because no such fields exist in the System Status GUI.

Question 9

In the Alerts dialog box in the System Status GUI, you'll find two checkboxes that let you configure how new alerts will be displayed when they arrive. What are those checkboxes named?

○ a. Play System Default Beep Sound, Show This Window

○ b. Send Email, Show This Window

○ c. Send Email, Play System Default Beep Sound

○ d. SNMP Trap, Send Email

○ e. SNMP Trap, Show This window

○ f. SNMP Trap, Play System Default Beep Sound

Answer a is correct. In the Alerts dialog box in the System Status GUI, you can configure Alerts to play the system default beep sound or show the Alert window. Answers b and c are incorrect because sending email is not a valid option. Answer d is incorrect because sending email is not a valid option and because an SNMP trap cannot be generated. Answers e and f are incorrect because an SNMP trap cannot be generated.

Question 10

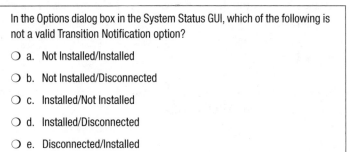

In the Options dialog box in the System Status GUI, which of the following is
not a valid Transition Notification option?

O a. Not Installed/Installed

O b. Not Installed/Disconnected

O c. Installed/Not Installed

O d. Installed/Disconnected

O e. Disconnected/Installed

O f. Disconnected/Not Installed

O g. All of the above are valid Transition Notification options.

O h. None of the above are valid Transition Notification options.

Answer g is correct. All of the choices are valid Transition Notification options
that can be configured in the Options dialog box in the System Status GUI.
Each of the answers represents a possible status change that the firewall can
incur, and notification can be sent if one of these situations occurs.

Need to Know More?

 Goncalves, Marcus and Steven Brown. *Check Point FireWall-1 Administration Guide*. McGraw-Hill, New York, NY, 1999. ISBN 0-07-134229-X. This book serves as a good bookshelf reference for FireWall-1.

 www.phoneboy.com is a great site that can address questions relating to troubleshooting FireWall-1 issues.

Sample Test

Question 1

What is the name of a generic, unmodified rule?

○ a. Base rule

○ b. Starter rule

○ c. Default rule

○ d. Blank rule

Question 2

The Connect Contol tab is used for configuring properties relating to which of the following?

○ a. Connection speed

○ b. User access

○ c. Access timeout

○ d. Load balancing

○ e. All of the above

○ f. None of the above

Question 3

Which GUI is used to modify network address translation (NAT)?

○ a. Policy Editor

○ b. Log Viewer

○ c. System Status

○ d. Real Time Monitor

○ e. NAT Editor

Question 4

Which of the following are types of authentication? [Check all correct answers]

❏ a. Client

❏ b. User

❏ c. Session

❏ d. Remote

Question 5

What is the benefit of hide mode in NAT?

○ a. Users can't see their valid IP addresses.

○ b. Each internal IP address is assigned an external IP addresses.

○ c. Hide mode can be activated only while using VPN-1.

○ d. All internal IPs are "hidden" behind a single valid IP address.

○ e. All of the above.

○ f. None of the above.

Question 6

What happens to the old log when a new one is created?

- ○ a. It is deleted.
- ○ b. Nothing—you cannot create a new log.
- ○ c. You are asked for the name of the file to which you want to save the old log.
- ○ d. A log is created with a name containing the date and time.

Question 7

Which is not a choice for creating a new security policy?

- ○ a. Rule Base Wizard
- ○ b. Rule base template
- ○ c. Empty database (manual)
- ○ d. Network discovery

Question 8

What three pieces of information do you need to log on to a firewall? [Check all correct answers]

- ❑ a. NT domain administrator access
- ❑ b. Username
- ❑ c. Password
- ❑ d. IP address (or hostname) of the firewall

Question 9

What file is needed in Windows NT to create permanent ARP entries?

- ○ a. fw1.arp
- ○ b. local.arp
- ○ c. ntarp.arp
- ○ d. arp.dat
- ○ e. local.dat

Question 10

What is a stealth rule?

- ○ a. A rule that makes the firewall hidden from administrators
- ○ b. A rule that catches all the traffic not handled by the rules above it
- ○ c. A rule for tracking down hackers
- ○ d. A rule used to block connections to the firewall

Question 11

Which of the following is not a method of network address translation?

- ○ a. Hide mode
- ○ b. Static destination mode
- ○ c. Static source mode
- ○ d. Selective hide mode

Question 12

What types of logs are available in Log Viewer? [Check all correct answers]

- ❑ a. System
- ❑ b. Security
- ❑ c. Accounting
- ❑ d. Application
- ❑ e. Active
- ❑ f. All of the above

Question 13

The order of the rules in a security policy is irrelevant.

- ○ a. True
- ○ b. False

Question 14

When does a workstation object become recognized as a firewall?

- ○ a. When Gateway is checked in the Workstation properties.
- ○ b. A workstation cannot become a firewall.
- ○ c. When anti-spoofing is enabled on the object.
- ○ d. When the interfaces for the object are defined.

Question 15

If a firewall examines only those packets leaving the firewall, in which direction is it said to be inspecting packets?

- ○ a. Inbound
- ○ b. Outbound
- ○ c. Eitherbound
- ○ d. The firewall always examines the packets as they travel both directions.
- ○ e. None of the above

Question 16

Only one administrator can have read/write access to an Enforcement Module at one time.

- ○ a. True
- ○ b. False

Question 17

FireWall-1 needs third-party software to scan packets for viruses.

- ○ a. True
- ○ b. False

Question 18

Does the number of years appear in a time object?

○ a. Yes

○ b. No

Question 19

What types of matching are available on URI objects? [Check all correct answers]

❏ a. Wildcard

❏ b. Content

❏ c. UFP server

❏ d. File

❏ e. All of the above

Question 20

What port is used for Telnet client authentication?

○ a. 21

○ b. 23

○ c. 800

○ d. 259

Question 21

What element helps you to identify object types?

○ a. Color scheme

○ b. Text

○ c. Port assignment

○ d. Rule order

Question 22

> How does selection criteria affect printing logs?
>
> ○ a. Only logs that meet the criteria are printed.
>
> ○ b. It does not affect what is printed.
>
> ○ c. You must select the criteria in order to print a log.
>
> ○ d. Both a and c.

Question 23

> What is another name for a proxy server?
>
> ○ a. Stateful inspection firewall
>
> ○ b. Microsoft Proxy
>
> ○ c. Application layer gateway
>
> ○ d. Packet filter

Question 24

> How do you designate a switch as having FireWall-1 installed on it?
>
> ○ a. Switches and routers cannot have FireWall-1 installed.
>
> ○ b. On the switch's General tab, select FireWall-1 to be installed.
>
> ○ c. You must set this in the FireWall-1 properties in order for the Enforcement Module to recognize switches that have FireWall-1 installed.
>
> ○ d. None of the above.

Question 25

> What must a user provide for transparent user authentication?
>
> ○ a. Nothing
>
> ○ b. The username and password on the gateway and destination machine
>
> ○ c. IP address of the firewall, username, password, and destination IP address
>
> ○ d. The username and password on the gateway

Question 26

Session authentication uses the least amount of system resources.

○ a. True

○ b. False

Question 27

Where would you place a cleanup rule?

○ a. At the top of a rule base

○ b. At the bottom of a rule base

○ c. In the middle of a rule base

○ d. None of the above

Question 28

What is it called when a packet's source IP address is altered to make it appear as though the packet came from a trusted network?

○ a. Thrashing

○ b. Impersonation

○ c. Stealth

○ d. Spoofing

Question 29

What are all the elements in a rule base?

○ a. Number, Firewall, User, Network, Destination, Source, Service, Action, Track, Install On, Time, Comment

○ b. Number, Source, Destination, Service, Action, Track, Install On, Time, Comment

○ c. Number, Source, Destination, Track, Install On, Time, Comment

○ d. Source, Destination, User, Authentication, Service, Action, Track, Install On, Time

○ e. Number, Source, Destination, Service, Authentication, Track, Install On, Time, Comment

Question 30

What are the advantages of packet filtering? [Check all correct answers]

- ❑ a. Inexpensive
- ❑ b. Strong security
- ❑ c. Good performance
- ❑ d. Application aware
- ❑ e. Application transparent

Question 31

FireWall-1 is built on _____ technology.

- ○ a. Proxy Server
- ○ b. INSPECT
- ○ c. Stateful inspection
- ○ d. Packet filtering

Question 32

An implicit rule is the same as a pseudo rule.

- ○ a. True
- ○ b. False

Question 33

Which of the following is not an encryption scheme?

- ○ a. IKE
- ○ b. Manual SKIP
- ○ c. SKIP
- ○ d. FWZ
- ○ e. Manual IPSec

Question 34

What options in an Alerts window are available in the System Status GUI? [Check all correct answers]

❑ a. Play Sound

❑ b. Show This Window

❑ c. Clear

❑ d. Dismiss

Question 35

You have created a rule in your firewall to block access to IRC services for all internal users. In the rule, you set tracking for long. In the Log Viewer, which column will tell you the destination port requested?

○ a. Port

○ b. Service

○ c. Proto

○ d. S_Port

Question 36

You have created a rule in your firewall to block access to IRC services for all internal users. In the rule, you set tracking for long. In the Log Vewer, which column will tell you the rule number that was applied to the packet?

○ a. Rule

○ b. Number

○ c. Service

○ d. A log file will not tell you a rule number.

Question 37

What is the default security policy?

- ○ a. All traffic is denied unless expressly permitted.
- ○ b. All traffic is allowed unless expressly permitted.
- ○ c. All traffic is denied.
- ○ d. The default security policy is the one that is installed when a firewall is restarted.

Question 38

What options are available for spoof tracking? [Check all correct answers]

- ❑ a. Short
- ❑ b. Log
- ❑ c. Alert
- ❑ d. None

Question 39

Which of the following internal authentication schemes does FireWall-1 support? [Check all correct answers]

- ❑ a. Radius
- ❑ b. Axent Pathways Defender
- ❑ c. VPN-1 & FireWall-1 Password
- ❑ d. OS Password
- ❑ e. TACACS
- ❑ f. S/Key
- ❑ g. SecurID

Question 40

Which of the following are external authentication schemes that FireWall-1 supports? [Check all correct answers]

❑ a. Radius

❑ b. Axent Pathways Defender

❑ c. VPN-1 & FireWall-1 Password

❑ d. OS Password

❑ e. TACACS

❑ f. S/Key

❑ g. SecurID

Question 41

What can a firewall not protect you from?

○ a. IP spoofing

○ b. External users

○ c. Internal users

○ d. Firewalls protect you from all of the above.

Question 42

The Management Server and GUI tools must reside on the same machine.

○ a. True

○ b. False

Question 43

What protocol does content security not work with?

○ a. Telnet

○ b. FTP

○ c. HTTP

○ d. SMTP

○ e. NAT Editor

Question 44

What is the minimum amount of memory necessary to install FireWall-1?

○ a. 32MB

○ b. 64MB

○ c. 128MB

○ d. Depends on the OS

Question 45

A "state derived from the previous communications" is the definition of which of the following?

○ a. Communication information

○ b. Application-derived state

○ c. Communication-derived state

○ d. Look-ahead state

○ e. None of the above

Question 46

You are the administrator for a large firm that is currently using a packet filtering firewall. Due to security breaches from the Internet, your boss has asked you to select a more secure firewall. You decide on FireWall-1, because it is a stateful inspection firewall. Your boss asks you to explain what stateful inspection means. How would you define stateful inspection?

○ a. A stateful inspection firewall can make control decisions for the handling of packets by manipulating information that has been derived from past communications and other applications.

○ b. A stateful inspection firewall is implemented on the Application layer. It takes the place of the source machine and sends requests for information to the intended destinations by using its own IP address.

○ c. Stateful inspection firewalls simply compare network protocols to a database of rules and forward the packets that meet the predefined criteria.

○ d. Stateful inspection firewalls break the packets up and examine them bit by bit. If all of the information meets the predetermined criteria, it is passed up the IP stack and must state its intended destination by containing the destination IP address.

Question 47

Your boss has agreed that FireWall-1 is the right firewall for your environment. While planning your firewall, you discover that you have 50 workstations, 12 servers, and 14 printers. Only 20 workstations and 1 server will be accessing the Internet. How many licenses must you purchase for your firewall?

- ○ a. 100
- ○ b. 50
- ○ c. 21
- ○ d. 76

Question 48

How do you determine the number of licenses you need to purchase for a FireWall-1 firewall?

- ○ a. FireWall-1 requires licenses for only the machines with IP addresses that will be using the firewall as a gateway.
- ○ b. FireWall-1 can be licensed only in certain amounts. You must purchase the license level that covers the necessary amount.
- ○ c. Only workstations need IP addresses. Servers and printers do not count.
- ○ d. You need one license for each IP address behind a firewall. Therefore, you only need enough licenses for each workstation, server, and printer.

Question 49

You receive the firewall software from Check Point. You are attempting to install it onto a Windows NT server with Service Pack 3. You have plenty of memory and disk space on the server. Why can't you install FireWall-1?

- ○ a. You have the wrong version of FireWall-1.
- ○ b. FireWall-1 will work only on Windows 2000, not NT.
- ○ c. You must be running Service Pack 4 or above for Windows NT.
- ○ d. Everything is fine. Call Check Point support.

Question 50

You are installing the FireWall-1 software. During the key hit session, a picture of a bomb appears. What has happened?

○ a. You are typing the same character twice or you are typing too fast.

○ b. The key you have pressed is not a valid character; only alpha and numeric characters are allowed.

○ c. You have a virus on your system. Stop the installation and run virus scan.

○ d. The character you typed was accepted.

Answer Key

1. c	18. b	35. b
2. d	19. a, c, d	36. a
3. a	20. d	37. a
4. a, b, c	21. a	38. b, c, d
5. d	22. a	39. c, d, f
6. d	23. c	40. a, b, e, g
7. d	24. b	41. c
8. b, c, d	25. b	42. b
9. b	26. a	43. a
10. d	27. b	44. b
11. d	28. d	45. c
12. b, c, e	29. b	46. a
13. b	30. a, c, e	47. a
14. a	31. c	48. b
15. b	32. a	49. c
16. a	33. b	50. a
17. a	34. a, b, c, d	

Question 1

Answer c is correct. The name for a newly created, unedited rule is *default rule*. This simply means that the rule has not had any modifications made to it after adding it to the rule base. Answers a, b, and d are incorrect because they are fictitious answers.

Question 2

Answer d is correct. The Connect Control tab is used to control the load agent port and load measurement interval that is used for load balancing traffic among servers in a network. Answer a is incorrect because Connect Control is used for load balancing, not connection speed; in fact, there is no tab in the firewall properties for connection speed. Answer b is incorrect because Connect Control does not handle user access; user access is controlled through the User Management tool. Answer c is incorrect because access timeout is a fictitious answer.

Question 3

Answer a is correct. The Policy Editor is the only GUI tool that you can use to modify NAT settings and NAT rules in FireWall-1. Answer b is incorrect because the Log Viewer does not control any firewall properties; it is used for viewing logs. Answer c is incorrect because the System Status GUI is used for obtaining firewall status data. Answer d is incorrect because the Real Time Monitor is used to view realtime data. Answer e is incorrect because NAT Editor is a fictitious answer.

Question 4

Answers a, b, and c are correct. There are only three ways that a client can authenticate with a firewall. The three options are client, user, and session authentication. Each of these methods handle authentication in different ways. Answer d is incorrect because remote authentication is a fictitious answer.

Question 5

Answer d is correct. Using hide mode for network address translation (NAT) allows you to hide all of your internal hosts with IP addresses behind a single valid IP address. Answer a is incorrect because NAT does not necessarily prevent users from seeing their valid IP addresses. Answer b is incorrect because hide mode NAT assigns a single address for multiple internal IP addresses. Answer c is incorrect because hide mode NAT does not require VPN-1.

Question 6

Answer d is correct. When a new log is being created, the log being replaced is saved to your hard drive with a file name that contains the time and date that the log was saved. This makes reviewing archived logs easier if the need should ever arise. Answer a is incorrect because the old log is not deleted. Answer b is incorrect because you can indeed create a new log. Answer c is incorrect because you are not prompted to enter a file name for the old log.

Question 7

Answer d is correct. Network discovery is not a valid option for creating a new security policy. Answers a, b, and c are incorrect because you can create a new security policy in the Policy Editor in one of three ways: by using the Rule Base Wizard, rule base template, or empty rule base.

Question 8

Answers b, c, and d are correct. You do not need domain administrator access to log on to a firewall. In fact, you don't even need a Windows NT domain. The only three pieces of information needed to log on to a firewall are the username, password, and IP address (or hostname). Answer a is incorrect because FireWall-1 does not require NT domain administrator rights.

Question 9

Answer b is correct. Because Windows NT cannot store permanent ARP entries, you must create the local.arp file in the x:\%systemroot%\fw\state directory in order for NAT to work properly. Answers a, c, d, and e are incorrect because they are fictitious file names.

Question 10

Answer d is correct. The stealth rule is used to block connections to the firewall and to make the firewall transparent to users. The stealth rule is placed at the top of the rule base in the security policy. Answer a is incorrect because the stealth rule is not hidden from administrators. Answer b is incorrect because the stealth rule is placed at the top of the rule base. Answer c is incorrect because the stealth rule cannot track hackers.

Question 11

Answer d is correct. Selective hide mode is not a method of network address translation. The only valid network address translation methods available on FireWall-1 are hide mode, static destination mode, and static source mode; therefore answers a, b, and c are incorrect. Hide mode hides many IPs behind one valid IP. The static modes are used for one-to-one address translation.

Question 12

Answers b, c, and e are correct. In the Log Viewer, three types of logs are available. Security logs show all security-related events, accounting entries show accounting entries and security information, and active connections show connections currently open with the firewall. Answers a and d are incorrect because System and Application log types don't exist in FireWall-1.

Question 13

Answer b is correct. This is unequivocally false. If rules are not applied in the correct order, they will conflict with one another and will cause the firewall to function improperly, if it will install at all!

Question 14

Answer a is correct. A workstation is considered a firewall after it is activated as a gateway. After it has been changed to a gateway, the FireWall-1 software can be activated on the object. Because a firewall must have at least two interfaces, it can not simply be a host in a real environment. Answer b is incorrect because a workstation object is used to create a firewall object. Answer c is incorrect because enabling anti-spoofing does not make a workstation become a firewall. Answer d is incorrect because the interfaces of the object do not need to be defined prior to becoming a firewall.

Question 15

Answer b is correct. If a firewall is examining packets only as they leave the firewall, it is said to be applying the rules in the outbound direction. Answer a is incorrect because inbound means that packets would be inspected as they came into the firewall. Answer c is incorrect because eitherbound means that packets are examined as they enter and exit the firewall. Answer d is incorrect because the firewall can indeed examine packets traveling in one direction only (as is the case with inbound and outbound).

Question 16

Answer a is correct. Although many administrators can have read access to a firewall at one time, only one administrator can have read/write access to the firewall.

Question 17

Answer a is correct. FireWall-1 cannot scan packets and files by itself. It must have a third-party application installed (and defined) in order to scan files.

Question 18

Answer b is correct. The Year field does not appear in a time object. Only time, days in a month, days in a week, and months can be specified in a time object.

Question 19

Answers a, c, and d are correct. When defining a URI (Uniform Resource Identifier) object, you can set the URI Match specification type to wildcard, file, or UFP (URL Filtering Protocol) server. The Match tab will change depending on the specification type you choose on the General tab. Answer b is incorrect because there is no content matching available when defining a URI object.

Question 20

Answer d is correct. When using client authentication, users must Telnet to port 259 or connect to the firewall with a Web browser using port 900 in order to be authenticated. The firewall will then ask for the ID and password to verify the user. Answer a is incorrect because port 21 is the port commonly used for FTP. Answer b is incorrect; although 23 is the port commonly used for Telnet, client authentication will work only on port 259. Answer c is incorrect because 800 is not a defined port, nor is it used for client authentication.

Question 21

Answer a is correct. To make administration easier, FireWall-1 has the ability to differentiate objects not only by icons but by colors as well. Answers b, c, and d are incorrect because none of these can be used to specifically identify object types.

Question 22

Answer a is correct. When you select criteria in the Log Viewer, only logs that meet the criteria you have chosen will be printed. All other logged information will be discarded for the print job. Answer b is incorrect because selection criteria is indeed used to determine what will be printed. Answer c is incorrect because you do not need to specify criteria in order to print a log. Answer d is incorrect because answer c is incorrect.

Question 23

Answer c is correct. Proxy servers are also known as *Application layer gateways*. Proxies take the place of the source machine and send the request for information to the intended destination using its (the proxy server's) own IP address. When the data is returned from the intended target, the information is then sent to the initiating source. Answer a is incorrect; a stateful inspection firewall, such as FireWall-1, makes control decisions for the handling of packets from past communications and other applications, and it is not another name for a proxy server. Answer b is incorrect because Microsoft Proxy is a firewall product put out by Microsoft. Answer d is incorrect because a packet filter is a different type of firewall from a proxy server. A packet filter simply compares network protocols to a database of rules and forward all packets that meet the predefined criteria.

Question 24

Answer b is correct. Only Xylan switches can be configured to be FireWall-1 enabled. To enable FireWall-1 on a Xylan switch, click the VPN-1 & FireWall-1 Installed checkbox on the General tab. Answer a is incorrect because you can specify a switch or router to have FireWall-1 installed. Answer c is incorrect because there is no setting for this in the firewall properties.

Question 25

Answer b is correct. For transparent user authentication, a user must provide the username and password on the gateway and destination machine. The word *transparent* can be a bit deceiving. Transparent user authentication is FireWall-1's default setting; it allows a user to initiate a connection directly to the server. That way, a user does not have to start a session for the service with the firewall and wait for the firewall to establish the connection with the destination. Answer a is incorrect because authentication information must be provided. Answer c is incorrect because the IP address of the firewall is not necessary. Answer d is incorrect because a user also needs to supply the username and password on the destination machine.

Question 26

Answer a is correct. The statement is true. Session authentication creates the least amount of overhead on a firewall. Session authentication is a transparent, per-session authentication process.

Question 27

Answer b is correct. The cleanup rule should be placed at the bottom of a rule base. All of the other rules need to be placed above the cleanup rule in order for it to serve its intended purpose, which is to catch all the traffic not handled by the rules above it. Answers a, c, and d are incorrect because the only place you should place a cleanup rule is at the bottom of the rule base.

Question 28

Answer d is correct. With IP spoofing, a host sitting somewhere on the Internet takes the IP address of another host as its own for a variety of reasons. IP spoofing is a popular way to generate denial of service attacks by generating packets from a nonexistent IP address and fooling the server into generating the SYN/ACK. Answer a is incorrect because thrashing is a type of attack that makes normal computer activity extremely slow because memory or other resources have become overwhelmed. Answer b is incorrect because impersonation is a method of attack that takes the identity of another computer that is trusted by a network. Answer c is incorrect because stealth means being furtive.

Question 29

Answer b is correct. The elements of the rule base, in order, are: Number, Source, Destination, Service, Action, Track, Install On, Time, and Comment. Answers a, c, d, and e are incorrect because each of these answers either has additional fictitious elements or is missing an actual element from this list.

Question 30

Answers a, c, and e are correct. The three largest advantages of packet filtering firewalls are that they are inexpensive, offer good performance, and are application transparent. Answer b is incorrect because packet filtering firewalls do not offer a strong level of security. Answer d is incorrect because stateful inspection firewalls do not filter packets to the Application layer.

Question 31

Answer c is correct. FireWall-1 is built on the stateful inspection technology. Answers a and d are incorrect because Proxy Server and packet filtering are other methods of firewalling. Answer b is incorrect because INSPECT is the name of the FireWall-1 inspection engine.

Question 32

Answer a is correct. The statement is true. An implicit rule (also called *implied rule*) is simply another name for a pseudo rule. Implicit rules are derived from the security (firewall) properties, and the explicit rules are found in the rule base.

Question 33

Answer b is correct. Manual SKIP is a fictitious name and not a valid encryption scheme in FireWall-1. IKE, SKIP, FWZ, and Manual IPSec are all valid encryption schemes for use with FireWall-1, so answers a, c, d, and e are incorrect.

Question 34

Answers a, b, c, and d are correct. Play Sound, Show This Window, Clear, and Dismiss are all options that are available on the Alert screen. Play Sound sends an audible tone when an alert is received, Show This Window displays the alert screen on an alert, Clear clears alerts, and Dismiss closes the Alert screen.

Question 35

Answer b is correct. The Service column shows the destination port requested. Answer a is incorrect because Port is not a valid column. Answers c and d are incorrect because Proto and S_Port are the communication protocol and source port, respectively.

Question 36

Answer a is correct. The Rule column is used to determine the rule that was applied to the packet. Answer b is incorrect the Number column shows the number of the log entry. Answer c is incorrect because the Service column tells you the destination port requested. Answer d is incorrect because the log file does tell you the rule number.

Question 37

Answer a is correct. All traffic is denied unless it is expressly permitted. In other words, if you don't state that you want traffic to be accepted in a rule, it will automatically be denied. Answer b is incorrect becacause all traffic is not allowed by default. Answer c is incorrect because traffic is denied only if it is not expressly permitted. Answer d is incorrect because the default security policy is not installed upon reboot.

Question 38

Answers b, c, and d are correct. Log, Alert, and None are the only valid options available for spoof tracking. Answer a is incorrect because Short is a method of tracking that is applied to a rule in the rule base.

Question 39

Answers c, d, and f are correct. VPN-1 & FireWall-1 Password, OS Password, and S/Key are all internal authentication schemes. Answers a, b, e, and g are incorrect because Radius, Axent Pathways Defender, TACACS, and SecurID are external schemes.

Question 40

Answers a, b, e, and g are correct. Radius, Axent, TACACS, and SecurID are all external authentication schemes. Answers c, d, and f are incorrect because VPN-1 & FireWall-1 Password, OS Password, and S/Key are internal schemes.

Question 41

Answer c is correct. Firewalls can protect you from external users and IP spoofing, but they cannot protect you from users and workstations that are inside the firewall and considered "friendly." Answers a and b are incorrect because a firewall does protect you from IP spoofing and external users. Answer d is incorrect because answer c is incorrect; therefore, all of the above cannot be correct.

Question 42

Answer b is correct. The statement is false. The Management Server and GUI tools can be installed on separate machines.

Question 43

Answer a is correct. Content security has no method of protecting a network or workstation from Telnet traffic. Answers b, c, and d are incorrect because content security works with FTP, HTTP, and SMTP. Answer e is incorrect because NAT Editor is not a protocol.

Question 44

Answer b is correct. FireWall-1 requires a minimum of 64MB for installation. However, Check Point recommends 128MB. Answer a is incorrect because 32MB is not sufficient memory for FireWall-1. Answer c is incorrect because, although 128MB is recommended, it is not the minimum requirement. Answer d is incorrect because the minimum amount of memory is constant across all operating systems.

Question 45

Answer c is correct. The communication-derived state is derived from the previous communications handled by the firewall. Answer a is incorrect because communication information is data obtained from the top five layers of a packet.

Answer b is incorrect because the application-derived state is derived from other applications. Answer d is incorrect because look-ahead state is a fictitious answer.

Question 46

Answer a is correct. A stateful inspection firewall makes control decisions for the handling of packets from past communications and other applications. Answer b is incorrect because this answer is the definition of a proxy server. Answer c is incorrect because this answer is the definition of a packet filter. Answer d is incorrect because it is a nonsense answer.

Question 47

Answer a is correct. FireWall-1 is licensed on certain levels—25, 50, 100, and 250 users. Because the network has a total of 76 nodes with IP addresses behind the firewall, answer a is the only possible answer. Answer b is incorrect because it does not provide enough licenses. Answers c and d are incorrect because licensing is not available in these amounts.

Question 48

Answer b is correct. The same reasoning applies here as it did to question 47. Because you have a total of 76 nodes with IP addresses behind the firewall, answer b is the only possible answer. FireWall-1 is not concerned with the number of internal users or workstations accessing the Internet; it is licensed based on the number of IP addresses it is protecting behind the firewall. Answer a is incorrect because any node with an IP address behind the firewall must have a license, regardless of whether it uses the Internet. Answer c is incorrect because workstations, servers, printer, routers, switches—any node with an IP address—needs a license. Answer d is incorrect because licensing can be purchased in certain amounts only; it is not based strictly on the number of nodes.

Question 49

Answer c is correct. At a minimum, FireWall-1 requires Service Pack 4 for Windows NT to be installed. FireWall-1 will install correctly on Service Pack 5, 6, and 6a, as well. Answer a is incorrect because you can purchase only the latest versions of FireWall-1. Answer b is incorrect because FireWall-1 will work on Windows NT or 2000. Answer d is incorrect; there is no need to call Check Point (and even if you were to call, you will not be helped unless you have a support contract!).

Question 50

Answer a is correct. A bomb will appear during the key hit session if you are typing the same character too many times or if you are typing too fast. Answer b is incorrect because you can use any character on the keyboard. Answer c is incorrect because FireWall-1 is not aware of whether viruses are present. Answer d is incorrect because a light bulb would appear if you typed an accepted character.

Glossary

access control list (ACL)
The ACL is a list of objects that have been granted or denied permission to perform operations on a particular object.

access control rights
Access control rights are used by security administrators for granting remote management administration privileges.

ACK packet
The ACK packet is the third step in the network handshake process. It is the response from the source host after a SYN/ACK packet has been sent from the destination host.

Action field
The Action field is the rule base element used to determine how a data packet will be handled in a firewall rule.

address range object
An address range object is a network object that is used to represent a range of IP (Internet Protocol) addresses as a single entity.

algorithm
An algorithm is a step-by-step problem-solving procedure used to determine the integrity of a message.

application-derived state
The application-derived state is information that is gathered from other applications previously examined.

Application layer
The Application layer is the top layer of the IP(Internet Protocol) stack.

Application layer gateway
See proxy server.

ARP (Address Resolution Protocol)
ARP is used by TCP/IP to map IP network addresses to the hardware addresses used by the data link protocol.

authentication
Authentication is the process of validating whether data being sent or received is being transmitted from the expected host.

Axent Defender

Axent Defender is an external authentication system that can be implemented with FireWall-1 authentication.

CA (certificate authority)

A CA is a trusted resource (usually third-party, such as VeriSign) that creates and validates certificate keys.

CCSA (Check Point Certified Security Administrator)

The Check Point Certified Security Administrator certification can be achieved using the material in this book. This is the first level of certification for Check Point.

CCSE (Check Point Certified Security Engineer)

Check Point Certified Security Engineer is the second level of certification for Check Point. This exam covers remote management, encryption, load balancing, tracking, and VPN (virtual private network) in much more detail than the CCSA certification exam does.

CCSI (Check Point Certified Security Instructor)

A Check Point Certified Security Instructor certification can be obtained only by employees of Check Point or any of Check Point's authorized training centers. The CCSI certification allows candidates to teach FireWall-1 and VPN-1.

certificate

A certificate is a digital signature used for data encryption.

CIDR (Classless InterDomain Routing)

Using CIDR, each IP (Internet Protocol) address has a specific *network prefix* that identifies either a collection of gateways or a single gateway. CIDR lets one routing table entry represent a collection of networks that exist in the forward path that do not need to be specified on that particular gateway.

Cisco

Cisco Systems develops network routers, switches, and other networking equipment.

Cisco PIX

Cisco PIX is a firewall developed by Cisco Systems.

cleanup rule

The cleanup rule is a rule that is placed at the end of a rule base to handle any of the traffic that is not specifically controlled by any of the rules that precede it.

client authentication

Client authentication is the method of authentication in which a client is granted access through a firewall by authenticating the client to a specific IP (Internet Protocol) address.

Comment field

The Comment field is the rule base element used to add additional comments for a specific rule.

communication-derived state

The communication-derived state is information gathered from previous communications.

Destination field

The Destination field is the rule base element used to define the intended recipient of a data packet in a firewall rule.

DMZ (demilitarized zone)

A DMZ is a computer or network that is located outside of the internal network but that is still protected behind the firewall from the Internet. DMZs are commonly used for servers that require access from users on the Internet but that should not be placed internally for security purposes.

DNS (Domain Name Server)

DNS is an IP (Internet Protocol)–related service that provides lookup capabilities for resolving IP addresses to fully qualified domain names.

domain name

In terms of a fully qualified domain name, the domain name is the name assigned to a specific set of computers. For example, in www.examcram.com, the examcram portion is the domain name.

domain object

A domain object is a collection or group of objects that is managed as a single entity.

eitherbound communication

Eitherbound refers to FireWall-1 inspecting packets when they enter and leave a firewall.

encryption

Encryption is a method of protecting data by altering it so that it is only usable by parties who have the ability to decipher the altered data.

encryption scheme

An encryption scheme is an algorithm and key management protocol used to pass secured keys. These keys allow the two ends of the VPN (virtual private network) tunnel to communicate with one another.

explicit rule

An explicit rule is a rule that is created manually using the Policy Editor.

firewall

A firewall is a resource (either software or hardware) that is placed between internal and external networks for the purpose of securing communications.

firewall daemon

The firewall daemon is responsible for passing communications between clients, hosts, and other modules.

Firewall Module

The Firewall Module is responsible for controlling the security policy, logging events, firewall synchronization, and user authentication.

FireWall-1

Check Point FireWall-1 is among the industry leaders in firewall technologies. FireWall-1 uses the stateful inspection method of network firewalling.

FloodGate-1

FloodGate-1 is a bandwidth-management solution used to resolve network congestion due to bandwidth-intensive traffic. FloodGate-1 works by prioritizing certain, more critical types of traffic over less important traffic.

FQDN (fully qualified domain name)

The FQDN is the full name of a host, consisting of its local hostname and its domain name, including a top-level domain. An example of a fully qualified domain name is **www.examcram.com**.

FTP (File Transfer Protocol)

FTP is a TCP (Transmission Control Protocol) protocol used to move files between two hosts.

FW1

FW1 (port 256) is the port used by FireWall-1 in remote management for the exchange of license keys.

FW1-log

FW1-log (port 257) is the port used by FireWall-1 in remote management for transferring log information.

FW1-mgmt

FW1-mgmt (port 258) is the port used by FireWall-1 in remote management for the loading and retrieving of a security policy.

fwstart

You can start FireWall-1 from a command line using the **fwstart** command.

fwstop

You can stop FireWall-1 from a command line using the **fwstop** command.

FWZ

FWZ is Check Point's proprietary encryption scheme.

gateway

A gateway is a device that sits between two networks and is used to facilitate communications between those networks. A gateway can be a firewall or a simple routing device.

GUI (graphical user interface)

A GUI is an application that uses graphics and menus for the management of back-end services. Examples of GUIs are the Policy Editor, Log Viewer, and System Status GUIs.

hide mode

Hide mode is one of the three address translation modes used by FireWall-1 (the other two are static destination mode and static source mode). Hide mode allows multiple internal (invalid) IP addresses to be represented by a single, Internet-valid IP address.

high availability

The concept of high availability is that a particular function—be it a firewall, server, router, or even a simple phone line—has certain cost consequences based on the amount of downtime it incurs.

hostname

A hostname is the name of a host within an FQDN. For example, in **www.examcram.com**, the **www** portion is the hostname.

HTTP (Hypertext Transfer Protocol)

HTTP is the protocol used to communicate over the World Wide Web.

ICMP (Internet Control Message Protocol)

ICMP is a protocol that is used between a host and a destination for message control and error reporting. The purpose of these control messages is to provide feedback about problems in the communication environment.

IKE (Internet Key Exchange)

IKE is a widely used encryption scheme that is used for communication negotiation between two hosts.

impersonation attack

Impersonation is a method used to take the identity of another computer that is trusted by a network. The purpose of this type of attack is to convince the other machines on a network to pass private information based on the fact that they assume the impersonated workstation can be trusted.

implicit rule

An implicit rule is a rule that is implied by the creation of the explicit rule base and firewall properties. Also called *implied rule* or *pseudo rule*.

inbound communication

Inbound refers to FireWall-1 inspecting packets only when they enter the firewall.

Inspection Module

The Inspection Module of the firewall is responsible for access control, auditing, authentication (client and session), and address translation.

Install On field

The Install On field is the rule base element used to define which gateway a specified rule will be installed on.

InstallU

InstallU is used on Solaris systems for installing files onto a machine in a standalone installation.

integrated firewall object

An integrated firewall object is used to manage third-party firewalls, such as CES, Timestep, and Cisco. These firewalls can be integrated with FireWall-1 to allow for the configuration of alternative security implementations.

Internet

The Internet is a very large, worldwide network of computers that use the TCP/IP protocol to exchange information.

IP (Internet Protocol) address

An IP address is a set of numbers used by computers to determine the location of a network host.

IPv4 (Internet Protocol version 4)

IPv4 is the current generation of IP addressing. Offers IP addresses that are 32 bits.

IPv6 (Internet Protocol version 6)

IPv6 is the next generation of IP addressing. IPv6, when fully implemented, will offer IP addresses that are four times as many bits as currently available in IP version 4 (128 bits versus 32 bits).

IP spoofing

IP spoofing is a method used by hackers to make data packets appear as if they are coming from another IP address.

ISP (Internet Service Provider)

An ISP is a company that provides access to the Internet.

LDAP (Lightweight Directory Access Protocol)

LDAP is used to access databases using TCP/IP. LDAP is a variation on the X.500 directory access standard.

load balancing

In terms of FireWall-1, load balancing is a process in which the traffic (load) is distributed evenly between two (or more) firewalls so that no one firewall is burdened with excessive amounts of traffic.

local.arp

The local.arp file is crucial for using ARP (Address Resolution Protocol) and NAT (network address translation) with Windows NT. You must create the file local.arp in the \%localhost\fw\state\ directory before NAT will function properly in Windows NT.

Log Viewer

The Log Viewer is a GUI that is used to view logged information that has been requested in the rule base of the Firewall Module.

logical server object

A logical server object is a network object in FireWall-1 that is used to signify a group of machines that offer the same type of service and are used in a load-balanced environment.

MAC (Media Access Control) address

A MAC address is a unique address that is associated with a network interface card (NIC). The MAC address identifies a specific machine; no two machines can have the same MAC address.

Man-in-the-middle attack

A man-in-the-middle attack is a form of an impersonation attack. In this case, a hacker sits between two computers that are in communication. When one of the computers opens communications with the other, the hacker intercepts the traffic.

Management Module

The Management Module is a GUI-based Management Module used to administer and monitor Firewall Modules.

Manual IPSec (Internet Protocol Security)

Manual IPSec is a widely used encryption scheme that uses fixed-length keys for the purpose of encrypting and decrypting data packets.

master

A master is the host that all of the FireWall-1 logs and alerts are directed to. The master also holds the rule bases for all firewalled systems that are in its control.

Meta-IP

Meta-IP is a central administration point for control over IP (Internet Protocol) services and network naming conventions. It automates IP addressing and eliminates duplicate IP address errors with DHCP (Dynamic Host Configuration Protocol), provides failover by replicating DHCP, and provides increased security and stability.

NAT (network address translation)

NAT is a method of translating an internal (invalid) IP (Internet Protocol) address into an Internet-valid IP address so that the internal IP address is never revealed to outside networks, such as the Internet.

network object

A network object is one of several objects that can be created within a network. Network objects include workstations, networks, domains, routers, switches, integrated firewalls, logical servers, and address ranges.

Network Objects Manager

The tool in the FireWall-1 Policy Editor used to manage the network objects in use by the firewall. Also called *Network Objects tool*.

NIC (network interface card)

A network interface card is a physical (or virtual) endpoint where an IP (Internet Protocol) address can be assigned. NICs rely on IP addresses and MAC (Media Access Control) addresses to maintain individuality within a network.

original packet

In terms of network address translation (NAT), the original packet section tells us information about the original, pre-translated packet.

outbound communication

Outbound refers to FireWall-1 inspecting packets only when they leave the firewall.

packet (data packet)

A packet is a collection of data that is transmitted across a network for an intended destination.

pkgadd

Pkgadd is a command-line utility used with Solaris for transferring the FireWall-1 installation files to the Solaris machine. Pkgadd is most useful when performing a distributed installation of FireWall-1.

proxy server

A proxy server is a firewall that is implemented on the Application layer. Proxies are an improvement over packet filtering, because they examine packets all the way up to the Application layer. They offer better security, because they are fully aware of the context of the information that is being passed between the networks. Another name for a proxy server is an *Application layer gateway*.

pseudo rule

See implicit rule.

RADIUS (Remote Authentication Dial-In User Service)

RADIUS is an external authentication system that can be implemented with FireWall-1 authentication.

RARP (Reverse Address Resolution Protocol)

RARP is the reverse of ARP. RARP is used to provide an IP (Internet Protocol) address when a physical address is supplied.

RFC (Request for Comments)
An RFC is a document that is used to discuss standards and concepts of the Internet.

RIP (Routing Internet Protocol)
RIP is used to enable communications and exchange routing tables between routers.

router
A router is a device that is used to determine the next hop (address in a network) to pass a data packet.

router object
A router object is a network object in FireWall-1 that is used to specify and, in some cases, manage external routers from within the Firewall Module.

routing table
A routing table is used to correlate network IP (Internet Protocol) addresses with the IP address of a network router.

RPC (remote procedure call)
RPC is a protocol that allows a program running on a source host to cause code to be executed on another host without the need to have the code written for this function. RPC is often found in the client/server model of distributed computing.

rule base
A rule base is a collection of individual rules created by the Policy Editor for securing communications.

rule base elements
Rule base elements are the individual fields of a rule that define the functionality of the rule. Rule base elements include Source, Destination, Service, Action, Track, Install On, Time, and Comment.

Service field
The Service field is the rule base element used to define the services (types of communications) of a data packet in a firewall rule.

session authentication
Session authentication is a method of providing transparent authentication for access through a firewall. Session authentication requires the session authentication client to function.

session authentication agent
The session authentication agent is a small yet crucial software package that must be loaded on individual workstations to enable them to use session authentication through the firewall.

SKIP (Simple Key Management for Internet Protocol)
SKIP is an encryption scheme and key management protocol used to securely share keys between two hosts.

SMTP (Simple Mail Transfer Protocol)
The SMTP protocol is used for the transfer of email between mail servers.

Solaris
Solaris is a Unix-based network operating system developed by Sun Microsystems.

Source field
The Source field is the rule base element used to define the originator of a data packet in a firewall rule.

stateful inspection
Stateful inspection is a type of firewall that stores information from applications and past communications and determines how a packet should be handled based on that information. A stateful inspection firewall will allow only traffic that it is programmed to allow.

static destination mode
Static destination mode is one of the three address translation modes used by FireWall-1 (the other two are hide mode and static source mode). Static destination mode translates an Internet-valid IP (Internet Protocol) address to an internal (invalid) IP address when a packet enters the internal network.

static source mode
Static source mode is one of the three address translation modes used by FireWall-1 (the other two are hide mode and static destination mode). Static source mode translates an internal (invalid) IP (Internet Protocol) address to an Internet-valid IP address when a packet leaves the internal network.

subnet mask
A subnet mask is a number used to divide a network into several subnetworks. A subnet mask looks similar to an IP address, because it is broken into four sections separated by periods. Also called *network mask*.

switch
A switch is a device used as a common communication point for networks. Devices such as routers, servers, workstations, and printers are connected to a switch. The switch knows the location of the devices and passes data packets to them as necessary.

switch object
A switch object is a network object in FireWall-1 used to specify and, in some cases, manage switches in a network from the Firewall Module.

SYN packet
A SYN packet is the initial packet sent by a host to begin a handshake, which will allow communications between two hosts.

SYN/ACK packet
A SYN/ACK packet is the second step in a network handshake. When a SYN packet is received from a source host, the destination host responds with a SYN/ACK packet.

sync.conf
The sync.conf file must be created in the $FWDIR/conf directory on two firewalls that will be synchronized. The sync.conf file contains the names of the remote firewalls that will synchronize with the local firewall.

synchronization
In FireWall-1, multiple firewalls have the ability to synchronize with each other. Synchronization creates the ability of one firewall to take over for another firewall, if the second firewall fails to communicate.

SYNDefender

SYNDefender is a feature of FireWall-1 that protects the firewall and internal network from denial of service attacks.

System Status GUI

The System Status GUI is a utility provided with FireWall-1 that is used to examine the status of firewalled objects.

TACACS (Terminal Access Controller Access Control System)

Terminal Access Controller Access Control System (TACACS) is an external authentication system that can be implemented with FireWall-1 authentication.

TCP (Transmission Control Protocol)

TCP is built on top of the Internet Protocol (IP) and is almost always seen in the combination TCP/IP (TCP over IP). TCP adds reliable communication, flow control, multiplexing, and connection-oriented communication. TCP is used to send and receive data, thereby guaranteeing transmission from the source to the destination.

Telnet

Telnet is a simple terminal protocol that can be used to access a remote host.

Time field

The Time field is the rule base element used to define the time that a firewall rule will be enforced.

Track field

The Track field is the rule base element used to determine how data packets will be tracked (if at all) in a firewall rule.

translated packet

In terms of network address translation (NAT), a translated packet tells the source, destination, and service information about a packet after address translation has occurred within the firewall.

UDP (User Datagram Protocol)

UDP can be defined as the Internet standard Network layer, Transport layer, and Session layer protocols that provide simple but unreliable datagram services. UDP is a connectionless protocol that is layered on top of IP (Internet Protocol).

URI (Uniform Resource Identifier)

A URI is a method for specifying resources on the Internet by name. Resources can be specified by their full name or by using wildcards.

URL (Uniform Resource Locator)

A URL is an address of a node on the Internet (or on an intranet).

user authentication

User authentication is a method of authenticating a host on a per-user basis. User authentication can function only with the FTP (File Transfer Protocol), HTTP (Hypertext Transfer Protocol), HTTPS (Secure Hypertext Transfer Protocol), Telnet, and rlogin services.

VLAN (virtual local area network)

Most switches allow you to configure a virtual local area network (VLAN). A VLAN is a local area network with a definition that maps workstations on some other basis than geographic location. A VLAN controller can change or add workstations more easily on a VLAN than on a physical LAN.

VPN (virtual private network)
A VPN is a technology that provides the ability to use public networks like the Internet rather than private leased lines for wide area network communications. VPN technologies implement virtual networks that use the same cabling and routers as the public network, without compromising security.

VPN-1 Gateway
VPN-1 Gateway combines the functionality of the FireWall-1 suite with advanced VPN technologies. VPN-1 Gateway provides connections to corporate networks, off-site users, and remote offices.

VPN-1 SecuRemote
SecuRemote is the client-side portion of Check Point's virtual private network implementation. VPN-1

SecuRemote is used to connect remote users to corporate networks through the Internet over secure connections.

Windows 2000
Windows 2000 is the network operating system developed by Microsoft after Windows NT.

Windows NT
Windows NT is the network operating system developed by Microsoft prior to Windows 2000. The latest release of Windows NT is version 4.

workstation object
A workstation object is a server or workstation or, more generically, any object that has an IP (Internet Protocol) address specifically assigned to it.

X.500
X.500 is a protocol used to communicate with a directory service or database system. LDAP is a spin-off of the X.500 protocol.

Index